*To the loving memories of my wife, Lisa Endig, and
my mother, Eva*
—DM

To Steve with love
—SGC

To Ila and Ivan, who taught me the value of cooperation
—TKB

Contents

Preface

Any project that has to deal with collective information has to make sure that all information can be spread out and used equally. It doesn't have to be music, it can be just whatever information.
—Ornette Coleman, jazz musician,
  explaining his theory of "harmolodics."

TEAMS AND INFORMATION TECHNOLOGY are two of the most important developments in organizations today. Vast amounts of time, money, and effort are spent with the expectation that their impact on the bottom line will eventually justify their costs. But many organizations are disappointed in the results. Few are getting the bang from the many bucks they spend each year to create teams and to develop new information systems. The challenge facing these organizations is how to fulfill the potential of these two promising and complex developments.

The premise of this book is that each is necessary to take full advantage of the possibilities created by the other—that is, information technology can make teams more effective, and teams can help fulfill the promise of new information technology. Together, teams and new information technology can catalyze dramatic improvements in organizational performance. How to make this happen is the subject of this book.

Like many collaborative efforts, this book grew out of the serendipitous convergence of ideas and people. Two of us—Don Mankin and Tora K. Bikson—had worked together on several research projects at the RAND Corporation in the early to mid-1980s. The projects dealt with the implementation of information systems in work settings, particularly on the role of the user in the development and implementation process. By the mid- to late 1980s the focus of this work began to shift, reflecting the dramatic developments in technology that were beginning to emerge at the time, especially the evolution from large, centralized, mainframe computer systems to client-server, networked architectures. Like many of our colleagues, we realized that to understand the impact of new technology on work and organizations we needed to shift our attention from individual users to collaborating users. The appropriate level of analysis for our work was now the team.

Chance, the Zeitgeist, serendipity, divine intervention—take your pick—then took over. Our social/professional network stepped in to help us understand the impacts of technology networks on organizations. Increasingly, we crossed paths at professional meetings and other events with Susan Cohen from the Center for Effective Organizations at the University of Southern California. We talked and liked one another well enough to continue talking past the niceties of casual conversations. We discovered a common interest in teams and information technology. Susan, however, came to this interest from the other side, from her research on team effectiveness and self-management. For the last several years she had focused on knowledge work teams and the design of team-based organizations. She recognized the potential of teams to improve performance and the elements needed to fulfill this potential—information technology, in particular.

The three of us had similar experiences in our research and consulting. We saw many organizations struggling with teams and new information technology. While they strongly believed that each offered great promise, fulfilling that promise was another story. What was needed, we felt, was a sound, pragmatic perspective on how to do just that— how to change organizations by integrating the design and implementation of teams and new technologies. True, there are a number of excellent books on creating effective teams—most notably J. Richard Hackman's *Groups That Work (And Those That Don't)* (1989) and Sue Mohrman, Susan Cohen, and Allan Mohrman's *Designing Team-Based Organizations* (1995)—and a few on implementing information systems—Richard Walton's *Up and Running* (1989), for example. But there is no book that pulls these two topics together. Furthermore, while the literature on groupware, new technologies that support cooperative work, is growing by leaps and bounds, the focus is primarily on the technology. The organizational change processes required to introduce the technology into work settings has been largely overlooked.

So we decided to write this book, primarily to help practitioners deal with the details of team-technology change as well as to help them think more conceptually and strategically about its longer-term implications. The book is specifically aimed at functional-area managers in all manner of organizations—large and small, public and private, not-for-profit, etc.—who are now engaging in these efforts or thinking about initiating them in the near future. It is also designed for the consultants and staff professionals and managers who may be called on to help them in this effort. Information technology professionals should find this book of particular interest. We also hope that it will inspire human resource professionals to seek out new opportunities at the leading edge of the technological frontier. Finally, while we did not write this book for an academic audience, we believe that teachers and scholars in organizational behavior, MIS, and other areas will find this book of interest as well.

PLAN OF THE BOOK

The book is organized into four parts. Part I describes the basic themes, terms, and concepts to be used throughout the book.

- *Chapter 1* introduces the subject of the book—how to develop and integrate teams, information technology, and high-level policies and structures to create more effective organizations. Much of the chapter previews the mutual design and implementation (MDI) framework, the perspective we use to understand and address many of the key issues facing organizations today.

- *Chapter 2* provides basic background information on the focus of the MDI effort—teams, technology, and organizations. This chapter lays the groundwork for later chapters by defining our terms and presenting critical concepts. Much of the chapter is devoted to a description of the different team types—work teams, project and development teams, parallel teams, management teams, and ad hoc networks—and a preview of the design approach to team effectiveness.

In part II we begin to explore the details of the MDI framework. The chapters in part II focus on the core of the framework—the MDI team, the name we use to describe the project team(s) of stakeholder representatives responsible for carrying out the MDI effort.

- *Chapter 3* explains how to identify an MDI opportunity and get the project started. After describing and illustrating the various kinds of projects that can benefit from an MDI approach, the chapter reviews how the stakeholders and others can initiate an MDI project and create an overall structure to help them integrate and manage the project.

- *Chapters 4 and 5* discuss the different stakeholders in detail. In these chapters we describe who they are, how to select individuals to represent their interests, what roles these representatives should play, and how they can be most effectively involved in the MDI process. These stakeholder representatives comprise the MDI team.

- *Chapter 6* addresses the design of the MDI team. This chapter will cover such topics as training, leadership, information resources, and linkages with the stakeholder groups they represent as well as with the rest of the organization.

The chapters in part III describe the process by which the MDI team designs and implements new technologies and the teams that will use them (user teams). The process can be roughly divided into three stages.

- *Chapter 7* describes the first stage of the process, in which the project is defined, objectives are identified, and various design alternatives explored until one is chosen.

- *Chapter 8* addresses the steps and activities involved in executing the technology portion of the design strategy chosen in stage 1. Much of this work involves the actual "building" of the systems the teams will eventually use. The chapter begins by describing the criteria and principles that should guide the design and build process; it then applies these criteria to evaluate one of the most promising and controversial technological developments of recent years, groupware. The chapter concludes by comparing traditional approaches to systems development with contemporary approaches more in tune with the MDI framework and the underlying themes of this book.

- ◆ *Chapter 9* is devoted to the design of the user teams—the other part of stage 2. During this phase—which can precede, follow, or run parallel to the building of the system—user-team designs take the form of proposals on paper rather than actual functioning work arrangements. It is not until they are implemented in the final stage of the project (chapter 10) that they become a reality. Chapter 9 reviews the design factors critical to each of the team types described in chapter 2, including the different kinds of information and information tools they require.

- ◆ *Chapter 10* deals with the implementation of the technology and user-team designs developed in the previous stage of the MDI process. The implementation process includes all of those activities concerned with how the systems and teams designed in the preceding stage are incorporated into the ongoing work flow of the organization.

These team and technology designs have implications for the overall organization, particularly for its structure and human-resource policies and practices. Organizations must adapt to their teams and technologies, just as these teams and technologies adapt to each other and to the constraints and culture of their organization. The two chapters in part IV focus on these higher-level issues of organizational change.

- ◆ *Chapter 11* describes the organization-wide changes that need to be made to support user teams and new technologies. Topics covered include human-resource policies for team-based organizations and the changing role of HR, corporate information technology, and senior management.

- ◆ After briefly summarizing the preceding chapters, chapter 12 presents a speculative look at the team-based, technology-enabled organization of the future. Integrating themes from recent work on emerging organizational forms with the themes of this book, we present a vision of work unbounded by such traditional constraints as time, place, authority, function, and formal organizational boundaries.

ABOUT OUR USES OF CASES AND EXAMPLES

The recommendations presented in this book are based on our research and consulting experience involving more than 100 organizations of all kinds—large and small, public and private, manufacturers and service providers, low tech and high tech. A partial, representative list includes Aid Association for Lutherans, ARCO, Aspect Telecommunications, Boston Edison, Digital Equipment Corporation, Encore Computers, Harris Computer Systems, Hewlett-Packard, Honeywell, IBM, the Los Angeles Times, the Office of Economic Cooperation and Development, Princess Cruises, Pacific Bell, the Public Service Company of Colorado, Scott Paper, the Seattle Water Department, Steelcase, the United Nations, the U.S. Forest Service, and the World Bank.

The cases and examples we use to illustrate our recommendations are drawn from the many organizations we have worked with in our research and consulting over the years. The cases and examples take two forms. The first is a continuing story (soap opera might be a better descriptor) about a team-technology project in a nonexistent organization. The story and the company are composites based on actual situations and organizations. We open each chapter with an installment of the story to dramatize the principal issues to be addressed, and we close each chapter by illustrating how the project team dealt with these issues. Within each chapter we also use brief examples drawn from actual organizations and situations to illustrate specific points. We have changed the names of the companies and identifying details to protect the confidentiality of the organizations and the individuals involved.

ACKNOWLEDGMENTS

Two organizations played a special role in the writing of this book—the Center for Effective Organizations at the University of Southern California in Los Angeles and The RAND Corporation in Santa Monica, California. Our colleagues and the research conducted at these organizations strongly influenced this book.

At the Center for Effective Organizations Ed Lawler deserves special mention not only for the impact of his work on our thinking and his unflagging support, but also for his comments on an earlier draft of the manuscript that significantly improved the final product. The four-year study of knowledge work teams completed in collaboration with Susan

Mohrman and Allan Mohrman helped shape many of our ideas about teams and designing team-based organizations. Jay Galbraith, Gerald Ledford, Ram Tenkasi, and Gary McMahan contributed to our knowledge of organization design, reward systems, and organizational learning. Dana Lee did an outstanding job in turning our chicken-scratch sketches into well-drawn figures and tables.

Several researchers and consultants at RAND also helped us develop the ideas and recommendations in this book. Cathy Stasz and Barbara Gutek were the other members of the research team that conducted the earlier studies on information-systems implementation. Sally Ann Law was always available to listen and critique ideas and drafts, and Terry West was a primary source of information on rapid application development. We also owe a special thanks to Albert P. Williams, corporate research manager of social policy at RAND, for providing Don Mankin with office space and administrative support to help get this project underway.

We would also like to thank the many managers and employees that have participated in our studies and worked with us in our consultations. This includes the corporate sponsors of the Center for Effective Organizations, the many organizations that participated in the RAND studies, and the twenty manufacturing organizations visited by Don Mankin in conjunction with a research study conducted by Ann Majrchzak at the Institute for Safety and Systems Management at the University of Southern California. We owe a great debt to all of them. Their experiences made an invaluable contribution to the knowledge on which this book is based.

Others provided ideas that helped shape the manuscript in its early stages and comments on later drafts that influenced the final product: J. D. Eveland, Kim Fisher, Jeff Hahn, Dan Heitzer, A. B. (Rami) Shani, Jay Shuster, Pat Zingheim, the anonymous reviewers, and the students in Don Mankin's teams and technology class at the Los Angeles campus of the California School of Professional Psychology, especially Jim Tidwell. We would also like to thank our editors at Harvard Business School Press, Carol Franco and Marjorie Williams. Carol gave us the encouragement to begin; Marjorie's patience and support gave us the space to explore and her gentle prodding ultimately gave us the push to finish. Last but very far from least, we would like to thank each other. We couldn't have found better teammates!

TEAMS *and* TECHNOLOGY

Part One

Developing a
Framework for Change

THIS FIRST PART OF THE BOOK introduces the concept of using teams and information technology to effect organizational change. Each element on the left side of this "equation" (the teams and the technology) is of equal importance in bringing about the "result" (organizational change); in fact, the synergistic relationship between teams and information technology makes them far more effective agents of change together than either could be apart. Chapter 1 makes clear the significance of this relationship and presents the basic components of the process intended to exploit it: the mutual design and implementation (MDI) of teams and technology.

Teams are a particularly important part of this equation. For this reason, chapter 2, part of which is devoted to defining all elements in the equation, focuses on the design of teams. The general information provided there on the different kinds of teams, the purposes for which they can be used, and the guidelines for designing them effectively should help organizations ensure that teams play the vital role they are intended to play in the MDI process.

1

Changing Organizations with Teams and Technology

6:00 A.M., late August, Los Angeles . . .

The desert wind blew all night. It was one of those hot, dry Santa Anas that come down through mountain passes and curl your hair and make your nerves jump and your skin itch.[1] *Mark Hoffman tosses fitfully in his bed. He hasn't slept all night. Just as he finally begins to fall asleep, exhausted, the phone rings. Mark answers, his sleepy voice barely masking his irritation.*

The voice at the other end chirps, "How come you're still asleep? What time is it out there anyway, twelve o'clock?"

Mark groans. "Six o'clock, you @#$%&*! It's three hours earlier here, not later. When are you going to get it right?"

"Whatever. Listen I got a great project for you. You'll love it, it's right up your alley."

It was Steve Newman, head of the information-technology practice for the East Coast office of Storm & Drang, a large management consulting company with offices worldwide. Steve is an old friend of Mark. Since their college days their careers have run parallel, Steve on the fast track with S & D and Mark as an independent consultant specializing in change management.

In spite of the early hour and his lack of sleep, Mark listens closely for the next hour and a half, interrupting only occasionally as Steve describes the project. He is intrigued. Besides he needs the work and is desperate to get out of town for a few days to escape the intolerable heat.

The project Steve describes is for Paws & Claws, one of the largest manufacturers of pet products in the world—dog and cat food, flea collars, pet toys, and the like. Paws & Claws has hired S & D to help develop a strategic management information system to be used by production teams in the company's factories located throughout the United States. The project is the brainchild and passion of a visionary, charismatic, and iconoclastic midlevel manager at Paws & Claws, Chris DeManconi.

Chris is the director of special projects reporting directly to the senior vice president for manufacturing for all of the Paws & Claws plants in North America. His job is a perfect match for his personality, essentially giving him free rein to explore innovative ways to improve manufacturing productivity. His latest idea, the one involving Steve and S & D, is his most ambitious and controversial to date.

According to Steve, Chris wants to reorganize the plants around "empowered" production teams with responsibility for producing different families of products. The production technology is different for each product family. For example, one production line can produce several different varieties of dry dog food—another, wet dog food—yet another, dry cat food—and so on for their entire product line. Each line is flexible and highly automated. By using different mixes of ingredients and raw materials the lines can shift from producing one product in its product family to another.

With the planned reorganization, the production teams would have responsibility for identifying cost-saving and revenue-generating "targets of opportunity" (as a former navy pilot, a "top gun," Chris is rather fond of military metaphors). The teams would then have the authority to implement whatever ideas they come up with to lower these costs. But Chris had an even more ambitious objective—to give the teams the authority and resources for making decisions about what products to produce, how much, and when. Marketing and sales would provide each team with a support person to help them make these strategic production decisions.

The information system—Strategic Information for Continuous Improvement in Manufacturing (SICIM)—is the principal resource to be used by the teams to analyze their costs of production and the potential profitability of different product mixes. Chris's idea is to create a system that provides each team with detailed, up-to-date information on their monthly production costs for everything they manufacture. It would also enable them to project costs, sales, and revenues for various product mixes so they could make strategic decisions about how much of each product to produce each month. His boss has reluctantly given him the go-ahead and allocated $5 million for the first phase of the project.

Chris has also managed to convince his boss to hire an outside vendor to develop the system instead of giving the job to the Paws & Claws MIS department. His reason for this end run is his belief, in his words, that "the technocrats in MIS haven't the foggiest notion of what I mean by 'empowerment via information.'" (He was going to put that expression—empowerment via information—on the T-shirts he was having made for the systems development team.) He just could not imagine the Paws & Claws conservative, traditional data-processing professionals being comfortable with the idea of putting information systems under the control of the people who most need them—the production teams and their managers. That is why he has contracted with Storm & Drang to develop the system.

This is where Mark comes in. Both Steve and Chris recognize that the critical factors in the success of this project are not exclusively technical. For one thing, the production teams need to be set up and trained to put their new roles, responsibilities, and technology to work. They also realize that Paws & Claws may have to change some personnel policies to bring them in line with the new, team-based work in the plants. Finally, they know that the systems development process itself will be difficult and potentially contentious, and they believe that they need someone like Mark to help them facilitate the project team meetings.

Once again, Chris decides to execute another end run—this time around the Paws & Claws personnel and human resources department. He has asked Steve to recommend an external consultant to help them with team building and with managing the change process. And that is why Steve is calling Mark at this ungodly hour.

In three days Mark is on his way to Paws & Claws corporate headquarters in Baltimore, trading the hot, dry southern California winds for the equally hot and unbearably humid East Coast of late summer. He is just as uncomfortable, but it doesn't seem to matter. He has work. The work sounds interesting and challenging. And he'll be in Maryland for the peak of the hard-shell crab season. What could be bad?

◆ ◆ ◆

THIS IS A BOOK about organizational change. But not just any kind of change. Our focus is on teams and information technology (IT)—two of the most important developments in organizations today. Year after year, organizations increase their investment in new information systems[2] and use teams to do more and more of their work.[3] The challenge these organizations face is how to fulfill the potential of these two promising and complex developments.

We will argue in this chapter and demonstrate throughout this book that each is necessary to take full advantage of the possibilities created by the other. Together, teams and new information technology can catalyze dramatic improvements in organizational performance. How to bring about this synergy, how to effect organizational change that integrates the two, is the subject of this book.

KNOWLEDGE IS THE KEY TO ORGANIZATIONAL PERFORMANCE

Knowledge work, knowledge workers, the knowledge society—these expressions reflect the growing recognition that knowledge is the key strategic resource of the postindustrial organization. To succeed in the fast-paced, intensely competitive global marketplace, organizations will have to learn how to generate, organize, manage, and apply knowledge more effectively. Whether solving production problems on the shop floor, creating new products in the laboratory, or mapping strategy in the executive suite, organizations need access to knowledge that is as broad as it is deep.[4]

That is why organizations are now so intensely interested in teams and information technology. The link between information technology, knowledge, and organizational performance is clear. Information technology provides access to diverse sources for specialized information and enhances our ability to analyze, manage, and apply this information to our work. While the link between teams, knowledge, and organizational performance may be less obvious, it is just as important. A team brings together different individuals who know and can do different things. It is a means of pooling and using the diverse "knowledges"[5] and skills of its members to accomplish mutual goals. When there is a synergy between teams and information technology, as pictured in figure 1–1, the contribution of the two to knowledge and organizational performance is greater than the sum of the parts.

Information Technology Can Make Teams More Effective

Teamwork is essential for organizational success. As Jon Katzenbach and Douglas Smith note in their book *The Wisdom of Teams,* teams are the "primary unit of performance for increasing numbers of organizations."

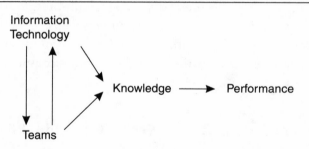

Managers can not master the opportunities and challenges now confronting them without emphasizing teams far more than ever before. The performance challenges that face large companies in every industry—for example, customer service, technological change, competitive threats, and environmental constraints—demand the kind of responsiveness, speed, on-line customization, and quality that is beyond the reach of individual performance. Teams can bridge this gap.[6]

If teamwork is the key to effective organizations, information is the key to effective teamwork. Consider for a moment Chris's project as depicted in the story that opens the chapter. He wants the production teams to use the new system to help identify ways to lower their production costs. The raw material for this analysis is information about costs associated with different stages and factors of production. The analytical process itself is also information based. And the result is information about where and how the teams can intervene to lower costs.

From this example, we can see that it is not enough to say that information is necessary for effective teamwork. In a practical sense, information *is* the work. Information is the raw material to be manipulated and transformed, and it is the basis for the process by which these actions occur. Information is what is exchanged by team members as they analyze and deliberate. Ultimately, it is the result of the process—the solutions they devise, the decisions they make, and the new information and knowledge they generate.

This is not just the case for work that has always been knowledge based, such as market research, engineering design, and systems development. As our story illustrates, all work is becoming more knowledge based, even the work of production teams. Therefore, team members need "tools" to help them gain access to this information, manage and analyze it, share it among themselves, and communicate it to others. These tools come in the form of new technology—it is what will enable teams to function effectively within the rich matrix of information that, from the executive suite to the shop floor, now comprises the very essence of modern work.

Teams Can Make Information Technology More Effective

In the late 1970s the personal computer sparked a wave of excitement about the promise of the information revolution. Optimists and futurists enthusiastically described the dramatic changes in our work lives that this revolution would engender. Developments in communications and network technology only reinforced their rosy picture of our future. Telecommuting instead of commuting, working at home in blue jeans rather than in the office in a suit, seamlessly integrating work into our busy personal schedules, all accompanied by productivity gains that have not been equaled since the introduction of the assembly line—these were the images that beckoned us toward the twenty-first century.[7]

Today, most of us still head out to work in the morning wearing something other than blue jeans. We fight mind-numbing traffic to get there and reserve our nonwork activities for what little time remains in the evenings and on weekends. And perhaps more disturbing for managers and many employees is that most organizations have little to show for their huge investments in new technology.[8]

But signs of a potentially dramatic "technology payoff" have finally begun to emerge. Blending redesigned corporate structures and work processes with the new technologies may be the key. Such integrated "sociotechnical" strategies are now helping more and more organizations fulfill the potential of their new technologies.[9] Unlike their less successful competitors, these organizations are not conducting business as usual; they are not using information technology to squeeze out incremental gains from existing tasks. They are using it to do new things, not just the same things in a better way.

Perhaps the most important "new" thing organizations can do with their new information technology is to integrate some of the very functions deconstructed by the division of labor. Since the earliest days of the industrial revolution, organizations have broken work down into well-defined sequences of separate tasks and functions and assigned these "pieces" to individual employees or departments. They then created elaborate control mechanisms—for example, formal policies, management hierarchies—to tie together these increasingly specialized functions. The end result was a highly bureaucratic organization with well-defined boundaries separating its many levels of authority and functional specializations. Information, work in progress, and decisions must sequentially pass through these boundaries, from one department or individual to another, before the final product or service reaches the customer.

By now, most everyone is aware of the limitations of this cumbersome design. Whenever problems or delays occur, as they often do, trying to identify the source of the problem and facilitate the process can tax the patience of even the most understanding customer. The problem-solving approach typically used involves passing the buck—or, more to the point, the customer—back and forth between one department or individual to another until the problem is finally solved. Ultimately, the process is costly to the organization and frustrating to the customer.

Work processes designed around new information technology can look quite different. Information technology makes it possible to integrate the various functions that make up the process. It opens up the boundaries so that pooled knowledge can be brought to bear on complex, time-critical issues. Everyone involved in the work process can have access to the same information and can therefore work together to serve customer needs. People can work as a team to accomplish their goals more effectively. Thus, the technology creates the potential, and teams help the technology fulfill that potential.

Organizational Change Supports Teams and Technology

Integrating teams and information technology is an important step toward high performance, but it is not enough. The growing use of teams and information technology has significant implications for the organization. The nature of the organization itself—its structures, policies, and technology platforms—must change to support the teams and their technologies as they operate within, and increasingly across, its boundaries.

Developing new technologies and team designs should be embedded within a broader effort to truly unleash their full potential.[10] Team-based, technology-enabled organizations need to create high-level structures, policies, and systems to support individual teams and the information tools they use. This "macrostructure" must be able to integrate team efforts and technology to serve overall organizational goals. In effect, this macrostructure should do for the organization what our skeletons and nervous systems do for our bodies—support and connect our muscles and organs.

We can now tie all of these theses into the overarching premise of our book: *Achieving high levels of organizational performance requires the integrated development of information technology, team structures, and the overall organizational context. The development processes should be interrelated so that designs in all three areas will be mutually reinforcing.* But how is this integrated development process to be carried out? This is where most change projects go awry. Designing a "good" technology is no guarantee that it will be used well, or even used at all.[11] Similarly, collaborative intentions are easier to state—as in, "we will now all work together as a team"—than to practice.[12] Implementing successful change in any one of these areas is difficult, but when it involves all three—technology, teams, and the overall organization—the challenges can be overwhelming. That is why we devote so much of this book to describing the details of this change process.[13] As we will see, nothing is as complex as the implementation of a seemingly straightforward vision.

THE MDI FRAMEWORK: A PREVIEW

In the chapters that follow we describe a framework for addressing team/technology/organization change and present specific recommendations on how to put it in place. We refer to this framework as *mutual design and implementation,* or MDI. Our definition of *mutual* reflects both of its meanings in everyday use: (1) correlations, connectedness, and reciprocal influence among things, events, and ideas, and (2) common interests and relationships among people.

The first meaning refers to the focus of this book—new information technology, the teams that will use this technology (we will hereafter refer to these teams as *user teams*), and the organizational context for this use. The mutuality describes the interdependency of all three, as shown in figure 1–2. This figure forms a triangle, which is also the Greek letter *delta,* the symbol for change.[14] Since a change in one corner of the

Figure 1–2   Mutual Design and Implementation Framework

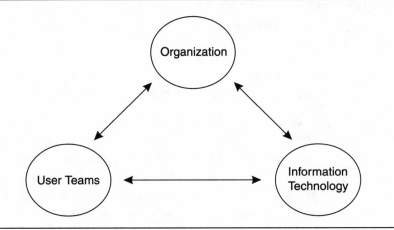

Note: To be precise, the technology and teams should be embedded in the
organization context. We have chosen to use a simpler figure to emphasize the
interconnectedness of the three.

triangle will necessarily influence the others, all three should be addressed to ensure that all changes will be complementary and mutually
supportive.

The second meaning of *mutual* reflects our emphasis on the many
diverse people and constituencies that need to collaborate in team,
technology, and organizational design. Integrated development of all
three is a difficult task that involves complex decisions and multidimensional designs. Trade-offs and compromises will have to be made and,
ultimately, designs linked and integrated. This process requires varied
high-level skills and knowledge, and many people will be profoundly
affected by the decisions made. A number of people with different kinds
of expertise and concerns will need to collaborate throughout the process of change.

This collaboration should include those people whose work will be
most affected by the changes, whose knowledge and skills are relevant
to the change effort, and whose commitment to the changes will play
an important role in their success. These people are the *stakeholders* in
the development process; they have a stake in the outcomes and are
critical to its success. Representatives from all stakeholder groups need
to be involved in the MDI process. The stakeholder representatives
make up the MDI project team (hereafter referred to as the *MDI team*).

Changing Organizations with Teams and Technology | 11

The members of the MDI team are the primary agents of the change effort. They will be responsible for designing the technology and the user teams, putting them in place, and recommending the organizational changes needed to support them.

UNDERLYING PRINCIPLES AND ASSUMPTIONS

Several principles underlie our framework and all of the recommendations we offer. Often, they are only indirectly reflected in the ongoing discussion; at other times, they emerge explicitly as we address particular issues and topics. They are important for a number of reasons. They hold together what might otherwise appear to be disparate topics. They also help to distinguish what we are proposing here from seemingly similar approaches and frameworks proposed elsewhere. But perhaps most important, they should direct the entire MDI process. Just as information technology professionals talk about system platforms to describe the technological base for specific applications, we can view these principles as a cognitive platform from which specific MDI activities can be most effectively approached. In effect, these principles are the platform on which our framework and recommendations rest.

Using Tension and Conflict Creatively

The first principle concerns the conflict and tension that inevitably arise when people work closely together. It redresses the relentlessly upbeat imagery employed in much of the popular literature and by many organizational development (OD) practitioners to describe teams and teamwork. Learning to work together effectively can be messy. It means that diverse viewpoints, positions, and goals need to be reconciled and that compromises and trade-offs need to be made. Compromise means that no one gets everything he or she wants and that everyone has to give up something he or she values. Conflict and tension are inevitable in these new working relationships, and resistance to moving in this direction is difficult to avoid.[15]

If individuals, teams, and organizations are not aware that some conflict and tension are inevitable, they may be unprepared to deal with them when they arise. They might then become discouraged and eventually abandon the effort altogether. By acknowledging and accepting conflict, teams and organizations can avoid being overwhelmed by it and instead use it as a source of creativity. To emphasize this potential, we choose to refer to these forces as *creative* tension and conflict and attempt to identify throughout this book how they can be managed and their potential fulfilled.

Designing for Surprises

A second principle concerns the importance of designing teams, technologies, and organizations for spontaneity, serendipity, and surprise. In recent years, the world has witnessed the failure of command-and-control economic planning systems, which require specific and immutable long-term goals and detailed and rigid plans to achieve these goals. Given the pace and unpredictability of change in their current social, economic, and technological environments, organizations would be foolish to pursue similar approaches to their own planning efforts, especially those involving their information systems.

An alternative approach to such inflexible planning is offered by the Italian organizational theorist Claudio Ciborra. He urges organizations to encourage and support *bricolage* ("tinkering" in French) by end users so that "new ideas from the bottom of the organization [can] bubble up."[16] The rationale is that "the more volatile the markets and the technologies, the more likely it is that effective solutions will be embedded in everyday experience and local knowledge. This is the petrie dish for tinkering; here creative applications that have strategic impact will be invented, engineered, and tried out."[17]

One of the prerequisites for productive tinkering is the use of information technology to *augment* rather than *automate* work tasks. Instead of designing systems that simply replace what people do with a computer routine or program, they can be designed so that they enable users to do what they have not been able to do before. The kinds of labor savings realized from systems that automate tasks are in any case rarely great enough to justify the costs of the systems themselves. On the other hand, systems that augment user capabilities and permit them to explore and tinker are more likely to lead to significant process improvements as well as new products and services. To use Ciborra's terms, the point is to design systems and organizations to support *bricolage,* thereby augmenting the capabilities and tapping the creativity of teams and their members.[18]

Taking a Multilevel Perspective on Change

Unlike other approaches to and frameworks for organizational change, such as reengineering, which call for change directed from the top down, the point of entry for application of our framework can come at most any level. Senior management can use MDI to make the organization more team based and information savvy. Cross-functional product development teams can use it to upgrade their information tools to help them with new projects. A manufacturing plant can apply the framework to reorganize around shop-floor production teams.

Regardless of where the process starts, other levels should eventually be involved. If beginning at the topmost levels of the organization or division, the ultimate point of action is with the teams that will be doing the work on a daily basis—in the words of an interviewee in one of our research studies, "where the rubber meets the road."[19] If beginning with the teams, high-level organizational change will eventually be necessary to integrate and support their work. Without this high-level change, team-based efforts are unlikely to succeed in the long run.

The key point is that organizational and technological change needs to be addressed at several levels—for teams (the micro level), for the overall organization (the macro level), and at levels in between. Furthermore, these changes need to be integrated. Individual teams should be aligned with and supported by the larger organization; the information systems they use should be compatible with other systems and link individual teams and other departments and units throughout the organization. Finally, carrying out these multilevel changes requires a multilevel approach. Integrating top-down and bottom-up approaches can be a powerful source of creative tension for those organizations that can manage this potentially incendiary combination.[20]

Creating Open-ended, Iterative Learning Processes

Effective organizations are open to change and committed to innovation. Instead of trying to minimize or resist change, these organizations encourage and nurture change and learn how to manage it so they can take advantage of the opportunities it presents. Therefore, all efforts to change should be viewed as ongoing and continual experiments that can produce learnings useful to the design and implementation of further change. This is a difficult and challenging perspective for most organizations to adopt, especially when significant commitments of effort and time and large sums of money are involved, as they typically are in most large-scale technological change. Organizations and managers often insist on "getting it right the first time." If so, "right" may well end up being far less than what could have been achieved and not enough to justify the costs of the effort.

To learn from their efforts to change, those involved should evaluate the effectiveness of their efforts frequently so they can modify designs and implementation plans as needed. As obvious as this might seem, this principle is far easier to state than to practice. While some of the difficulty arises from the technical and methodological nature of this activity, the problem is largely political and psychological. Many people, work units, and organizations feel threatened by the prospect of having their performance assessed and evaluated. They are afraid that they will appear inadequate and incompetent. The ability to overcome this fear and replace it with a willingness to take risks, occasionally fail, and learn from the experience is the hallmark of innovative employees and effective management.

Furthermore, it is a mistake to view this process as a linear progression from a defined beginning to a defined end. Since technology and organizational environments are constantly changing, the process is never complete. It continues indefinitely as the organization strives for a competitive technological advantage and adapts to (or tries to shape) an increasingly turbulent environment. What usually happens, according to social science researcher J. D. Eveland, "is that about two-thirds of the way through the project, things have changed—either the company, the environment, or the technology—to the point where backtracking, or even restarting the process is a necessity."[21] And the outcomes that are eventually produced may look quite different from what was originally intended.

The only way to deal with these open-ended, iterative learning processes is to make them an intrinsic part of the way organizations do business. Starting from scratch with each new attempt at change is prohibitively difficult, inefficient, and expensive. Organizations need to develop the capability to deal with change on an ongoing basis. This can be accomplished by adopting and institutionalizing a framework, process, or approach—such as the one presented in this book—that offers an experience-based means for dealing with change as a positive aspect of organizational life. Doing so will enable organizations to learn from previous efforts and to improve on these efforts in subsequent projects.

CONCLUSION

Both teams and new information systems can be powerful engines of organizational change and performance; each is necessary to realize the full potential of the other. How to create these teams and the information systems they will use is the focus of this book.

In the chapters that follow we describe a framework for change that is integrative, proactive, collaborative, and concrete. We offer specific recommendations on ways to use information technology to make teams more effective and to use teams to fulfill the potential of new technologies. We demonstrate how organizations can develop and integrate team-based work, new technologies, and organizational change to create smarter work units and more effective organizations. But we first need to know more about the focus of the MDI effort—the technology, the user teams, and the organization. The next chapter discusses the concepts, issues, and trends that are critical to understanding the MDI framework and the recommendations that follow from it.

◆ ◆ ◆

LATE MORNING, early September, Chris DeManconi's office at Paws & Claws corporate headquarters, Baltimore . . .

Mark's first meeting with Chris is winding down. For the last hour and a half he has listened, fascinated, as Chris laid out the specifics of the project. The sources of Chris's inspiration varied widely—from Frederick W. Taylor to chaos theory, seasoned liberally with new age metaphysics and emerging management paradigms. The range of his references and ideas made Mark's head swim as he tried to follow the frequently elusive thread of the largely one-way conversation. What emerged, however, was impressive—an expansive vision, in Chris's words, of "a technology-enabled, team-based, high-performance organization."

The details of Chris's vision were equally impressive, particularly his view of the information system that would be the core of the project. He described several different modules planned for the final version of the system. One module would provide comprehensive, fine-grained cost breakdowns for each product. Two modules would be expert systems; one would project the profitability of different product mixes within each product family, the other would enable each team to evaluate their competitors. Another module was designed to be an E-mail system connecting all of the plants and corporate headquarters. Mark lost track after that, but Chris had described several other modules. Chris and Steve had also already worked through many of the details of the human-computer interface—how users would navigate through the system, what information would be presented on each screen, and how it would be presented.

On the other hand, Chris's vision concerning the teams that would be using the system was rather vague. He mentioned several times that he expected the technology to "drive the teams." He also expected to use his considerable experience and skills in group facilitation and team building to create teams in the plants. "Once we've got the system built, you and I will work with the production workers to get them working together as a team. I've done a lot of team building and group facilitation so it shouldn't take us long to get these teams into shape," he boasted.

His idea was to use the SICIM project team members as guinea pigs to try out some new team-building techniques he could then use with the production teams. He described several of the techniques he had in mind. Mark recognized a number of them, the others were clearly of Chris's invention, relying heavily on flip charts, colored markers, and Chris's dramatic flair. "This is what I'm really interested in these days. When this project is finished, I'm going to become a consultant, like you," he confides. Mark winces, hoping Chris doesn't notice. Chris's plan is to organize a retreat for the project team to get them working together more effectively while trying out some of the techniques he hopes to use in the plants.

"I'll need your help with this. What are your plans? Can I talk you into hanging around for a couple of weeks so the two of us can organize this thing?"

"Sure." ("Great. I can taste those crabs already.")

"How about if we start tonight over dinner? Do you like Mexican?"

("Mexican? In Baltimore?") "Love it. Just tell me where and when and I'll meet you there."

2

Cornerstones of the MDI Process

Two weeks later, the Paws & Claws Conference Center in the woods of Western Maryland . . .

It had been a grueling day. Chris had everybody up at 6 A.M. for a three-mile run. It was still dark, the trail was rocky, and the revelries of the previous evening had run late. Not surprisingly, many walked. The real fun began in earnest after breakfast. First, most everyone struggled with the ropes course—to build confidence, according to Chris. Then came the rock climbing, also to build confidence as well as develop trust. Unfortunately, trust could hardly describe what the climbers felt. Who could blame them given the bewildered looks on the faces of their climbing partners holding the ropes that were supposed to prevent their certain death in case of a fall. Finally, they broke down into teams for a problem-solving exercise. Finding a way to safely cross a wide, chilly, and fast-flowing stream was supposed to build teamwork and test their ability to work together. From the number of shouts, splashes, and angry outbursts, one could reasonably surmise that few passed that test.

Now they were adjourning to the conference room for their first meeting as the new SICIM project team. Actually, the membership of the new team was the same as the former team, mostly technical consultants and systems developers from Storm and Drang. But their responsibilities were about to be significantly expanded. Besides designing the system, they would also be responsible for developing and trying out the team-building techniques the production teams would use to help them work together more effectively. "You can adapt some of the techniques we used today" [several people audibly groan] "plus some of the techniques I'll show you tonight as we develop a mission statement for the project.

*Don't worry, I know that's not your thing, but I'll work closely with you on it."
Either he doesn't notice or chooses to ignore the skeptical looks on their faces.
"Let's get started!"*

*For the next three hours, Chris is a whirlwind of activity. Working the room
like a borscht-belt comic on speed, he alternately cajoles, prods, and harangues the
members of the team. He massages their responses and comments, feeds it back
to them for elaboration or critique, resolves differences and conflict, and summarizes their sometimes awkward contributions with clarity and flair. The handful
of particularly reluctant participants get special attention from Chris. At first
withdrawn and even sullen, they are masterfully drawn out by Chris, and before
long they are talking and arguing with the rest. Mark, who has the job of
recording their work on flip charts, can barely keep up. Chris's energy seems
boundless.*

*Later that evening, Chris, Mark, and Steve adjourn to the bar to discuss what
has happened so far. The glow brought on by several drams of a very old and
expensive single-malt whiskey seems to have finally loosened Steve from his
normally professional reserve. He begins to tell his client what he really thinks
of this dramatic shift in the focus and approach of the project.*

$$\blacklozenge \ \blacklozenge \ \blacklozenge$$

Before describing how to initiate and conduct an MDI project,
we need to know some basics. In this chapter, we define, describe, and
otherwise clarify what we mean by teams, technology, and organizations—the cornerstones of the MDI process. Because teams are not only
a focus of change (as in user teams) but are also the agents of change (as
in MDI team, the vehicle by which MDI projects are carried out), much
of this chapter is devoted to providing fundamental knowledge about
what teams are and how to make them more effective.

TECHNOLOGY

In this book, the term *technology* refers to the information and communications technologies, systems, and tools used by individuals and teams
in their work. It does not refer to production technology that is controlled directly by a computer and does not require direct human
involvement. As Shoshana Zuboff notes in her book *In the Age of the
Smart Machine,* however, "The devices that automate by translating
information into action also register data about those automated activi-

ties, thus generating new streams of information."[1] This process of "informating," as she calls it, can be used to indicate potential problems, provide diagnostic data on the source of these problems, and help project future demand and production. For these uses, human operators must be brought back into the loop to analyze this information and make judgments and decisions based on these analyses.

Our definition therefore refers to information systems in which humans are in the loop, in which knowledge-based, human interactions are critical to the way the technology performs. It excludes robotics and highly automated, numerically controlled manufacturing processes, but it does include the "informating" systems that help human operators troubleshoot the process. From this discussion we can see that the focus of our book is not the production technology used to manufacture Paws & Claws consumer products but the systems that monitor the production process and provide operators with information about the process (how fast the production line is moving, conditions out of tolerance, etc.). SICIM, the system that provides them with information about their costs of production, also falls within our use of *technology*.

A final note about terminology: the terms *tools* and *applications* are used interchangeably to describe systems used by teams or individuals to meet their particular needs. In contrast to these microlevel systems, we use the term *infrastructure* to describe the information technology hardware, platforms, software environments, networks, and the like that serve the entire organization.

Increasingly, information technology infrastructures are designed to enable individuals and teams to communicate and work with other individuals and teams. With respect to teams, linking and coordinating technologies are the most important. Otherwise the issues of development and implementation are not all that different from what they are for individual, noncollaborating users. So when we talk about information technology and systems, often we are referring to the networks and client-server systems that enable people to work together and share information even if they are not located in the same office, department, or site.

Of these systems, none has more potential impact than the networks that link different organizations and thereby help potential collaborators transcend the geographic, cultural, or political distances that separate them.

Whether they are referred to collectively as the National Information Infrastructure (NII)[2] or the information highway, interorganizational communications networks may be the most important technological development of the transmillenial era. As telephone, cable TV, computer, entertainment, and publishing industries continue to merge, access to information and people—anytime, anywhere—is no longer just the fevered dream of science-fiction writers and futurists. It is an emerging reality for more and more organizations and individuals connected via their local area networks (LANs) to external networks, which are connected in turn to networks of networks such as the Internet.[3]

As a result, it will soon be possible to team up with almost anyone, regardless of where they work and who they work for. Furthermore, the quality of the interactions within a team need not be compromised by distance. Because of the expected broad bandwidth made possible by the NII, relatively inexpensive, full-motion videoconferencing will be able to capture the nuances of face-to-face interactions that might otherwise be lost in the ether. If the NII actually lives up to its promise, it will offer these geographically dispersed teams just about all of the information and analytical tools they could possibly want.

The implications are profound. Networked information and communication technologies permit entire firms to reconsider traditional boundaries and invent new organizational forms. Equally significant, such technologies also make organizational boundaries more permeable. Successful examples of customer and supplier firms linked via networked computers are by now widely familiar; many such linkups have influenced entire industries. American Hospital Supply, which linked pharmacies directly to its order departments, and American Airlines' SABRE system, which linked flight schedules and reservations systems directly to travel agencies, are probably two of the best known.[4]

The payoffs from a national information infrastructure may well result as much from its use by organizations and their employees as from its use by consumers for entertainment and various other services. Its immediate potential was illustrated in the aftermath of the January 1994 Northridge earthquake, which devastated critical segments of southern California's freeway system. For several months following the quake, telecommuting offered many people an alternative to jammed streets and frayed nerves.[5] But its potential goes well beyond its role as a transportation alternative. The ultimate success of the NII will rest in part on its ability to provide access to the people, information, and applications needed to generate innovative ideas, make informed decisions, and implement effective plans, programs, and policies.[6]

The success of the NII will also rest on the ability of organizations to take advantage of this access. No doubt there will be "haves" and "have-nots"—those who have access to communication networks and the skills to use them to their advantage and those who do not. When talking about organizations, however, the "class" distinction arises not just from socioeconomic disadvantage but also from a lack of vision and commitment. What will distinguish the organizational haves from the have-nots is a network culture. Organizations that are successful in creating this culture will reap the benefits of the NII; those that do not will become the new organizational underclass.

ORGANIZATIONS

We use the term *organization* in two ways. Our general use casts a wide net and includes large and small manufacturing and service businesses, government agencies at all levels (local, state, regional, federal), and nonprofit firms of all kinds, to mention some of the most obvious categories. When we refer to an organization as a focus for mutual design and implementation, however, it most often means something less than the entire firm, agency, or institution. During the MDI process, the MDI team may identify issues over which it has little authority. For example, it may decide that existing compensation systems cannot effectively reward team performance. The compensation structure is usually set at a higher level for the entire company or some semiautonomous business unit (division) within the company. Or the work redesigns and technologies the MDI team develops may span the boundaries of several teams and units and require a significant redesign of larger organizational work processes.

Therefore, the MDI team may need to address its recommendations for organizational change to the level that can approve and implement them. In some companies, this may be at the highest level, where policy is set for the entire company; in other companies, large ones in particular, this may be at the division level or even lower. So, *organization,* as we use it within the context of MDI, usually refers to the level within the larger body that has the authority to implement the kinds of systemic changes needed to support individual teams and to integrate the activities of many.

There is another sense in which our use of *organization* is unusual, a sense that reflects the ongoing evolution of organizational forms. During the hey-day of mergers and acquisitions in the 1980s, our notions of what constitute organizational boundaries began to change. The emerging era of transnationals, alliances, and metaorganizations may finish the job, assisted to a considerable degree by internal and external communications networks. As a result, organizational boundaries have grown increasingly permeable and difficult to identify. With access to networked systems, these boundaries need no longer be barriers to cross-organizational collaboration. Teams made up of individuals and groups from different organizations can work together on projects that exceed the resources and capabilities of any single organization. Identifying the appropriate "organizational context" for instituting cross–organizational change through teams and technology will challenge the ingenuity of even the most resourceful and creative MDI team.

TEAMS

When it comes to organizational effectiveness, no topic is more important than teams. Moreover, no topic is more popular or more widely misunderstood. We have all worked in teams, so we all figure that we know something about them. Many of us played on athletic teams in our youth, and just about all of us have been on work teams as adults. It is probably not surprising then that almost everyone thinks they know a great deal about them. In many cases this knowledge seems to boil down to the core belief that effective teamwork requires little more than commitment and a willingness to make personal sacrifices in the service of team goals. Exhorting people to pull together and facilitating interpersonal interactions are the favored means for eliciting this commitment and sacrifice.

A number of misconceptions underlie this belief. Shortly, we will attempt to correct these misconceptions and replace them with a sound, pragmatic perspective on teams and effective team performance. But first we need to define what we mean by *team*. Calling a group of people a team does not necessarily make them one. The characteristics that define a team are task interdependence and a shared goal or purpose—that is, the work of each team member is dependent on the work of at least some of the others. For example, in a production team one member may pass on the product of his or her work for another member to work on. Or the interdependence may be more interactive, such as in a writing team, where the members go back and forth in rapid, overlapping succession creating complex concepts and searching for ways to express them. By this definition, a word-processing pool or a department of field engineers who work on separate projects are not teams. They work independently of each other except for the occasion when one has to back up another because of work overload, absence, or poor performance. For the most part and most of the time, they are not interdependent. Therefore, they are not, for our purposes, teams.

"A team is a team is a team," Gertrude Stein might say if she were reincarnated today as a manager or an organizational consultant. Like most people, she would probably assume that all teams are pretty much the same. Though this view is widely held, it is inaccurate and tends to overlook important differences in the various ways people can work together. Organizations that fail to recognize these differences run the risk of creating, designing, and managing teams inappropriately.

Five types of teams can be found in organizations today: (1) work teams, (2) project and development teams, (3) parallel teams, (4) management teams, and (5) ad hoc networks.[7] These types define a continuum of sorts. At one end are the work teams, which tend to be formal, ongoing, and have permanent members. At the other end are the loose, informal collections of people we call ad hoc networks (to distinguish them from technology networks). They are less bound by time, and their membership is more fluid and diffuse. The other team types fall somewhere in between.

Work Teams

The work team is the type team most people think of when talking about teams. They are essentially continuing work units responsible for producing products or providing services. Unlike the other team types, they perform regular, ongoing work. Membership is typically stable, full-time, and well defined. As a result, it is easy to identify who is on the team and who is not. Figure 2–1 illustrates this team type.

Traditionally, work teams have been directed by supervisors who

Figure 2–1 Work Teams

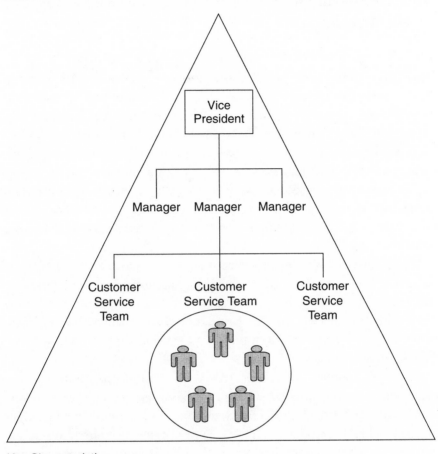

Key Characteristics:
• Permanent Work Units
• Produce Products or Provide Services
• Ongoing Work
• Stable Composition

Source: S.A. Mohrman, S.G. Cohen, and A.M. Mohrman, Jr. *Designing Team-Based Organizations: New Forms for Knowledge Work.* (San Francisco: Jossey-Bass, 1995). Copyright 1995 by Jossey-Bass Inc., Publishers. Reprinted by permission of the publisher.

make most of the decisions about who does what and how. Lately, an alternative form—referred to by a variety of labels, including *self-managed, self-directed,* and *empowered*—has attracted the enthusiastic attention of many managers and consultants. The hallmark of the self-managed work team (SMWT) is the participation of all team members in decisions that were formerly the exclusive province of supervisors and managers.

The SMWT is just the most recent reincarnation of a work-team alternative that has actually been around in one form or other since the late 1940s.[8] This time around, the concept appears, as they say in Hollywood, "to have legs." The reasons probably can be found in increased concerns over global competition and the accumulating evidence that SMWTs may actually be an effective alternative to traditional work teams in many situations.[9] More and more companies, managers, and consultants now believe that SMWTs can improve the quality of products and services. Since SMWTs typically take on supervisory and in some cases managerial responsibilities, many companies also use them to reduce their need for managers and supervisors and thereby cut costs.[10]

While the jury is still out concerning the effectiveness of SMWTs, more and more organizations are moving aggressively in this direction and reporting positive results.[11] Procter & Gamble, General Motors, Texas Instruments, and the Aid Association for Lutherans, a Wisconsin-based insurance firm, are just a few of the companies that have successfully implemented SMWTs.

These examples illustrate the SMWT's wide applicability. These teams can be used in many situations where people work interdependently and can be made collectively responsible for producing a product for or providing a service to an internal or external customer. While the concept has most frequently been used in the design of production and assembly teams in manufacturing settings, it is increasingly being applied to administrative and professional support teams and customer sales and service teams. Indeed, wider and more intensified penetration into white-collar and knowledge-based work seems a logical next stage in the evolution of SMWTs. This kind of work requires greater flexibility and informed point-of-action decision making. The SMWT concept is a natural fit for these emerging needs.

Project and Development Teams

Knowledge workers drawn from different functional units typically make up the project and development team. They are brought together to produce one-time outputs, such as a new product or service to be marketed by the company, a new information system, or a new plant (see diagram A in figure 2–2). When their work is complete, project teams usually disband and the individual members either return to their functional units or move on to other project teams. Because these teams are temporary and cut across functions, organizations can use them to create the right mix of knowledge and skills needed for particular projects without giving up the advantages of functional specialization. Some companies, particularly in high-tech industries, are even going so far as to discard functional organization entirely and structure all of their work around project teams (see diagram B in figure 2–2).

Since they produce a one-time output, project teams are charged with tasks that are less predictable and routine than those of formal work groups, which produce the same product or service over and over again. As a consequence, project teams tend to have broad mandates and considerable authority to make point-of-action decisions. Typically, they are responsible for defining the conceptual framework for the project and identifying objectives and methods for accomplishing their tasks. Thus, project teams are self-managing. Teams cannot solve non-routine problems or create innovative products and processes without having the authority to make key decisions. Their autonomy is not unlimited, however. They do need to function within the strategic parameters set by the organization and maintain linkages with the stake-holder groups and departments they represent.

Project and development teams have been on the organizational scene for quite some time. They have been widely used in the aerospace and defense industry since World War II. In recent years their use has spread to all kinds of organizations. As work continues to grow more complex, requiring greater breadth as well as greater depth of knowledge, project teams will become even more widespread and commonplace than they are today. Since the MDI team is a project team, we discuss this team type in considerable detail in the next several chapters.

Parallel Teams

Parallel teams are similar to project teams in several respects. They literally exist in parallel with the rest of the organization, pulling to-gether people from different work units or different jobs to perform tasks or functions that can not be accomplished within the existing formal structures. The difference is in the nature of their tasks and the intensity

Figure 2–2 Project and Development Teams

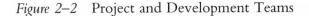

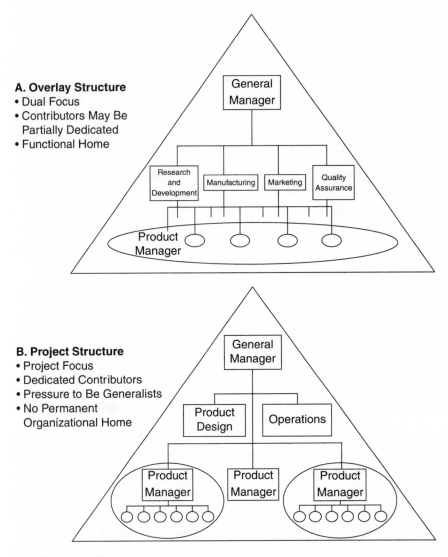

A. Overlay Structure
• Dual Focus
• Contributors May Be
  Partially Dedicated
• Functional Home

General Manager

Research and Development | Manufacturing | Marketing | Quality Assurance

Product Manager

B. Project Structure
• Project Focus
• Dedicated Contributors
• Pressure to Be Generalists
• No Permanent
  Organizational Home

General Manager

Product Design | Operations

Product Manager | Product Manager | Product Manager

Key Characteristics:
• Temporary Structures
• Produce One-time Outputs
• Diverse, Specialized Expertise
• Broad Decision-Making Authority

Source: S.A. Mohrman, S.G. Cohen, and A.M. Mohrman, Jr. *Designing Team-Based Organizations: New Forms for Knowledge Work.* (San Francisco: Jossey-Bass, 1995). Copyright 1995 by Jossey-Bass Inc., Publishers. Reprinted by permission of the publisher.

Figure 2–3   Parallel Teams

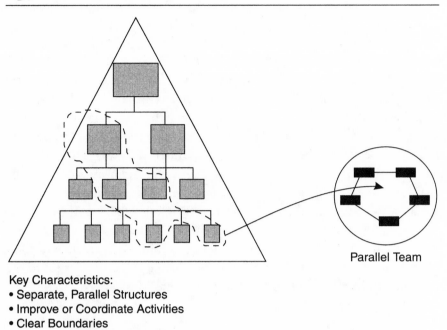

Parallel Team

Key Characteristics:
• Separate, Parallel Structures
• Improve or Coordinate Activities
• Clear Boundaries
• Make Recommendations

of effort needed to perform their tasks. Rather than creating new products, systems, or other complex and unique outputs, parallel teams perform coordination, problem-solving, and improvement-oriented tasks (see figure 2–3).[12] Therefore, parallel team members do not need to be as intensively involved as project team members. Typically, they will meet for a few hours every couple of weeks or so while continuing to do their regular jobs. The authority of such a team over issues with impact extending beyond itself is typically limited. If so, the team can only make recommendations to be considered by others higher up the organizational hierarchy.

Specific examples of parallel teams include:

♦ a team of trainers from different plants within the same company formed to plan and coordinate training programs across the company;

♦ several members of a work team that meet regularly to discuss and solve production problems; and

◆ a task force made up of employees from various units and levels organized to make recommendations on how to improve service to internal and external customers.

While these teams have been around for some time, the recent surge of interest in "quality" has dramatically boosted their appeal. It is hard to find an organization of midsize or larger that has not implemented several of these teams in the last few years.[13] The widespread popularity of parallel teams can be explained by a number of factors. First, they are easier to implement than other team types. In addition, unlike self-managed work teams and project teams, they require no shifts in managerial power and authority and are therefore less threatening. Finally, as noted earlier, they require no change in the structure of the organization. Because of these factors, as well as accumulating evidence of their beneficial impact on organizational performance,[14] we can expect to see continued growth in the use of this team type in the years to come.

Management Teams

As the name suggests, management teams are composed of the managers responsible for integrating the activities of the units that report to the individual members of the team (see figure 2–4). As Susan Mohrman, Susan Cohen, and Allan Mohrman describe these teams, they are "responsible for the coordinated management of a number of sub-units (teams, work groups) that are interdependent in the accomplishment of a collective output, such as an entire process or product."[15] The subunits are often linked within an overall process. The role of the management team is to provide the individual units with direction and resources as well as to manage the larger unit or process these units make up (a division or strategic business unit). Management teams also play a critical role in the MDI process, as the steering committee responsible for overseeing the overall project (to be discussed in chapter 3).

The use of management teams, like that of all the team types, is growing, especially the use of executive teams at the highest levels of the organization. Their collective expertise and shared responsibility are often the best way to deal with the complexity and turbulence of the global business environment. Management teams are also playing an increasingly important role at the level of the strategic business unit, as

Figure 2–4 Management Teams

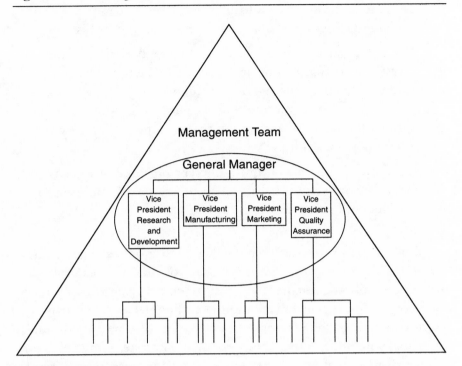

Key Characteristics:
• Permanent Structures
• Provide Coordinated Management of Subunits:
 (1) Provide Direction, (2) Allocate Resources
• Hierarchical Authority

the means for accomplishing the lateral integration of interdependent units across key business processes.

Ad Hoc Networks

The fifth team type is a collaborative form that most people might not even think of as a team. Consider the following examples:

◆ The members of a cross-functional quality improvement team, after completing their work and making recommendations to senior management, decide to continue to keep in touch to help each other with other issues and problems that might come up in their work.

- A group of workshop attendees from different locations within the same company decide to use the company's E-mail system to continue discussions on the topic raised in the workshop.

- A high-tech manufacturer creates a "dispersed learning network" to disseminate information about successful and unsuccessful innovation practices throughout the company. The network is designed "to overcome the tendency for innovation to be an isolated phenomenon and to foster peer consulting as a learning and support mechanism."[16]

- A number of individuals from different organizations, many of them anonymous, participate in an online discussion group on flexible work schedules on the Internet.[17]

Ad hoc networks consist of individuals and groups connected by a shared interest or purpose. Members join voluntarily and usually participate on a part-time basis. They may work in separate locations and even work for different organizations—ad hoc networks in many organizations may include customers, suppliers, and/or peers with similar professional interests. As the above examples illustrate, ad hoc networks can be created intentionally or they can emerge spontaneously as work-related tasks and responsibilities bring people into unplanned contact with each other. Informal relationships may result from these contacts, defined in part by their shared concerns and objectives. The relationships are then maintained and strengthened by phone calls, newsletters, meetings, memos, casual conversations in hallways, or E-mail communications. (Figure 2–5 illustrates this last team type.)

Probably the most important defining characteristic of this team type, the characteristic that distinguishes it from the others, is the lack of clear boundaries between the ad hoc network and the rest of the organization. Membership tends to be fluid and diffuse, with members joining and leaving as the defining purpose of the network evolves and the needs and interests of the members change. Therefore, individual members often are not able to identify all of the other members and may be aware of only those participants with whom they have current and direct links. The loosely bound, fluid nature of ad hoc networks is also the source of their unique advantage—the flexibility to respond rapidly to changing conditions.

Figure 2–5   Ad Hoc Networks

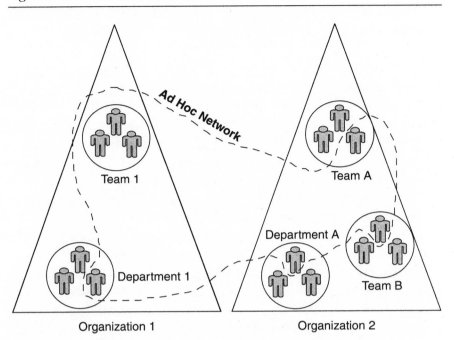

Key Characteristics:
- Temporary, Collaborative Forms
- Individuals and Teams Connected by Shared Interests
- Part-Time
- Fluid and Diffuse Membership
- Loosely Bound

Even though the nature of their boundaries distinguishes ad hoc networks from other team types, this difference primarily reflects a difference in perspective and time. In effect, the network bears the same relationship to the other team types that the "primordial soup" did for the first life on earth: it can act as a broad, amorphous, preexisting structure from which more defined types of teams can evolve. For example, in one large computer company the sales and customer service organization is designed as an ad hoc network of people with responsibilities for either particular systems or major customers. They use this network to create project teams to respond to the opportunities presented by particular customers. From this example, we can see that the factor that transforms the informal, amorphous nature of an ad hoc network into another team type is an explicit defining goal, usually to develop or produce something such as a system, a product, or a set of recommendations.

After decades of trying to ignore or actively suppress these informal, and often contrary social organisms, managers are beginning to view ad hoc networks as productive complements to regular, ongoing work. As a result, some companies are exploring ways to make these informal, spontaneous collaborations more explicit, intentional, and effective. Most notably, many organizations are now implementing new communications networks to link people and groups, regardless of location and schedule. The promise of collaboration across boundaries is now a reality because of these modern communications systems. They provide the infrastructure that makes ad hoc networks viable. They are the catalyst for transforming these social networks into the building blocks of revolutionary new intra- and interorganizational forms.

Despite the recent enthusiasm and optimism about the promise offered by networking people with network systems, the reality remains less than the hype. What may ultimately make the difference is the growing role of diverse, specialized knowledge in contemporary work. Ad hoc networks offer easy, flexible, and spontaneous access to knowledge. Teams can be formed rapidly in response to changing needs, and everyone can share the pooled knowledge and experience of the entire organization. The learning organization creates the need, employees networked via new communications technologies provide the means. No wonder many writers and management gurus see networked organizations as the wave of the future.[18]

It Takes All Types

As we have seen in the last several pages, teams can take many forms. At one end of the spectrum we find the spontaneous, informal interactions of several coworkers who meet by chance in a hallway and end up discussing an issue of mutual concern. At the other end might be a self-managed production team going through a highly structured problem-solving exercise to reach a decision about its work. In between, we find task forces, committees, project teams, and system design teams. Furthermore, new technologies have made it possible to team up in previously unlikely ways. Team members in different locations, on different schedules, and in different organizations may rarely meet in person and only occasionally communicate in real time, swapping messages instead via E-mail. At any given time, any of these collaborative forms may be operating within the same organization, frequently overlapping in membership, converging in purpose, and competing for resources and time.

Despite the differences described in the last several pages, the distinctions among these team types are not always unambiguous. For example, the ongoing work of many high-tech companies takes the form of projects. Moreover, parallel teams can evolve into project teams and then work teams (for instance: when an information-systems task force turns into a systems-development project team and eventually becomes a business-systems department). And, as we noted earlier, other team types can evolve from ad hoc networks. Nonetheless, the differences between these team types are important. Recognizing these differences and designing and managing teams accordingly are critical to maximizing their effectiveness. In the next section we turn to the issue of team performance and the ways these differences can be used to design more effective teams.

"BUILDING" VERSUS "DESIGNING" EFFECTIVE TEAMS

As more and more organizations recognize the rapidly expanding role of work groups and teams in organizational performance, interest in methods for enhancing team effectiveness has grown apace. Most of the methods used in organizations today fall loosely under the rubric of *team building*. Unfortunately, this is one of those organizational buzzwords used so often and so indiscriminately that it encompasses almost everything and therefore means almost nothing. If defined appropriately, however, it can be a convenient label for a host of practices in wide use in organizations today.

We use the expression to describe those approaches and techniques that focus on internal team processes and dynamics. This would include group facilitation methods used in most organizations to enhance team effectiveness: techniques for resolving conflicts; improving interpersonal communications; building trust, commitment, and cohesiveness; and generally encouraging team members to respect each other, get along, and work as well together as possible. This is essentially the approach Chris took with the SICIM project team in the Paws & Claws story segment that opened this chapter. The way in which most people use the expression, *team building* does *not* include approaches that focus on the structure and design of the group and its relationship to the rest of the organization (its goals, distribution of authority, rewards, etc.).[19] These "design" issues will be introduced later in this chapter and discussed in detail in upcoming chapters.

The conventional wisdom in most organizations is that internal team dynamics and processes are the keys to effective teams. Therefore, the conventional wisdom continues, team building interventions should be particularly useful for improving their performance. But as with so many human resource and team development practices in wide use today, support for the conventional wisdom remains elusive. Since the early days of "sensitivity training" to more recent interest in team building in wilderness settings, a meaningful link between internal processes and group performance has yet to be demonstrated.[20] Employees who participate in these interventions generally enjoy the experience and report all kinds of positive feelings toward their fellow team members following the programs. The problem is that these feelings often fade when team members return to the same old jobs, policies, and organizational settings. Furthermore, the good feelings do not necessarily translate into improved performance. That old saw—"happy workers are more productive workers"—is another piece of conventional wisdom that does not hold up to close scrutiny.[21]

The problem with team-building interventions is that they are essentially reactive; that is, they typically come into play when problems emerge and do not address the fundamental reasons why destructive conflict and other group-process problems occur in the first place. If a team's goals are not clear, if its members do not have the resources or skills to do their jobs effectively, if individual members feel they are not being paid fairly in comparison with others on the team or elsewhere, if relations with the rest of the organization are problematic, then engaging in team building will be like rearranging the deck chairs on the *Titanic*. No amount of role playing, conflict resolution, trust building, or communications training will have a significant and lasting impact on employees' ability or desire to do their job well.

Because of the limitations of team building, many managers, organizational researchers, and consultants are taking a more proactive approach to improving team effectiveness. This approach focuses on *team design* (an expression we will use throughout the book to include not only the design of new teams but the redesign of existing teams). Team design involves several steps.[22]

Identify Team Type and Goals

There are actually two parts to this first step. The first is to identify the type of team to be designed. In most cases this will be fairly straightforward and will involve little more than thinking through the nature of the work to be done and, therefore, the function of the team. Listed below are the possible functions in general terms and the team types that correspond to these functions:

- to produce a particular product or service on a regular, ongoing basis (work team);
- to develop a one-time output, such as a new product or service, new information system, or new plant (project team);
- to address special issues without fundamentally changing the structure of the organization (parallel team);
- to provide higher-level coordination and integration of different units and to provide direction and resources to these units (management team); and
- to create informal collections of individuals and groups who share similar concerns, interests, and purposes from which other types of teams can later be formed (ad hoc network).

Once the type of team has been identified it is then possible to define its mission and develop clear and explicit team goals that are linked to overall business strategy. This is an important design factor in its own right, which, unlike the others we will discuss, applies to all team types.[23]

Determine Team Structure

Determining the desired structure of a team involves several considerations.

Define Team Composition Identifying the tasks to be performed by the team should determine who is to be included on it. Critical to this determination is interdependence—that is, the activities to be integrated, the people who need to communicate to address ongoing issues, and the work that should be coordinated to produce a relatively whole product or perform a service. These analyses will help identify the roles, tasks, and responsibilities that should be included within the boundaries of the team—boundaries that can increasingly cut across departments and organizations. But ultimately, teams are made up of people, not roles. This means identifying the kinds of people who should fill these roles and how. What kinds of skills do the team members need? Should they be full- or part-time members, temporary or permanent, colocated or not? The answers to these questions vary for different types of user teams.

Define and Fill Leadership Roles There is probably little that can be said about team leadership that applies to all situations and team types, besides the obvious statement that teams need leadership. Whether that leadership is provided by one person for the life of the team or by different people at different times or for different tasks, the determination of who should fulfill these roles and how should they fulfill them depends on the type of team and other circumstances. Whatever the case, these issues should be addressed as soon as possible after the composition of the team has been determined.

Develop External Connections Our discussion till now has focused on drawing the team's boundaries and designing what happens within those boundaries—who is on the team, what is the nature of their involvement, and how the team is managed and led. With this step the team is linked to the rest of the organization and beyond. In particular, the team that is being designed needs to be connected to those individuals, teams, and units that will either be most affected by or have the greatest impact on their work. This issue is critical for all team types; exactly who these individuals and units are will vary depending on the type of team being designed.

Develop Team Capabilities

Once the basic structure of the team has been designed, the dominant issue becomes how to enhance the team's ability to perform its tasks. There are two primary means of accomplishing this.

Provide Access to Information Resources One of the most important means for developing team capabilities is to increase its access to critical resources, especially the information it needs to do its work and the tools it needs for managing, analyzing, and communicating this information. Regardless of team type, collaborative work in contemporary organizations involves capturing, pooling, and using expertise and information from many different sources. Information technology is not the only means for doing this, but it is certainly one of the most promising.

Provide Training A universal principle of team design is that team members should possess the skills required for their roles and tasks. Team members also require good interpersonal skills, regardless of role, task, or team type. Whenever possible, teams should be staffed with members who possess these skills. But even under the best of circumstances, some training will be needed to compensate for the lack of critical skills and knowledge among some or all team members. In addition, as teams and their members learn from their work, gain experience, and move up the learning curve, they will need advanced training to further enhance their capabilities so that they can take on more difficult challenges. The need for training is universal; the details vary by type of team, where the team is in its development, and the specific domains of its work.

A Role for Both Team Building and Team Design

In spite of the increasing emphasis on proactive design approaches to team effectiveness, team building still has an important role to play. Conflict is inevitable, even in well-designed teams, perhaps even more so if team members are highly motivated and come from diverse backgrounds and functions. The participation and commitment of all members need to be encouraged. Many teams need help in keeping focused on their goals as they work on their tasks. Members need to communicate with each other, regardless of how the team is designed.

Team building can even be a valuable tool in team design. Like all group processes and tasks, the processes involved in the design of teams are frequently marked by tension and conflict, loss of focus, and distrust and insensitivity among team members. When these difficulties emerge—or better yet, to mitigate their negative impact before they do—team-building interventions can be used to facilitate the design process just as they are used to facilitate other team processes and activities.

Thus, team building and team design are complementary, not competing approaches. Good design creates the conditions for effective interpersonal interaction and group dynamics. Indeed, the very expression *team building* implies design, and many practitioners are beginning to integrate the two into a more comprehensive approach. An old cliché illustrates this relationship—team building can "grease the skids" of the well-designed team by keeping it on track and running smoothly.

But even that is not enough. The ultimate goal is not *team* effectiveness, but *organizational* effectiveness via teams. Organizations need to integrate team activities, create macrostructures that will support these activities, and ensure that all of this is aligned with overall organizational strategy and goals. To repeat the theme of this book, what is really necessary is an integrated focus on teams, technologies, and the organizational structures and policies that will support them.

COMMON MISCONCEPTIONS ABOUT TEAMS

Before leaving the topic of teams, we offer several cautionary notes about teams and their role in organizational performance. Some have to do with idealized misconceptions about teamwork. Others reflect our concern about trends, fads, and fashions in the methods used to improve team effectiveness and the pitfalls of pursuing easy, cookbook solutions to complex issues.

The first note concerns the misconception that teams are invariably a good thing. Teams are hot. Self-managed work teams are even hotter. Consultants and managers enthusiastically tout their benefits. Almost every organization is looking for ways to organize its employees into teams, self-managed or otherwise. Because of the almost messianic attention paid to teams in recent years, particularly SMWTs, the expression has been overused, misused, and abused by managers and consultants in their rush to jump on the empowerment band wagon. But teams are not always appropriate. They require a lot of time, and their costs are not always offset by the savings and gains they produce.

Furthermore, creating teams means much more than the platitude, "We should all work together and help each other out." The defining characteristics of teams are interdependence and shared goals and purposes. If tasks and people are not interdependent, and if the benefits of restructuring their work to make them interdependent (assuming it is even feasible to do so) do not justify the costs, then it is best to leave things as they are. In that case, looking at ways to enhance individual performance, rather than trying to artificially create a team where it does not make sense, would reap greater rewards for the company and the individuals involved.

Another misconception is that teamwork and individual work are incompatible. But too much togetherness can have the same effect on teams as it does on marriages. In even the most cohesive teams, individual members will have to go off on their own to accomplish a task or solve a problem. Group tasks proceed more efficiently when individual team members have done their homework and are well prepared to contribute to the team effort.

Organizations and units should also be cautious about adopting intact team designs because they have worked elsewhere. What works well in one context may not fit another. Organizations need to *adapt* rather than *adopt* team designs, modifying designs used elsewhere to fit their particular circumstances.

The final note concerns the complexity of team-related issues, a complexity that cannot be managed by introducing a few flashy exercises or techniques. Too many organizations look for simple approaches to the complex issues of collaboration and team effectiveness. "Feel good" sensitivity training, technically elegant and sophisticated "groupware" (more about this in chapter 8), and managerial exhortations and admonitions to "work together as a team" can occasionally play an important role. But creating effective teams requires much more—careful planning, often tedious effort, considerable patience, and, most important, knowledge about what really makes them work.[24]

CONCLUSION

In this chapter we defined, clarified, and discussed the focus of the MDI effort—teams, technology, and the organization (figure 2-6 summarizes these definitions). We also introduced the design approach to creating more effective user teams. This design approach is applicable to the MDI team as well. The more effective the MDI team is, the more effective will be the user teams it designs, the technology it develops, and the organizational changes it helps create. Designing more effective MDI teams is critical to the MDI effort.

◆ ◆ ◆

Figure 2–6   Key Definitions

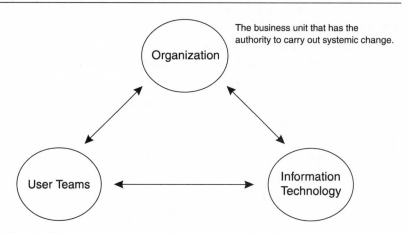

The business unit that has the authority to carry out systemic change.

A group of people interdependent in their tasks who need to work together to fulfill a common purpose or goal. They will be the principal users of the technology to be developed.

The information and communications technology, systems, and tools.

SEVERAL MINUTES LATER, the same evening . . .

Chris bristles defensively in response to Steve's initial comments, then visibly softens as the validity of what he has to say begins to sink in. Besides, he can already see how to address Steve's concerns and keep the project moving forward. The main thrust of Steve's comments is that, "as an unrepentant techie nerd, I take all of this airy-fairy team-building stuff with more than a grain of salt."

"Surely," he continues, "we need to do something more substantial to create teams on the production floor than what we've been doing here all day. They'll never put up with this! Besides, even if it does work with the project team, and I have my doubts about that, it won't necessarily work with the teams in the plant. They are different, what they do is different, and working in a plant is a helluva lot different from working in an office."

Mark is impressed by Steve's clarity and directness. Apparently, so is Chris. He sips his whiskey pensively. "Well, you've made your point. What exactly do you propose we do?"

"For one thing, I think we're getting ahead of ourselves. We haven't even decided the scope of what we're trying to do. I know you want to use the system in your reorganization of all seven plants across the country, but do you intend to do this all at once? I think we need to define the boundaries of this project." His voice gets higher as he picks up speed in his litany of concern. "What are we doing first? Are we implementing everything throughout the system at the

same time, or are we going to start with a bite-size chunk first. What's in that first bite—which plants, which teams . . ." He's almost breathless.

"Whoa, there, Steve," Chris interrupts, "you've convinced me. It sounds like we have some work to do. I hope you guys don't have any plans for this evening." Without waiting for a response from either, Chris signals the bartender for refills all around.

"This is gonna be a long evening, so let's get started," he adds, as they hunch over their notepads and go to work.

Part Two

Laying the Foundation

THE PRIMARY FOCUS OF PART II is the design of the team that will do the designing—the MDI team. The chapters in part II deal with such critical issues as who should be involved in the MDI process and how they can best work together as a team. Before we address these issues, however, we need to know more about what constitutes an MDI project and how it is started. The first chapter in part II—chapter 3—addresses these issues by offering concrete examples of the kinds of projects and situations that fit, or do not fit, the MDI framework. The chapter then describes how these projects can get started, how the MDI team is initially formed, and how the overall project structure is created.

Chapters 4 and 5 address the next step in the team design process as it applies to the MDI team: determining who should be on the team. In these chapters we will describe who are the stakeholders in the process and how to find the right people to represent their interests and participate as members of the MDI team. Once the right people have been identified and brought into the project, the MDI team is formed. Then the team needs to continue designing itself so that it can carry out its mission effectively. The remaining steps in this self-design sequence are the subject of chapter 6, the last chapter in part II.

3

Getting Started with MDI

THREE HOURS LATER, Paws & Claws Conference Center bar . . .

Chris, Steve, and Mark are still at it. The good cheer and single-malt whiskey have long since been replaced by weary irritation and strong black coffee. They seem to be no closer to defining the scope of the initial phase of the project than they were when they started.

Not surprisingly, Chris is arguing for what he calls a "galactic, total immersion approach. Let's implement everything, everywhere, all at once. Total reengineering, top to bottom, right to left, inside out. Sort of like shock therapy. One day they're doing things the old way, the next day they're doing it the new way. Don't give them a chance to fall back or retreat to the old ways of working. Every plant, every team, everybody, and all of the policies reinforce each other."

Steve, on the other hand, is surprisingly reticent. After all, what Chris has in mind could mean big bucks for S & D. "I've already had my share of meltdowns," Steve argues. "I've worked on too many projects that collapsed under their own weight, and I've developed too many systems that were obsolete before they even reached the shop floor. I'm more interested in small successes that can lead to steady, long-term business."

His preference is to develop the system for one team in one plant, try it out for a while, and then, if it seems successful, roll it out to the rest of that plant and eventually to the other six plants around the country. Initially, at least, this would make for a fairly straightforward project. Steve proposes that a couple of representatives from the SICIM project team work directly with whatever production team Chris selects to pilot the new system. The representatives would periodically visit the team at the plant, observe their work, interview the members, and report back to the project team. The project team would then convert the work needs of the production team into a usable system.

"This isn't that complicated," says Steve. "We're just building a new system for them. One team is the same as another. We just try it out with one and pass it on to the others. No need to get cosmic here."

Mark has been silent for much of the discussion. He can barely keep his eyes open. The coffee isn't helping—it's so bad he can hardly stomach it. ("What I wouldn't give for a decent latte," he thinks.) Finally, they turn to him.

"Mark, what do you think?" Chris asks. "You've had a lot of experience with projects like this, haven't you? What have they done in other companies?"

"Served better coffee, for one thing," he begins.

◆ ◆ ◆

MDI PROJECTS—projects that involve the mutual design and implementation of teams and technology—don't just happen. Some knowledge and considerable effort are needed to recognize the opportunity, define the project boundaries, and get it started. That is the purpose of this chapter—to describe what needs to be done to initiate an MDI project and keep it moving until the project is completed. While many of these issues will be covered in detail in the chapters that follow, a preview at this point will help provide the context, the big picture, for the more detailed discussions to come.

RECOGNIZING AND DEFINING MDI PROJECT OPPORTUNITIES

Before starting, it is important to know what kinds of projects are most appropriate for an MDI approach. There is no sense in applying the framework and recommendations to projects that do not fit these prescriptions. At best, there is the risk of overkill from using complex approaches to address simple issues. At worst, the wrong issues will be addressed or the right problems will be made worse by the wrong treatment. The first section of this chapter, using real-world examples, should help the reader to recognize and define the kinds of projects the MDI framework will fit and the kinds it will not fit. Once we are able to recognize and define an MDI opportunity, our attention will shift to getting the project started and creating the overall project structure.

Bad Fits

In our opening story segment, Chris and Steve express preferences for two different approaches to the SICIM project. Steve wants to develop the new information system for use by just one team, try it out for a while, then roll it out to the other teams and plants. Chris, on the other hand, wants to develop and implement the system throughout the company all at once. As we will see, neither approach fits the MDI framework well; in fact, neither is a wise strategy to follow regardless of the methodology or framework used. First, let's take a look at Steve's preferred approach.

Single Teams, Limited Impact, Modest Change Some projects may be too small to require the complex structures and processes we recommend here. This is the case, for example, if:

- the project involves only the development of an isolated application or tool for a relatively small, single team, or
- the impact of the project will be confined to the user team, or
- the design of the team is not likely to be significantly changed.

Under these circumstances, a separate MDI team is not needed. Since there is only one relatively small user team, it can work directly with an information technology expert[1] to develop an application that will focus specifically on meeting its needs, and its needs alone. In effect, the user team, plus an information technology expert, *is* the MDI team. The following example, a project conducted at the production and manufacturing plant of the Apex Corporation's Computer Systems Division, illustrates this situation.

> The project involved the inventory team, a seven-member cross-functional team with the responsibility for determining appropriate inventory levels based on projected production schedules. The team was made up of representatives from several departments within the manufacturing operation, including production, planning, and materials.
>
> The team needed information on inventory levels for parts used in the production process to forecast future inventory levels. Although these data were already being captured by existing information systems, they could not be pulled out easily from the inventory data base in the desired format. The team asked the information services department (ISD) to help it develop a report that could be generated by the existing systems

to provide the data the team needed, when it needed them, and in the form it desired.

A user consultant from ISD was assigned to the project. She attended team meetings on a regular basis and talked with individual members. From these meetings and conversations, she learned about their work and what they required. She was then able to help them clarify their needs by asking them how they expected to use the data and the reports. During this process, she helped the team members focus on what was feasible. At appropriate times, she also presented various alternatives and sample reports for consideration by the team.

This highly interactive and iterative process was conducted primarily within the context of regularly scheduled team meetings. Other people—from purchasing and procurement, for instance—were brought in as needed. The project did not lead to any permanent changes in the team's composition, structure, or process, but it did lead to a relatively minor change in work procedure that had little impact on anyone outside the team.

As it was conceived at Apex, this project was not an appropriate candidate for an MDI approach. The new data reports would have no impact on anyone outside of the inventory team, and they were unlikely to lead to significant changes in the team's composition and structure. Perhaps most important, since only one small team was involved and it was possible for the ISD representative to work with the entire team and its members, a separate MDI team was not required. In sum, the scope of the project was small, the issues to be addressed were not particularly complex, and the means for involving all of the stakeholders—the team members and the ISD representative—were straightforward and easy to implement.

This project would have been a better candidate for an MDI approach under different conditions and circumstances; if, for example,

1. the team had been significantly larger,
2. the entire team could not afford to devote large blocks of time to this project, or
3. the impact on other units had been significant—if, say, they had been linked in a common work process.

Any one of these conditions could create the need for a project team made up of representatives from the user team, ISD, and other stakeholders—in other words, an MDI team to take responsibility for the information technology application. Under these conditions, the framework and recommendations we will describe would apply.

But there is another way to look at projects that initially appear too small for an MDI approach. In some cases the issue is not the size of the project but the scope of the vision. Rather than asking whether a project is large enough for MDI, the question should be whether it is large enough to achieve significant results. While small projects involving only minor changes for individual teams can enhance the effectiveness of these teams, the overall organizational impact is likely to be modest at best. This is especially true if they are part of a larger process that involves other units and teams (see figure 3–1 for a definition and illustration of *process*). In fact, working on only one component of a larger process may actually lower overall performance.

We recommend that projects be defined broadly enough to address significant opportunities with potentially greater impact—*if* such an opportunity genuinely exists, and *if* the resources and time are available for a more sweeping and expansive project, and *if* the organization is in a position to put up with the level of disruption that such projects inevitably produce.

These are the kinds of issues that need to be addressed when deciding what projects to pursue and how to pursue them. The decision will rarely be clear-cut. Both approaches—defining the project in terms of immediate, narrow needs versus defining it in broader and more ambitious terms—may be possible for the same project. In most cases, this is a judgment call. The ultimate decision will involve the weighing of costs against potential benefits and reaching agreements on difficult but necessary trade-offs.

"Galactic" Change, All at Once At the other end of the spectrum is Chris's preference for "galactic, total immersion." But the project he envisions may be too big, not only for MDI but for any other approach. A recent study conducted by the National Academy of Sciences concludes that projects of excessive scope and scale—"'bet-the-company' IT projects"—are likely to be "overly complex, over budget, delayed, and mismatched to customer needs by the time they are implemented."[2] According to the study,

> For many years, IT vendors and popular journals overemphasized the importance of large-scale "system solutions." Managers too often responded by seeking to install mega-projects with high visibility. Such

Figure 3–1 Definition of *Process*

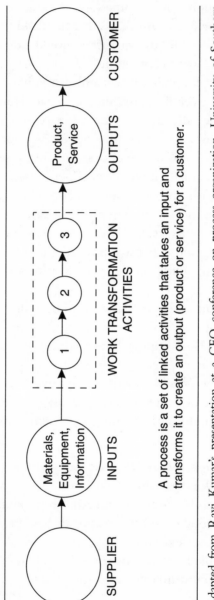

A process is a set of linked activities that takes an input and transforms it to create an output (product or service) for a customer.

SUPPLIER   INPUTS   WORK TRANSFORMATION   OUTPUTS   CUSTOMER
                          ACTIVITIES

Adapted from Ravi Kumar's presentation at a CEO conference on process organization, University of Southern California, Los Angeles, November 30, 1994.

projects generally have multiple objectives that must be reconciled and integrated across several divisions. Mega-projects tend to be very complex. And they often take inordinate amounts of time, investment risk, and political compromises to bring into being. As a result, even companies with well-established track records for innovative uses of IT have experienced difficulties with large-scale projects.[3]

The study cites several reasons for this lack of success, including the costs and inherent delays typically associated with projects of such large scope and complexity. By the time an organization completes a large project, the needs the system was designed to meet may have changed. In addition, competitors may have beaten the organization to the punch with similar, or even better, technology that was not available when the project was initiated.

For these reasons and others many of the companies interviewed for the study said that they now break down overly large projects into smaller, more discrete or modular segments. Each segment or subproject must be individually justified and aligned with overall project goals. These subprojects can be designed globally, but they should be implemented incrementally and tested on a small scale or in a single operating company. If successful, they can be integrated for testing with other successful projects. Feedback from these subprojects, as well as from those that are less successful, can be used to guide those that come later. They are then integrated, project by project, into an overarching system architecture. The companies reported that this approach led to significantly lower project costs, faster paybacks on investment, and reduced political resistance. In the words of one interviewee, James Stewart, the executive vice president and chief financial officer of CIGNA Corporation: "Increasingly we are shortening the planning time frame [from 2 to 3 years down to 6 months]. We are focused on shorter-term paybacks rather than building galactic systems."[4] The difference between this modular approach and the "single teams, limited impact, modest change" approach described earlier is that the modules are not designed as standalones but as pieces of a larger, more comprehensive design into which they will eventually have to fit.

Good Fits

Now that we have a handle on the kind of projects that do not fit an MDI approach, what can we say about those that do? In other words, what are the kinds of issues and problems that call for an MDI project? What are the conditions and circumstances that make the MDI framework an appropriate approach?

Ideally, MDI projects should be viewed from the beginning as involving both technology development and team or task redesign. These projects should strive to integrate information technology and team/task design in a coordinated and mutually reinforcing process from the very beginning. This was the original intent of the SICIM project at Paws & Claws. But this is the exception. Real life in real organizations often precludes starting a project with such a comprehensive, radical, and politically risky mandate.

Therefore, most MDI projects are either information technology or team driven when they begin. In *IT-driven* projects, an existing team (or set of teams) wants a new information tool or application to help members do their work better. Even though the original intent of the SICIM project was to integrate simultaneous changes in information technology and teams, it quickly became an IT-driven project. A *team-driven* project is initiated as a team or task (re)design—for instance, a decision to convert an existing supervisor-led team into a self-managed work team or to create a new team from separate individuals involved in the same work process.

What makes them MDI projects is that they eventually focus on both information technology and teams, regardless of the original impetus for the project. In the technology-driven case, the team should be redesigned (perhaps a new work flow) to respond to the new opportunities the technology creates. In the team-driven case, redesigned teams will often need new or different information resources to support their new missions, structures, and designs. Both will fall within our domain of application, as long as those conducting the projects recognize that eventually—sooner, rather than later—they have to look at the other side of the sociotechnical coin if they want their efforts to succeed.[5] Let us now look at some examples that illustrate each of these cases.

An Example of IT-driven MDI Following is an example of an IT-driven project at Apex Corporation, the same site from which we drew the earlier example of a project that did not fit the MDI framework.

Most IT projects of the last several years consisted of enhancements to existing systems, particularly to the 1980 vintage MRP system. But as of this writing Apex managers were planning a much more ambitious project, called Information Systems for the Year 2000.

One of the main drivers of this new, bigger system is the impending millennium. The reasons are eminently practical and have little to do with a metaphysical anticipation of the "new age." Existing systems will treat 1999 as coming after 2000 because it only reads and sorts on the last two digits of the year. Unless the system is changed the transition to 2000 will foul up production scheduling and planning. Apex managers figure they need to update by 1996 so that they can make five-year projections into the next century.

They could make the necessary adjustments to the existing system. But because of their "ancient IT platform," in the words of the manager of ISD, they can not take advantage of the "incredible opportunities in the microworld." So they are looking into a new client-server platform, a PC-based network, perhaps in a UNIX environment, using canned software when possible.

The structure of the overall organization is decidedly team based. Almost all work processes are organized around teams. In place of the traditional functional hierarchy, there is a hierarchy of teams in which cross-functional management teams oversee, coordinate, and integrate the work of the cross-functional teams that report to them. The new information system is seen as a platform to support team-based work. It will provide all teams—existing and new—with integrated systems and data bases that they will be able to adapt to their needs. Not only will individual teams be able to develop specific applications but the cross-functional team structures will make it easier to develop applications that integrate processes across individual teams.

The challenge of this project will be to manage the involvement of many user teams in the development process. Most of the company's projects to date have been modest, focusing primarily on small, local enhancements to the existing platform for single, relatively small user teams. As we saw in the inventory team example described earlier, Apex's development approach has been relatively straightforward, typically consisting of a single consultant from information services working with the entire user team within its existing structure and scheduled meetings.

The Information Systems for the Year 2000 project will require a much more complex and potentially contentious structure—a project team consisting of representatives from the different user teams debating system features and trade-offs. The complexity of this project calls for application of an MDI approach.

Two Examples of Team-driven MDI Our next two examples illustrate the team-driven case. The first is drawn from Premier Computers, a manufacturer of midsize computers used for complex training simulations (for commercial pilots, for example). We begin with the creation of a new team.

> Until recently, new product development at Premier was a sequential, "over-the-wall" process. Engineering would pass on new product designs to production. Production would then pass back recommendations for engineering changes based on its assessment of the product's "manufacturability," given the existing design.
>
> Premier has now switched to a concurrent engineering process in which design engineering, process engineering, and manufacturing work together as a team to develop designs for new products. The problem is, production facilities are more than 150 miles from the engineering division. While this distance was not a serious problem under the old design process, it is an obstacle to the new concurrent, team-based approach. Premier solved the problem by developing a video-conferencing system that linked specially designated and equipped conference rooms at both facilities. Weekly team meetings now take place via videoconference. During these telemeetings, participants work on the release process for every new product they develop, including phases, deliverables, and dates.

A different illustration of team-driven MDI can be seen in the following example from the gas distribution division of SouthWest Power and Light (SWP&L), a regional gas and electric utility company. This example involves the redesign of existing teams.

> The division manager had recently decided to reorganize the gas distribution division around self-managed work teams. He wanted to start with the gas emergency response field technicians responsible for checking out suspected gas leaks and doing repairs. Customers would call an SWP&L customer service representative (CSR) to report the possible leaks. The CSR would then pass on the information to dispatchers, who were responsible for assigning technicians in the field—each driving his or her own repair vehicle—to respond to each report.
>
> The division manager wanted to replace the present dispatcher-controlled process with self-managed work teams of field-service techni-

cians. As a team, they would assign the reports among themselves, and individual team members would decide on the order in which to respond to each report. Since the technicians were in the field most of the day, they could not meet face to face once their shifts began. Therefore, they needed technology-based linkages to make this process work. One link already existed, the two-way radio phones used by the dispatchers to communicate with the trucks. All they needed to do was change the work process and use the phones for a different purpose—to enable the technicians to communicate with each other.

If they were going to be truly self-managed, the technicians also needed to receive information about the gas leaks directly from the CSRs without it first going to the dispatchers. This problem was solved by using a technology that had been recently developed to serve another purpose. Originally, the mobile data terminal system (MDTS) was to be installed in the service trucks to replace the cumbersome map books the technicians used to look up the locations of reported leaks. By modifying the purpose, function, and use of both the MDTS and the radio phone system, the gas distribution division was able to create self-managed work teams.

Principles for Defining Projects

From the examples of Apex, Premier, and SouthWest Power and Light, we can extract some principles that can be used to recognize and define MDI project opportunities. The first principle is probably the most straightforward and follows directly from the introduction to this book:

1. MDI projects include both team and technology changes. The original impetus for the project and the order in which these issues are addressed—IT or team-driven or both simultaneously—are irrelevant as long as the other is introduced early in the project.

The remaining principles have to do with the scope and scale of the project. They all reflect the most appropriate range of application of the MDI framework—midrange projects that lie between simple changes for single teams and galactic changes for an entire enterprise.

2. The scope and scale of the project should be as simple as possible to attack the problem to be addressed.

3. On the other hand, the project should also be large enough to

include other teams and individuals who may be affected by the changes to be made.

4. If other teams within the same organization, division, or plant are dealing with similar issues, the project can be expanded into a multiteam project as long as doing so does not make the project overly complex and cumbersome.

If the project is expanded to include other stakeholders and teams, structures and mechanisms will have to be created to ensure that all activities, stakeholders, and players are coordinated and fully integrated into the project. How to get the project started and create these integrating structures are the issues we look at next.

INITIATING AN MDI PROJECT

MDI can be initiated at any level of the organization, from individual units or teams to senior management. Just as the conditions and circumstances that can get a project started may vary, so can the people who recognize these conditions as an opportunity for change.

- ♦ Supervisors or managers may see team-based collaboration as a way to improve the performance of the units reporting to them.

- ♦ Innovative, technically oriented, unit-based system users (sometimes referred to as local experts or gurus) recognize an opportunity as they experiment with a new system and learn how it might be adapted and applied to their team's work.

- ♦ The corporate IT department may initiate the MDI effort to develop a new end-user system or to take over responsibility for a project initiated by a technically sophisticated user-team member.

- ♦ Senior management may decide to use MDI to reengineer the organization as part of a strategy for increasing innovation, cutting costs, and getting new products to market faster.

Figure 3–2 illustrates what typically happens from the point of initiation on. First, initiators find one or more management sponsors for the project, unless the initiators themselves are able to fulfill this role. One of the most important responsibilities of the sponsors is to provide budgetary support and other resources throughout the project. Other

Figure 3–2 The Evolution of the Mutual Design and Implementation Project

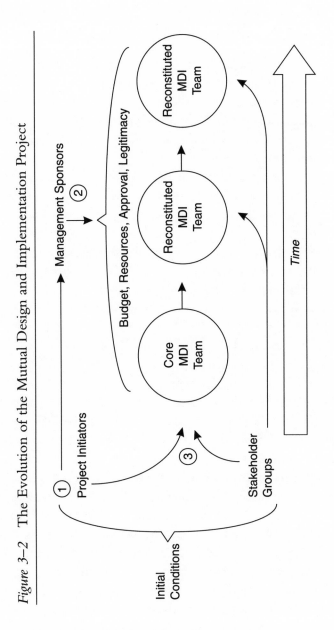

responsibilities include signing off on design and implementation plans and acting as a liaison with other relevant organizational units. The sponsors may also fulfill an important symbolic role, legitimizing the project and sending a clear signal to others that it is an important activity that may require their support as well. In effect, the sponsors provide the umbrella under which the project can proceed. Often the project sponsors belong to a project steering committee, a cross-functional management team made up of the sponsors and other key players identified by sponsors, project initiators, and members of the MDI team. The steering committee, when it is in place, performs much the same function as the sponsors.

The project initiators, sponsors, and the steering committee will then form the MDI team. This project team will be responsible for the design and implementation of the new technologies and the work structures in which these technologies will be used. It will also be responsible for recommending changes in the organizational context. For practical reasons, the MDI team usually cannot include all potential stakeholders—all the technical experts who might be called on to support the new system, all those who might use the system, and anyone else who might have a stake in the project. The size of the MDI team would be too large and cumbersome to work effectively. Project initiators need to work with the various stakeholder groups to select individuals who can represent their interests and expertise.

Initially, this may involve only those stakeholder groups that are most central to the process—the future users and the information technology experts who will be responsible for the technical aspects of systems development. These core members can then "bootstrap" the rest of the MDI team as the process unfolds, consulting with other stakeholder groups and adding representatives from their ranks as their expertise and involvement are needed. The MDI team, like other project teams, can be quite fluid to reflect the changing dynamics and agenda of the MDI process. As the team moves from issue to issue, new representatives may be added, others may drop out, some may rejoin as earlier issues are revisited and decisions reconsidered. Frequently, the project may have to be partitioned into component tasks and separate MDI teams created to focus specifically on each subtask. In effect, while designing the technology, teams, and organizational context, the MDI team is also designing itself.

CONCLUSION

The purpose of this chapter was to present a wide-angle view of the MDI process—the kinds of projects that are most suitable for MDI, the way to get started, and the overall structure within which the principal activities are carried out. With this basic understanding of how to define and initiate the MDI process, we can begin to look more closely at the details of the process itself.

◆ ◆ ◆

ONE BLEARY HOUR LATER . . .

Finally, they are finished. They have decided to take the middle road—pilot the first two or three modules of the system and the new team structures with all of the production teams in the plant on the outskirts of Baltimore, less than 15 miles from corporate headquarters. After six months or so of testing, evaluation, and modifications, the system and team designs will be rolled out to the other Paws & Claws plants. The same process will be followed for all of the other system modules as they become available.

As they fold up their flip charts and pack their briefcases, Chris asks in a gently mocking tone, "Anything else on your mind, Steve?"

Steve, apparently not noticing Chris's verbal equivalent of a wink and a friendly poke in the ribs, begins to lay out his remaining concern. The others groan, but they do stop and listen to what he has to say. He is worried about the lack of "buy-in" from the production teams. Like everyone else involved in the project, he has heard the grumblings from the plant. The workers there didn't know much about the system and the other changes that were being planned, and what they had heard did not impress them. They didn't see the need for the system and were suspicious about the reasons for restructuring the production teams.

In a comment that echoes his earlier concern, Steve notes, "I've been involved in too many projects that produced systems that cost too much and were used too little. S & D's reputation—hell, my reputation—is at stake, and I don't want to repeat past mistakes here. We need buy-in from the eventual users as soon as possible. And the best way to get it is to involve them in the project, maybe by putting a representative or two on the project team.

"We need to reconsider the entire make-up of the project team. Who needs to

be on the team and who doesn't. Then we have to think about what the team members will need to do their work, how they will be organized, what things they will have to do, and how they will do them. We need to think of building the project team like we think about building the system—it's a design task."

Chris and Mark nod their heads in drowsy agreement. "Steve, you're right," Chris responds, "but frankly I'm too tired to even think about this now. How about if we pick it up tomorrow morning?"

"Sure. How about we meet at seven over breakfast?" Steve grins. Chris glares back. "Why so late?" he replies. "Sleeping in?"

They all laugh weakly and shuffle wearily off to bed.

4

Selecting User Team Delegates

THREE WEEKS LATER, Paws & Claws plant on the outskirts of Balti-more . . .

Bill Marcel walks around his office, distractedly picking up objects from his desk and bookcase and placing them carefully in a brown cardboard packing box. Later that afternoon he will unpack the box in his new office in the corporate head-quarters building downtown. As he reaches for each object, his large, bulky body strains the seams of his ill-fitting suit. "When was the last time I wore this suit, anyway?" he wonders. "My nephew Matthew's communion, I think. Gained a few pounds since then, I guess. I'll have to get a couple of new suits for this project." That was one of several misgivings he had about joining the SICIM project team. Slacks and an open collar shirt were fine in the plant, but they wouldn't work downtown.

Bill has worked for Paws & Claws for more than twenty years. His first job was on the production line. This was followed by a promotion to supervisor a few years later. After several other promotions over the years, he has become one of the highest ranking production managers in the plant. Despite his rapid ascent through the managerial ranks, he is still in touch with his roots. He regularly joins the production workers for a few beers after work and is one of the stalwarts on the plant's bowling team. He really hates to leave the camaraderie and informality of the plant, but his new position as a full-time user representative on the SICIM project team would last only until the project is finished. Besides, he saw it as an opportunity for a major career move. If the project is successful, he could be in line for a major promotion, to plant manager perhaps or even eventually to an executive position. Apparently, his ambition and drive override his concerns about uncomfortable suits and unfamiliar colleagues.

On the other hand, if the project is not successful, he has a lot to lose. And he is not at all convinced that the project will be a success. Bill is particularly concerned about why he was asked to join the project team. The reason, according to Chris, is that he is well liked and respected by the plant workers he will be representing.

"Your credibility in the plant is unsurpassed," Chris said in their brief meeting several days ago. "You have that rare ability to get along with all kinds of people—supervisors, managers, and production workers in the plant, as well as with the 'suits' at corporate headquarters." Furthermore, Chris noted, he was the most computer literate of all the managers in the plant and the most prolific user of the new system applications developed for them.

But Bill is not sure that these are the real reasons. Until he joined the project team, he had been its most outspoken critic in the plant. Like everyone else, he had been kept pretty much in the dark, but unlike everyone else, Bill was willing to go public with his concerns—and how! "What makes them think they can design a system for us without asking us what we want?" he would ask anyone who would listen, every chance he had. "They're developing a system we don't need!" It was his incessant criticism, Bill suspects, that ultimately led to his selection for the project. Maybe they were just trying to shut him up.

Or worse, Bill fears that many of the key decisions have already been made. If he's right, then his involvement on the project team will be nothing more than window dressing to convince the people in the plant that they will have some say in the design of the system they will eventually use. His greatest concern is that Chris and the others are trying to co-opt him to get his buy-in and eventually the buy-in of the others in the plant. If so, his participation in the project could do serious damage to his credibility with his former coworkers. In that case he might as well forget about a promotion. Hell, he would be lucky to get his old job back!

His suit begins to feel even tighter. He tugs on his necktie, trying to loosen its noose-like grip on his throat. He gulps. "I better get this packing finished and get out of here before they think I've changed my mind," he mumbles to himself as he reaches for his bowling trophy with one hand and an empty box with the other.

◆ ◆ ◆

SUCCESSFUL CHANGE requires the knowledge, skills, and commitment of many people. This is especially true for MDI. Numerous voices from different areas, expressing diverse interests and concerns, need to be heard during the MDI process. They all can contribute to the rich tapestry of knowledge that is essential for instituting broad, complex change.

Some of the most important voices belong to those most affected by the changes—the user teams. They will use the new technologies and work together in new ways within a redesigned organizational context. They know the most about the work to be modified, redesigned, or transformed. They possess essential knowledge about the intimate, hands-on, day-to-day details of the work that cannot be provided by any other means.

They should also "own" the changes being made. In other words, they should help shape the changes and commit themselves to making them work. This involves more than overcoming fear and resistance to change—exaggerated and short-lived problems in most cases.[1] It means that individuals and groups should understand that their new work forms, technologies, and organizational policies are means of extending their capabilities. With these new capabilities they will be able to do things and work in ways not previously possible. The challenge for organizations then is not so much overcoming resistance to change as it is establishing conditions that enable their employees to embrace the opportunities it creates.

People outside the user teams will also be affected by change and possess critical knowledge or skills relevant to change. They include:

+ the managers to whom individuals and teams report;

+ the technical experts who can translate user needs into new systems, support the systems once they are implemented, and integrate them into the organization's IT infrastructure;

+ human resources (HR) staff who can help facilitate the MDI team, develop training programs, and advise senior management on changes in HR practice and policy to support team-based work;

+ customers and suppliers, both internal and external, who work closely with the team and use the same systems; and

+ senior managers, who can use their authority to support the

Table 4–1 Stakeholder Matrix

Focal Area	Stakeholder Group	Role	Key Characteristics
Teams			
Technology			
Organization			

project. They also will be responsible for implementing new policies concerning overall organizational change that emerge from the MDI process.

All of the above parties are "stakeholders"; they literally have a stake in what happens and need to feel a sense of ownership over the outcomes. Their commitment, skills, and authority are needed to create new work forms, technologies, and organizations. The word *mutual* in the name for our framework means that all of these groups should participate in the design and implementation of any and all changes.

Let us now look more closely at one of the first and most important steps in the project: identifying and defining the stakeholder groups and selecting representatives from among them to serve as MDI team members. Who are these stakeholder groups? What is the role of their representatives? How should they be selected? What are the implications of their involvement in the MDI process?

Table 4–1 provides a guide to the discussion in this chapter and the next. The three focal areas for MDI—teams, technology, and the organization—are listed in the first (left-hand) column. They help define the groups that should participate in the design and implementation process. Who they are and why they should be involved are the subject of the second column. Not everyone who is in a stakeholder group can participate directly in the MDI process. Representatives from each group need to be selected. The third column addresses the roles of these representatives in the MDI process. The fourth lists the key characteristics to look for when selecting individuals to fill these roles. In essence, most of the discussion in this chapter and the next will fill in the cells of the matrix. We begin this discussion with the stakeholder group that is the principal focus of the MDI effort, the one for whom new systems are developed and new organizational policies are meant to support: the intended user teams.

THE VALUE OF USER TEAM INVOLVEMENT

Among the most important stakeholders in the MDI process are the teams that will be created or redesigned—the eventual users of the new systems they help create. We refer to them as *user teams*.[2] User teams should not be confused with the MDI team—the group of people whose primary responsibility will be the actual design and implementation of team, technology, and organizational changes. Typically, one or more representatives from the user team are selected to serve on the MDI team. If more than one user team is to be the focus of the MDI effort, representatives from each may need to be involved. How to select these user team representatives is what this chapter is all about.

Although users are now widely considered to be legitimate stakeholders in systems development, this has not always been the case. Until the early to mid-1980s, "user involvement" was the often futile battle cry of a handful of systems professionals, managers, researchers, consultants, and users themselves concerned with the proliferation of technically sophisticated but underutilized systems. User involvement was the answer, they felt, to the growing list of stories about ambitious projects yielding disappointing results.

The argument was so persuasive and the experiences so pervasive that user involvement is now part of the conventional wisdom, even if this wisdom is not often carried out effectively in practice.[3] Consequently, the argument in support of user roles in systems development does not need to be made as often or as strongly as was once the case. Still, the rationale bears restating so that we do not lose sight of why user involvement is important and what that tells us about how to implement it successfully.

Resistance to change is often cited as a reason why many information systems fail; user "buy-in" is typically seen as the solution, and user involvement is usually viewed as the best means to that end. While the means of achieving user buy-in are sound, this interpretation of the problem and solution overlooks an even more important reason for user involvement: the intimate, in-depth knowledge of the details of the work possessed only by those who perform the work on a regular basis. Buy-in is important, but the best way to achieve it is to build a system that meets the needs of the people who will use it. The best way to meet their needs is to incorporate their knowledge by involving them in the process by which design decisions and implementation plans are made.

These distinctions may not seem important on the surface. The problem is that focusing on buy-in often leads to superficial involvement in unimportant decisions. This is the very issue that Bill faces in the story segment that opens this chapter. And just as he suspects, users are rarely fooled in these cases. They realize that the reason for their involvement has little to do with their knowledge and expertise. They may then end up resenting the time they put into the project and either expend little effort or refuse to participate altogether.[4] The design and implementation effort then will not benefit from their legitimate expertise, and an inferior system is likely to be the result.

THE DUAL ROLE OF USER TEAM DELEGATES

While the importance of user involvement is now widely accepted, there seems to be little agreement on how to accomplish it effectively. This is one of the reasons why so many information technology development projects fail to fulfill their promise. The first and most important step in creating effective user involvement is to choose the right people to participate in the MDI process.

When teams are too large they become cumbersome and inefficient. The MDI team is no exception. Rarely can it accommodate all potential user team members. Therefore, representatives should be selected from among them to serve on the MDI team. While there are no rules about how to select representatives, project initiators and user teams should look for certain characteristics in the individuals who will serve on the MDI team. To better understand what these characteristics might be, we must first examine the various roles user representatives play in the MDI process. Successful user representatives will have the characteristics that best fit these roles.

So far, we have referred to these individuals as *user representatives*. The term *user participant* is also frequently employed to describe this role. These expressions actually correspond to different but closely linked roles—*representation* of the users' perspective and task-related expertise and *participation* in the design and implementation process. These roles overlap. While these delegates to the MDI team participate in the process, they also represent their "constituencies"—the user teams to which they belong.

Despite the overlap, each role requires different skills and characteristics. How well individuals function as representatives depends on how similar they are to those they represent, how much they know about their work, and how able they are to identify with a wide range of users. Their effectiveness in this role also depends on the degree to which the people they represent see them as being similar, knowledgeable, and empathetic.

Effective participation requires different qualities. Among them is the ability to deal with the change and uncertainty inherent to the MDI process. Another is being able to work well with people of dissimilar functional backgrounds, perspectives, knowledge bases, and objectives. It is these differences that make the job of representative/participant so challenging—and important. People selected for these positions must be able to pull off a difficult balancing act. While maintaining connections with their "roots," they must move beyond the boundaries of the familiar to collaborate with near strangers on creating the unknown.

To convey the combined roles of representative and participant, we refer to these MDI team members as *user delegates*. By examining the characteristics associated with both user team representation and MDI team participation, we can better understand the requirements of the combined role and the kind of individual most suited for it.

Representation

There are five qualifications specific to the effective representation of the user team.[5]

1. User Delegates Should Reflect the Collaborative Relationships that are Critical to the Effectiveness of the User Team. The process of representation usually involves partitioning a larger population into meaningful categories and selecting individuals to represent these categories. If this book were about information systems for individual, independent users, we would recommend that user representatives be chosen to reflect the various job categories, levels, and departments found in the user population.

When users work closely together as part of a team, the picture gets more complicated. Individual tasks, activities, and users may not be as important as the relationships they share. Under these circumstances, selecting representatives on the basis of specific job categories, levels, or departments would not capture what is most integral to the team and essential to its performance—the interdependent relationships critical to achieving the team's goals. These are the relationships most intrinsically involved in serving the team's customers, both internal and external.

With new communications capabilities, these collaborative relationships can cut across functional, organizational, and geographic boundaries. This has a number of consequences. First, collaboration is less dependent on face-to-face interactions than it has been in the past. Second, the technology increases the number of people who can be effectively involved in a collaborative relationship. Third, since the limits of time and space are removed, people can potentially participate in a large number of different collaborative relationships. Both the size and the number of relationships are limited only by members' ability or inclination to handle the added chaos, complexity, and coordination involved.

In conclusion, *user delegates should be selected to represent the collaborations that are critical to the team's performance.* They should also be intimately familiar with the activities and tasks involved in these relationships and knowledgeable about what makes them work. In other words, the focus should be on activities, not formal work units; on knowledge and expertise, not formal authority; on actual task interdependency, not physical proximity. Let us return to the example of the SWP&L gas emergency response team from chapter 3 to see what this can mean in practice.

The division manager, the field service technician who developed the initial mobile data terminal system (MDTS) application, and his supervisor decided that they needed to assemble a project team to work out the details of the team and technology redesign. They created a project team made up of the supervisors of the field service technicians, the supervisors of the dispatchers, and a telecommunications specialist. Their objective was to redesign the overall gas emergency response process—including the jobs of the technicians and the dispatchers—and to adapt the MDTS to improve the effectiveness of this process.

In their first meeting, those gathered realized that they were not necessarily the right people to be on the project team. One problem was that their knowledge of the work activities was secondhand and dated. Before being promoted to supervisor, each had worked as either a technician or dispatcher, but that was some time ago. Those people now working in these positions were far more knowledgeable about the intimate details of the work than the supervisors on the project team. These "performance-level" employees were, therefore, more appropriate choices to serve on the team.

These first team members also realized that they had overlooked one of the most critical collaborative relationships in the new emergency response process they would be developing—the one between the customer service representatives and the field service technicians. Under the redesign, the representative would communicate directly with the field service team, and the technician responding to each call would in turn keep the representative informed as to when he or she expected to arrive at the location of the suspected leak. This latter information could then be passed on to the customer who had reported the leak and was waiting—somewhat anxiously, in most cases—for the field service technician. Since customer service was in another division and representatives never met face to face with field technicians, it was easy to see why the project initiators did not initially recognize the importance of this collaborative relationship.

The project team decided to reconstitute itself with customer service representatives and field service technicians. The initial work of the group would be to focus on the two most critical collaborative relationships: among all of the field service technicians on the one hand and between the technicians and the customer service representatives on the other. At some point, the supervisors and dispatchers would have to be involved as well. Until then, they would be kept informed and consulted on a regular basis and would be invited to sit in on the project team meetings whenever they wished.

As this example illustrates, the MDI process should begin with the critical collaborators. It also demonstrates that individuals do not need to interact face-to-face to be part of a team, especially when technology is available to tie team members together.

2. User Delegates Should Typify Their Community. For Richard Walton to typify the community means to "represent the attitudes, skills, and orientations that will characterize the system's normal operating environment."[6] So, for example, if a delegate is responsible for representing the field service technicians who will be part of the gas emergency response team, he or she should have a field technician's job and hold attitudes, skills, and orientations similar to the other technicians on the user team.

3. User Delegates Should Be Especially Expert in User Team Functions, Operations, and Tasks. As a group, user team representatives need to be collectively familiar with and highly knowledgeable about all of the collaborative relationships and the tasks and activities that comprise these relationships. They also should be familiar with the critical connections between the team and other individuals and groups outside the team as well as with the information and resources needed by the team to work effectively.

Paradoxically, as both Walton and Dorothy Leonard-Barton note, the more expert delegates are in the tasks being "automated or informated," the less likely they are "to typify their community."[7] By definition, experts are exceptional, not typical. This apparent conflict leads us to propose the next characteristic.

4. User Delegates Should Be Able to Empathize with the User Population They Represent. The *American Heritage Dictionary* defines *empathy* as "Identification with and understanding of another's situation, feelings, and motives."[8] Robert Hogan describes it as the ability to put oneself in another's place.[9] We would add that empathy implies patience with those who are less knowledgeable, a quality that can be hard to find among experts. Clearly, delegates who are highly empathetic as well as "especially expert" should be able to "typify their community" at the same time they provide the expertise that is so essential to the success of the project.

5. User Delegates Should Have Credibility with the People They Represent. User teams must be able to respect and trust their delegates. They should feel confident that the individuals chosen to represent them will be strong advocates for their interests and concerns and will keep them informed of important developments early enough in the MDI process to allow the user team to influence these decisions.

Participation

Following are the three qualifications specific to the effective participation of user delegates in the MDI team.

1. User Delegates Should "Develop a Sophisticated Understanding of the [New] Technology."[10] To appreciate both its strengths and its limitations, user delegates need to understand the basic language and core concepts of project-relevant information technology. If they do not possess this knowledge when they join the project team, they should at least have an initial interest in and curiosity about it so they can acquire this critical knowledge early on in the project. They need to be comfortable talking to information systems experts whenever the discussion turns to the technical aspects of the system under development. Not that they have to know a great deal about hardware platforms, communications standards, or software, but they should know enough to understand how decisions made in these areas will affect the work of the individuals and teams that will be using the new systems. They need a minimum level of technical knowledge to at least recognize what they do *not* know and be able to ask the right questions. They should also have the ability to learn quickly about the technology being explored as the MDI process unfolds.

According to Walton and Leonard-Barton, this guideline may be incompatible with the role of user representative. They argue that it "is unlikely that user participants who acquire the developer's sophisticated understanding of the technology will retain the perspective of users."[11] It is not difficult to see how this can happen. Initially, because of their different backgrounds, perspectives, and goals, user representatives and technical experts may have relationships marked by conflict and disagreement. But as they learn to work together and begin to see the system as a mutual product of their collaborative efforts, the interests of the user representatives and the technology experts will grow more closely aligned. The user representatives may become increasingly intrigued by the technical challenges of the project—challenges that are markedly different from those they typically deal with in their jobs. As the technical challenges become their primary focus, their connection with the daily concerns and interests of the users they are supposed to represent may diminish.

The fundamental problem is the potential conflict between the roles of user team representative and MDI team participant. User team delegates can not afford to neglect their participant role in their determination to fulfill their role as user representative. If they do, they can seriously compromise the entire MDI process.[12]

What, then, is the solution to this apparent dilemma? First, it's not necessarily an either/or issue. The same interpersonal skills are necessary for both roles, and empathetic user delegates should be able to maintain the dual perspective of user representative and MDI participant. But even the most empathetic delegates will lose the user's perspective if they do not keep in touch with the people they represent. That is why members of Congress often undertake extraordinary efforts to maintain their link with their constituents, via frequent mailings and trips home, for example. Similarly, user team delegates need to work closely with their "constituents" to develop activities and mechanisms (E-mail, newsletters, meetings) that will keep them in touch with each other. We will address this issue more thoroughly in chapter 6.

Ultimately, the issue is broader than MDI. With the growth of cross-functional teams and strategic business alliances, employees with multiple roles are rapidly becoming the norm in modern organizations. External communications networks will accelerate this growth and expand the number and range of these cross-organizational collaborations. Organizations will need to learn how to create a culture and implement policies and mechanisms to support these multiple roles. MDI can become the crucible in which these new cultures and practices are forged.

2. User Delegates Should Possess Good Interpersonal Skills. Like all members of the MDI team, user delegates should be able to work well with others. They need to be assertive enough to present their points of view when appropriate and flexible enough to compromise when necessary.

3. User Delegates Should Be Open to Change. The MDI process can be extraordinarily unsettling for those who participate in it. Rather than progressing in a more or less straight line from beginning to end, most projects will travel down a far more erratic, unpredictable path. Two steps forward, one step back, then off in a completely different direction is the typical course. Being a participant in an MDI project is like exploring new territory where the ground is constantly shifting under your feet, where the destination, like a mirage, keeps slipping out of reach. To make matters worse, the members of the expeditionary force barely know one another and have different backgrounds and experience.

This is why we recommend that the "explorers" chosen for this journey be flexible, future oriented, tolerant of uncertainty and ambiguity, willing to take risks, and able to learn from mistakes. This is what we mean by "being open to change." These qualities are necessary for dealing with the cross-functional, open-ended, nonlinear, learn-as-you-act nature of MDI. Specifically, user delegates need to be comfortable working with people who possess knowledge and expertise very different from their own. As they become more familiar with other delegates' domains of knowledge, they should be able to relate what they have learned to the interests and concerns of the user team. Likewise, they should be able to convey to MDI team members the implications of user team constraints on systems design and task restructuring. Essentially, the user delegate needs to be "bilingual," capable of translating the language of the user team to the MDI team and vice versa.

Initially, many user delegates may feel overwhelmed by the challenges of their task, particularly the technical aspects of systems design. Unless they have some technical background or are otherwise familiar with the technology, they may be defensive about their limited technical knowledge and reluctant to participate fully for fear of appearing incompetent. What they may not realize is that the other stakeholder representatives are in the same boat—they are all experts in their own areas and relative novices in areas represented by other participants.

As we will see in the next chapter, the MDI process must be viewed as a mutual learning experience in which everyone starts with knowledge of limited scope. Each participant's expertise gradually expands as the team members work together, share what they know, and encourage each other to test the limits of their knowledge. In the process, they will create a shared language and new knowledge as a team. This knowledge will be embodied in new systems, new ways of working, and new organizational forms. Therefore, those individuals selected to participate in the process should be comfortable with its inherent risk, ambiguity, and uncertainty.

This process also requires the kind of people who can shift their focus from immediate concerns and problems to future needs. This is not an easy task, especially if, as Leonard-Barton notes, they lack the technical understanding to have such vision.[13] Flexibility and tolerance for uncertainty may compensate for the absence of such prescience, however.[14] Effective user delegates are those who can participate patiently in an ongoing, iterative MDI process that at times seems like it will never end. They can develop a vision of their future needs as they learn from the process. They are able to respond and adapt to changing needs, knowledge, circumstances, and technology.

Representation and Participation

One last characteristic, which is relevant to the roles of representative and participant, may be the most important. It is also the most obvious characteristic and therefore the easiest one to overlook.

1. User Delegates Should Be Motivated Enough to Expend the Time and Effort Needed for Effective Representation and Participation. The involvement of disinterested user delegates, or worse, resentful ones who view their MDI team responsibilities as a burden that takes time away from their "real" work, may be worse than no user involvement at all. The best delegates enjoy the challenges of involvement; they perceive it as an important responsibility and a valuable experience that can contribute to their career development. They do not require close supervision and direction, and they thrive in situations where they can exert influence and *some* control (a need for too much control would conflict with the compromises and trade-offs that are the hallmark of productive collaborations).

But motivation does not thrive in a vacuum. It is not just a quality inherent to certain individuals or teams but a product of management and corporate human resource practices and policies. Management and the HR function are responsible for providing the rewards and resources and creating the conditions necessary for motivating user delegates to work hard and perform well.

IMPLICATIONS OF USER TEAM TYPE

Most of the research on user involvement in systems development has been conducted on work teams. As noted in chapter 2, user teams can be of any type—project teams, parallel teams, management teams, or ad hoc networks, as well as work teams—but different types present special challenges for those selected to represent them in the MDI process.

- ◆ *Project teams:* The MDI project may outlast the particular project teams from which the user representatives are drawn. This can present the MDI team with a choice. If it replaces the project team representative with someone from a new user team, the MDI team risks losing continuity. If it does not, the MDI team puts the representative in the potentially ambiguous and awkward role of representing a user team to which they no longer belong. One possible solution to this problem is to choose delegates who represent project teams engaged in similar efforts—for example, product development teams working on the same family of products.

- *Parallel teams:* Participation in these teams is typically an "add-on" to the member's usual job responsibilities. As a result, participation on the MDI team can be a double add-on of responsibilities that might stretch user delegates well beyond their limits. Project sponsors therefore need to make clear to all delegates why the project is important and why their participation is so critical to its success.

- *Management teams:* Selecting a management team delegate to serve on the MDI team can pose an especially difficult challenge. First, managers often do not see themselves as team members but as individuals who occasionally meet to discuss issues of mutual concern. In addition, most senior managers prefer not to participate in the kind of detailed, operational-level work required in the MDI process. They are used to delegating such tasks. To compound the problem, they are often computer illiterate and technophobic.

  The solution is to remind them that they need to walk the walk as well as talk the talk if they expect other stakeholders and their representatives to take the project seriously. Besides, if they really believe that information technology is critical to the firm's competitive position, they should act as role models for the rest of the organization. In any case, as with any other group, one person is likely to have more technical interest and aptitude than others. Unless there are good arguments to the contrary, that is the individual who should represent the management team on the MDI team.

- *Ad hoc networks:* Given the amorphous and fluid nature of ad hoc networks, user representatives may be less than certain about their boundaries and the network and its key collaborative relationships. It is especially important that they have a clear understanding of why the network exists and how it relates to the goals of the organization.

Finally, different types of teams may even be involved in the same project. This should be approached with caution, however, since there are different critical design factors for the different team types (see chapter 9). Mixing team types in the same project can add burdensome layers of complexity to an already complex process. To keep such projects from collapsing under their own weight, special care must be taken to break down the project into meaningful chunks and create the integrating mechanisms to tie it all together.

CONCLUSION

Finding delegates with all of the characteristics outlined above can be a daunting task. Most of the time project initiators and user teams will have to settle for mere mortals who possess many but not all of the qualities they desire. In any case, those with the responsibility for selecting representatives should resist the temptation to focus on specific characteristics. Individually, these characteristics are less important than a delegate's overall profile. The most effective delegates are bright, motivated, flexible, highly regarded, and socially skilled. They possess an expansive and interdisciplinary vision and are willing and able to work with and learn from other individuals with different functional backgrounds, perspectives, and agendas. In short, the MDI team needs user delegates who can keep in touch with their roots while embracing the unfamiliar and the unknown.

Furthermore, as we will see in chapter 6, the design of the MDI team itself can be structured to compensate for those characteristics that may be lacking and reinforce others that may be particularly important. For example, training in information technology fundamentals early in the process will provide user team delegates with the technological sophistication they need to work effectively with information technology experts. In addition, creating strong connections between user team delegates and those they represent can go a long way toward maintaining their user perspective even as they become more technologically sophisticated. We will have much more to say about these issues in the chapters to follow.

◆ ◆ ◆

Two weeks later, the SICIM project team conference room at the corporate headquarters of Paws & Claws . . .

This is the second meeting of the project team that Bill has attended since joining the project. Aside from some introductory comments, Bill's participation in his first meeting the week before was minimal. But this week he was ready to raise the concerns that have been troubling him since he was asked to join the project team a few weeks ago. He is anxious to get it over with, but he will have to wait since he is last on the agenda.

After the others have presented their reports it's Bill's turn. He expresses his concerns with surprising passion, in contrast with his usually taciturn demeanor. "The people in the plant are really pissed. I can't even get anyone to go out for a beer with me anymore. They think the project's a waste of time, that it has nothing to do with what they need. I'm just a management toady, they say. They think you brought me into the project to make it look as if they can have some influence, but they know that all of the important decisions have already been made. They think you're just trying to buy us off and don't really care about what we think. Worse than that, it looks as if you don't value our experience and knowledge. We have a lot to offer. We know a helluva lot about the work we do, damn it, a helluva lot more than you do." Bill visibly gulps as he realizes what he just said.

He continues for several more minutes, building up to a climax of frustration and unexpected excitement. In spite of his anxiety about the impact of what he has to say, he enjoys the attention and the opportunity. He finishes and looks around. A stunned silence fills the room.

Chris tilts back in his chair, puts his fingertips together, and purses his lips. He is deep in thought. Bill looks anxiously at Chris. "He doesn't look happy," he thinks. "Maybe I went too far."

Finally, Chris breaks the silence. "Well, it sounds like we got a lot of work to do. Bill, I'm really glad you're on the team. By the way, is that a new suit? It looks great on you!"

For a moment, Bill forgets the pinch of his tie and the weight of his suit. "Bill," Chris continues, "what kind of systems help do the users need? Do you know? Have any ideas about how we can find out?" As Bill begins to talk, Chris grabs a handful of markers and moves toward the whiteboard at the front of the room.

5

Selecting Information Technology Experts and Others

Mid-November, SICIM project conference room, Paws & Claws Corporate Headquarters . . .

Mark has left the project and returned to Los Angeles. When he announced his decision at the last meeting, he explained, "Crabs are no longer in season, the leaves have turned brown on the trees, and the weather is getting decidedly nippy. Besides, you really don't need me anymore. I think you can handle the rest of this project without me. In any case, I'll be available whenever you need me."

Although the project team meeting has just begun, the first since Mark's departure, the tone of the meeting is already belying his overly optimistic assessment. Leading off the meeting is Ann Cunningham, the lead delegate from marketing and sales. She joined the team just a couple of weeks earlier, after Bill and Mark convinced the others that someone from her department should be added to the project team. Marketing and sales will use the new system, Bill and Mark argued at the time, and will work closely with the production teams to help them identify the most profitable product mix. Since this collaborative relationship is critical to the success of the project, representatives from all parties to the collaboration should be on the project team. The logic of their argument won the day.

Ann begins her comments by raising a serious concern. Her boss, the department manager, is becoming a problem. Apparently, the VP he reports to has warned him that the project has only lukewarm support from the senior executives. Chris has been keeping them in the dark about the project because he didn't want them to interfere. As Chris noted with some pride on more than one occasion, "That really takes some chutzpah [his mangled pronunciation making Steve wince], considering I've managed to get them to commit a significant sum of money to the project."

"And that's exactly the problem," Bill thought. He had heard through the grapevine that the senior execs were beginning to resent Chris's "chutzpah." Besides, most of them viewed Chris as a bit of a loose cannon. None of them wanted to be too closely associated with the project in case it "went down in flames," to use one of Chris's favorite expressions. But then again, nobody was willing to write Chris off completely. He was too bright, too creative, and had a good track record. As a result, the senior executives were hedging their bets, trying to look supportive but ready to bail out at the first sign of trouble.

Their ambivalence was reflected by management at all levels. Ann's manager was no exception. He was putting pressure on Ann and the other design team members from his department to spend less time on the project and more time on their departmental responsibilities.

Steve is next on the agenda. He is concerned that several other critical stakeholder groups are not involved in the project. The cost accounting department is one. It will produce the data that will be on the system and will also use the system for its own work. Surprisingly, he is most concerned about the exclusion of the MIS group. The people in MIS are angry at being passed over for the project in favor of Storm and Drang, and Chris was planning on "teaching them a lesson on how to work with their internal customers." But they need to be involved, Steve feels, since they will eventually be responsible for systems support and maintenance. He didn't want to see the results of Storm and Drang's considerable efforts go to waste because of stubborn arrogance and hurt feelings. Some of the senior executives' ambivalence about the project, he suspects, could be directly tied to their concerns that the involvement of external contractors far outweighed participation by the company's own people.

After some heated discussion, Chris is finally convinced by Ann and Steve's arguments. He is only momentarily humbled by the implied criticism—he has heard much worse in his years at Paws & Claws. He dramatically crumples up the printed agenda and, without even a glance in the direction of the wastebasket in the corner, expertly sinks a hook shot off both walls. "I guess we need to change our agenda. Any thoughts about which issues we should address first?"

◆ ◆ ◆

User teams are just one of several stakeholder groups that may be affected by new technology and workplace designs and that bring knowledge and expertise to the MDI process. In this chapter we describe these other stakeholder groups and, as we did in the preceding chapter on user teams, discuss why and how they should be included on the MDI team.

We begin by looking at the information technology experts who will help develop the systems that will eventually be an integral part of the user teams' work. These two parties, user teams and IT experts, are the most important participants in the MDI process. The quality of the collaborative relationship between them is one of the best predictors of a system's ultimate success.[1] But this relationship is complex and often highly problematic. Selecting the right people to provide information technology expertise is critical to the success of the project.

INFORMATION TECHNOLOGY EXPERTS

Just as one could argue that user participation was one of the most important systems development issues during the 1980s, the role of the information technology expert may be one of the defining systems development issues of the 1990s and beyond. The issues are different, of course. No one has ever had to argue, for example, that information technology expertise is essential to systems development. But who provides this expertise, how they provide it, and what their relationship should be with users and the corporate IT function are very much in dispute. Dramatic changes in the nature of the technology—including greater emphasis on personal computers and distributed architectures—have produced equally dramatic changes in where information technology experts are located and what roles they can play in the MDI process.

Sources of Expertise

Organizations today draw their information technology expertise from three different sources: (1) their internal, centralized IT department; (2) their internal, team-based, "local" experts; and (3) external vendors, contractors, and consultants. Most large organizations employ all three, individually or in combination, depending on the project, corporate culture, availability of resources, and the perceived quality of the sources on which they can draw.

Internal, Centralized IT Departments Typically, a corporation's internal, centralized, information technology department is responsible for developing IT-based business applications. In this approach, systems analysts or consultants from the corporate IT department work with the user team to develop the appropriate information systems and tools. At their best, IT departments blend state-of-the-art technical expertise with firsthand knowledge of the culture and overall business of the organization. Using internal IT departments as the primary source of technical expertise also ensures that what is developed will be compatible with the corporate-wide information infrastructure and will be supported and maintained by the department.

The problem with this approach is that many systems professionals do not understand the specific needs of the intended users or the details of their work tasks and processes. Unless they themselves have similar work experience their substantive knowledge is bound to be limited and secondhand. They often cannot communicate with users, tend to subordinate user desires to broader, corporate imperatives, and view corporate management, rather than end-user units, as their client.

Compounding the problem is the fact that their clients, the system users, have reached a level of sophistication that enables them to recognize when they are not being served well by the systems they use. They are increasingly dissatisfied with the services and expertise provided by the IT departments they have become so dependent on. As a result, a consensus is emerging that "IT applications are best led by line managers who thoroughly understand the business situation."[2]

More and more, line managers and the units that report to them are developing their own applications and tools. This leaves corporate information technology departments with the responsibility for "infrastructure planning at the corporate level"[3] and the development of generic applications and tools that will be widely used throughout the organization. Where then will business units and user teams find the technical expertise they need to develop the applications they will use?

Internal, Team-based Experts In an increasing number of cases, the answer to the question posed above is that the expertise will be "home-grown" (or if you prefer, "home-brewed"); that is, it will (and, increasingly, already does) reside within the unit or team itself. The source of this expertise is the one or more individuals in every department or team who show more interest and facility with information technology than the others. They are the ones who come to work early or stay late to "play" with a new system. They master the basic operations of the system before anyone else and then move on to more advanced functions and applications. These "local experts" or "gurus" often think of new ways to use the system and modify it to do new things. Increasingly, their coworkers turn to them for help in learning how to get the most out of their new technology. In time, the local experts will be the first to recognize the limits of the existing system and begin to think of additions and upgrades, or even new systems, to meet the evolving needs of their units.[4]

Homegrown expertise may not always be available.[5] If it is not, teams can hire individuals to fill this role either as permanent team members or as consultants. Whatever the case, the important point is that they have expertise in both information technology and the teams' tasks. Whether homegrown or hired, team-based experts can help create a better fit between the team's information tools and business needs. As part of the team, they will have a better understanding of its work and functions than corporate IT experts or external contractors hired by corporate management. They can act as "translators" between these experts and their coworkers on the user team when they themselves do not possess enough technical expertise to be the primary information technology expert on the MDI team.[6,7]

In any case, their relative lack of technological sophistication is no longer as serious a limitation as it used to be. The technological empowerment of the nontechnical workforce that began with the introduction of the personal computer continues with more recent developments in user-modifiable software, modular programming, and high-level languages and procedures for applications development. These advances enable local experts to move rapidly up the applications development learning curve—perhaps faster than corporate information technology experts or external contractors can learn about the work of the team. And with the increased availability of modifiable, off-the-shelf software and end-user application development tools, user units are less dependent on custom-built applications that are costly to maintain, upgrade, and extend. As a result, user teams are more and more likely to nurture or hire their own information technology experts to help them develop their new systems and tools than to rely on the centralized, internal sources they have turned to in the past.[8]

Relying exclusively on local information technology experts does have its problems. Specifically, it excludes the corporate IT department from many important decisions that are often made early in the MDI process. Whether or not they understand user needs, the corporate IT experts know the technology infrastructure—its limitations as well as its capabilities. In addition, they are legitimate stakeholders in the process since they are responsible for:

- ensuring connectivity and compatibility among team-based systems and the IT infrastructure of the overall organization;

- standardizing across different applications and functional units when "reengineering" creates cross-functional teams and processes; and

- ensuring that work units throughout the company know about information resources created for specific units and can access or adopt these resources for their own uses when appropriate.

Just as user buy-in is often the primary justification for user involvement, representation of the internal information technology department on the MDI team is necessary to ensure its buy-in as well. If only team-based experts participate, corporate-wide information technology interests and concerns may not be well represented, if represented at all. The likely result? Conflict between team-based experts and the information technology department and, from the perspective of the overall organization, suboptimal systems.

External Vendors, Contractors, and Consultants The lack of buy-in and support from corporate information technology can also be an issue when systems development is outsourced to external vendors, contractors, or consultants. Initially, this approach was used primarily by small organizations that could not afford the expense of maintaining their own IT departments. But in recent years many larger corporations have also turned to external sources for their information technology expertise. Individual units, teams, and departments sometimes use outside vendors as well, especially if their internal IT department has neither the time nor the skill to meet their needs.

The major impetus for this move is twofold: controlling overhead by eliminating or downsizing the IT department, while increasing access to "world class" services.[9] With respect to the latter, external sources can often offer a combination of depth and breadth of experience and expertise that cannot be matched by internal information technology departments. Many vendors, consultants, and contractors focus on specific industries and have worked with a variety of companies and applications within those industries. They bring a broad perspective on industry-specific applications to the needs of particular clients within that industry. In addition, since many of them have experience in developing cross-organizational systems (for example, linking organizations with their suppliers), they can provide the kind of integrative perspective so much in demand by forward-looking organizations.

Organizational politics is another driving force behind the growing use of outside vendors, contractors, and consultants. Information technology development projects, especially those involving large-scale process reengineering, often lead to highly unpopular changes—some departments, for instance, end up with fewer employees, reduced budgets, and narrower scopes of responsibility. External sources can be handy scapegoats, taking the conflict and resentments with them when they are finished, so that those remaining can work together without the unpleasant residues left behind by a contentious process of change.[10]

There are a host of other reasons why more and more companies and user teams are turning to outside sources. In some cases, their intent may be to create competition for their internal information technology department in the hope of challenging it to develop particular competencies and improve performance. In other cases, the decision makers may feel that the culture of their corporate IT department is incompatible with the project (for example, too technocratic to develop user-empowering systems). Sometimes the reasons may even be punitive. Like Chris in our story, executives or managers may wish to teach their IT department "a lesson" for an earlier failing, either real or imagined. Outsourcing is also relatively easy to do these days. Since information-based work can be taken apart and reconfigured to generate new task structures, organizations have the option of farming out some of these reconfigured tasks to external vendors.[11]

Whatever the reason, the potential downside consequences are similar to those cited earlier with respect to the use of local experts. Corporate IT departments may be responsible for integrating vendor systems into the organization's IT infrastructure and for supporting and maintaining these systems once the contract with the external sources has ended. If representatives of corporate IT are left out of the process, destructive conflict and suboptimal system solutions may be the ultimate result.

Choosing the Right Person

All of the sources outlined above have their limitations as well as their advantages. Some of the limitations can be overcome by carefully choosing the particular individuals who will actually serve as members of the MDI team. Effective IT experts possess particular qualities and characteristics, which are in many respects similar to those of user delegates. But identifying who they represent is less straightforward, so defining the roles and, consequently, the characteristics of effective IT experts is somewhat more complicated.

Internal, Centralized IT Departments The role of IT department-based technical experts is similar to that of their user team counterparts. First, they are responsible for representing the expertise and interests of their stakeholder group, the IT department. Therefore, like the user delegates they should be experts—but in their case, in the technology to be developed and the technology infrastructure with which it will be integrated. They also need to typify their community and empathize with the people they represent so that the MDI team does not develop a system that the IT department will be able to support and maintain only with difficulty. In addition, just as the user delegates need credibility with the user teams they represent, IT experts on the MDI team should be respected and trusted by their colleagues.

To participate effectively on the MDI team, they should have characteristics and skills similar to those of the user team delegates. All members of the MDI team should possess good interpersonal skills and be adaptable and open to change. They must be capable of listening to and learning from users. For IT experts, the counterpart to the user delegates' need to "develop a sophisticated understanding of the technology" is the need to develop a sophisticated understanding of the work requirements and tasks of the user team. Again, all members of the MDI team, IT experts included, should be highly motivated to represent their stakeholder groups and participate in team efforts.

Effective IT experts differ from user delegates in one particularly significant way. In addition to representing the internal information technology department, they must also view user teams as their customers and serve their needs. In recent years, "customer service" has become the rallying cry for firms concerned about improving or maintaining their competitive position in the global marketplace. The focus on the customer goes beyond the individuals and organizations that buy a firm's goods or services. It also includes the internal customer, the person or unit within the firm served by other people or units within the same firm. The assumption is that the customer service perspective, when applied to internal relationships and transactions, should improve the effectiveness of these individual transactions and, ultimately, the overall effectiveness of the organization.

Nowhere is the potential of this perspective more revolutionary than when applied to the relationship between internal IT departments and the business units and teams they serve. Successful adoption of this perspective by information technology departments and their personnel might accomplish more to salve this frequently prickly relationship than any other single factor. A customer service orientation is one of the most important qualities the IT expert on the MDI team can have. In practical terms, this means that the expert should be genuinely committed to working with user teams to find the best way to meet its needs within the constraints imposed by budgets, technology, and organizational context.

To illustrate this point, let us return to our earlier example, SWP&L's gas emergency response team project.

As the project proceeded, the team realized that the technical challenges were pushing up against the knowledge and skill limits of the field service technician who had initiated it. Besides, he was beginning to feel overwhelmed by the combined weight of responsibilities from this project piled on to his regular job. They decided to ask the information services department (ISD) for help.

ISD sent one of its most personable, articulate, and user-oriented systems consultants to the group's next meeting. He helped them out with a number of technical issues. More.important than that, however, was his offer to serve as an ongoing technical consultant to the project. He would attend all meetings, offering advice and technical assistance as needed, and work closely with the local expert in between meetings to ensure continued progress.

From his experience with another, similar project he recognized that the technician needed some relief from his rapidly growing job demands. He encouraged the project team to ask the division manager to revise the technician's job description to reflect his current project responsibilities. He also suggested that they ask the division manager to download some of the technician's other responsibilities to the other field service technicians or to hire someone to take over these responsibilities. He offered his support and the support of his department to help make the strongest possible case for this proposal.

His last suggestion was particularly intriguing—to create a dotted-line relationship between the technician and ISD. Among other things, this would give the technician access to ISD's professional development seminars. By attending these seminars he could enhance his present knowledge and skills and be better prepared to serve the division's IT needs in the future. He would also develop a working network of collegial contacts he could draw upon to help him in this new, continually evolving role.

Internal, Team-based Local Experts Since user teams rarely have an excess of local experts from which to choose, selecting one is not usually an issue. If there is a choice, then the same characteristics as described for the internal, centralized IT department expert would apply. Probably the more important issue is how to develop and nurture this expertise in the first place and then integrate it with corporate-wide information technology functions, departments, and expertise. Since this issue is addressed in later chapters, we will defer discussion until then.

External Vendors, Contractors, and Consultants Information technology delegates from external sources require many of the same qualities and characteristics as those from internal, corporate IT departments. There is one important difference, however. MDI team delegates from the same organization are influenced by the same organizational culture. Whatever other differences may exist among them, all such team members are familiar with the dominant values, images, and policies of the organization. Their shared culture acts as an integrating mechanism, binding them together and enabling them to communicate using the same jargon, concepts, and stories.[12]

Because external delegates lack this common frame of reference, other binding mechanisms, such as their personal characteristics, are even more important than when internal sources are used. For example, the ability to work well with others and move easily between different settings and colleagues can help compensate for the lack of a shared culture.

On the other hand, the lack of a shared culture can be turned into an asset. External sources can often introduce to the MDI process the balanced, unbiased perspective of the outsider as well as fresh ideas and new knowledge. Because of their experience in responding to the needs of the marketplace, effective external sources are also likely to possess a genuine customer orientation.

Another important issue in choosing an external source is trust. Given the nature of the business, it is more likely than not that the vendor, contractor, or consultant an organization works with today will be offering similar services to that organization's competitors tomorrow. Therefore, outside sources should be chosen carefully. Some of the issues to be addressed when considering external contractors include the following:

- ◆ Do they have a reputation for integrity and a history that demonstrates an ability to maintain confidentiality?

- ◆ Have they worked successfully for the organization on other projects?

- ◆ Are they selling a specific system or application that may bias the recommendations and solutions they offer?

- ◆ Are they now working on a similar project for a competitor? This is especially important if the project involves the development of an application that is strategically critical for the organization's core business competencies and processes. It is less important if the application is generic—indeed, recent or even concurrent experience with similar projects in other companies can be very helpful. In any case, a clear understanding and agreement on these issues should be written into the contract.

- ◆ Do the personal characteristics of the people who would be working with the MDI team inspire confidence and trust?

An Ongoing Role for Corporate IT The use of team-based experts and external sources is clearly on the rise, and all indications are that these trends will continue into the future. Communication networks can accelerate these trends by connecting external sources more closely to their clients and by increasing local experts' access to the information, applications, and tools that can best serve the needs of their teams.

One might conclude from both of these trends that there is little reason for the continued involvement of internal, centralized information technology expertise in the development of systems and applications for use by teams. That would be a mistake. For reasons outlined earlier, the growing use of local experts and external contractors—plus the complex information architectures in which the applications they develop will reside—makes it even more important that corporate information technology departments be either included in or closely linked to the MDI process. We will talk about these linkages in more detail in the next chapter.

OTHER STAKEHOLDER GROUPS

For all of the remaining potential stakeholder groups, the characteristics of effective delegates are similar to those described for user delegates and information technology experts. Specifically, they should typify the stakeholder group they represent and be expert in the knowledge and skills characteristic of their group. They should also be highly regarded and trusted by the stakeholders they represent and able to put themselves in the place of these stakeholders (that is, be empathetic). They should be familiar with the user team's technology and work as well as with the technology to be developed. Finally, they need good interpersonal skills and should be open to change. Other characteristics specific to each group are noted in the following pages.

Immediate Supervisors and Managers

While managers at all levels have a stake in teams, technology, and organizational change, the level of management likely to be most affected by new systems and team designs are the immediate supervisors and managers to whom the user teams report. Their jobs and roles may be profoundly changed, or even eliminated, by new technologies and designs. They should therefore be represented as well.

Their representatives may belong to the MDI team or the project steering committee, depending on how critical their knowledge is to the project and how much they will be affected by the outcomes. If involved in the MDI team, their role is to represent other user team supervisors and managers, not the user teams themselves. In other words, they should participate *in addition to* the user team delegates, not in place of them. This is a frequent error that can lead to serious misrepresentation of the user population on the MDI team and, eventually, to systems that do not match their needs.

Whether they are on the MDI team or not, unit supervisors should make it clear to the user teams that report to them that their participation is mandatory. They need to send the message that user experience and expertise are essential to the project and that they expect the user teams to make the commitment and expend the effort required for effective participation. To the extent possible, immediate supervisors and managers should be prepared to support and reward this effort.

Helping in the selection of user team delegates is one of the first opportunities supervisors and managers have to demonstrate their commitment to the project. Employees' time is finite. How supervisors and managers allocate their employees' time to different activities is an indication of the importance they assign to these activities. Assigning a qualified, experienced, highly regarded, and well-paid employee to serve as a user team delegate is an unmistakable signal that the MDI project is to be a high priority.

This can also be a selection criterion for choosing supervisor and manager representatives. Project initiators or the MDI team should work with managers and supervisors as a stakeholder group to select representatives from their ranks. Those supervisors and managers who are willing to give up valued employees and support their participation in the project would be particularly good candidates if they also possess the qualities and characteristics generally desired of MDI participants.

Project Sponsors and Senior Managers

Project sponsors should be higher up in the management hierarchy than unit supervisors and managers; how high depends on the complexity, cost, and significance of the project. The rule of thumb is that they need to be high enough to symbolize the scope and importance of the project and to authorize the level of resources and budget it requires. Their role is more to legitimize and fund the project than to be involved in its ongoing tasks and activities. Therefore, they usually will not be part of the MDI team itself. Being connected to the process while remaining somewhat removed from the details and daily dramas enables them to play the essential role of advisor and mediator. As such, they can provide objective guidance and counsel, adjudicate conflicts, and break ties when consensus is not possible.

In some situations, other levels of management may need to be involved in the MDI project. For example, when:

- recommendations from several different MDI teams and projects need to be integrated and coordinated;

- the recommendations require changes in overall organizational policy or corporate IT infrastructure; or

- the MDI or user teams are cross-functional and therefore require representation of this cross-functionality at the levels of the organization that can establish appropriate priorities, make trade-offs, and resolve differences.

One caution: When successive layers of management teams are added on to oversee and coordinate multiple MDI projects, the organization runs the risk of re-creating the kind of bureaucratic structures it is trying to leave behind. Whenever possible, therefore, we recommend that project sponsors and senior managers be combined into a single management steering committee with the resources and authority needed to address the issues outlined above.

Human Resources

Representatives from the HR department should also be involved in the MDI process. They will be affected by many of the designs and changes that will be implemented. They may be asked to help develop programs to train users in the operation and application of new systems. They may need to rewrite job descriptions and reclassify jobs that are changed because of new technologies, tasks, and team designs. They will probably be involved in the development of team-based assessment and reward systems. And they may be asked to develop team-building exercises and programs for the MDI team and user teams. Indeed, the very nature of their jobs may change as new human resource information systems enable teams to do for themselves many of the things that HR personnel used to do for them.

The irony is that while most people would agree that HR departments and professionals should in principle play a significant role in systems development, they rarely do.[13] As Peter Keen notes, their role is usually reactive, and most of them become involved only after implementation, "mainly to deal with consequences of the new system such as increased turnover, job dissatisfaction, stress, and a mismatch between available and needed skills and resources."[14] Like Keen, we recommend a more proactive role for HR departments and professionals. With their wide-ranging expertise and skills, they can contribute to the MDI process in numerous ways:

- initial design of the MDI team itself and ongoing facilitation of its meetings;
- development of the technology, particularly design of the interface and the functions and tasks to be augmented by the technology;
- design of user teams and the overall organizational context (for example, training, job design, career development, and assessment and reward systems);
- plan for the implementation of new systems and associated changes in work flow, task design, and organizational structure and policy; and
- remind all participants of the important role user team members can play in technological and organizational change and of the need to balance social and technological objectives and issues.

Many of these actions may well need the blessing of senior management via organization-wide policy decisions and structural changes. We will return to the roles of human resources and senior management in MDI in chapter 11.

All Others

Depending on the nature of the project, the MDI team may identify other individuals and stakeholder groups that should participate in the process as particular needs or issues arise. This might include customers and suppliers, both internal and external, as well as special experts or key functional groups that are knowledgeable about relevant business issues or that will be affected by decisions, designs, and plans. The rule of thumb as to when representatives of these groups should be involved is, *early enough to participate in the decisions that will affect them or that call for their relevant expertise.* If as a result of the project they end up more interdependent with the user team, boundaries may have to be redrawn to include them as members of the redesigned team.[15]

CONCLUSION

In this chapter and chapter 4 we have described each major stakeholder group in some detail. These stakeholders are depicted in figure 5–1. The roles and characteristics of the people who will represent their interests and expertise are summarized and compared in table 5–1. All of these groups and their representatives have important roles to play in the MDI process, though when they will be involved, to what degree, and concerning which issues may vary widely.

From the discussion in these two chapters we can reach a number of conclusions specific to each major stakeholder group. For user teams, the dominant issue is no longer whether user involvement works. Instead, the focus is now on the factors and conditions that can make it

Figure 5–1 Stakeholders

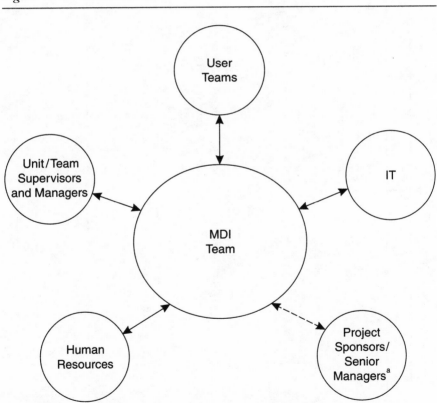

a Project Sponsors/Senior Managers are key stakeholders, but are more likely to serve on a steering committee than directly on the MDI team.

Table 5-1 Completed Stakeholder Matrix

Focal Area	Stakeholder Group	Role	Key Characteristics
Teams	User Teams	Provide functional/business expertise Represent users' collaborations Participate in design and implementation	Understand work processes Exhibit interpersonal skills Exhibit empathy, credibility Be open to learning
Technology	Information Technology Experts	Provide IT expertise Represent technology community Participate in design and implementation	Understand technology Have a customer service orientation Exhibit interpersonal skills Exhibit empathy, credibility Be open to learning
	Unit Supervisors/Managers	Provide functional/business expertise Represent supervisors/managers Select user team representatives Participate in design and implementation	Understand management processes Exhibit interpersonal skills Exhibit empathy, credibility Be open to learning
Organization	Project Sponsors/Senior Managers	Legitimate project Authorize resources Serve on steering committee	Understand management processes Exhibit interpersonal skills Exhibit empathy, credibility Be open to learning
	Human Resources	Provide HR expertise Facilitate team meetings Represent HR community Promote HR values	Understand HR function Exhibit interpersonal skills Exhibit empathy, credibility Be open to learning
	Others		

work—in other words, what the concept of user involvement really means and how it can be most effectively implemented in practice. The problem is that calling a set of activities "user involvement" does not necessarily make it so. As with most everything else, the issue is too complex to be captured in a phrase. The expression "user involvement" tells us little about who is involved, how they are involved, and what are their roles and responsibilities in the process. But these are exactly the considerations that can make the difference between a project that is successful and one that is not.

Other stakeholders besides user teams are critical to the success of systems development projects. Of these other stakeholders, information technology experts are the most important. Indeed, as we mentioned earlier, research studies have consistently demonstrated that the quality of the relationship between user teams and information technology experts during systems development is one of the best predictors of eventual systems success. As this chapter and the preceding one illustrate, this relationship can be enhanced by picking the right people to participate in the process and striking a balance between the needs of the organization and the needs of the user teams.

Focusing too heavily on the user/IT expert relationship, however, can lead project initiators and the MDI team to overlook another important group of stakeholders: senior managers. Ironically, their very status and influence would seem to make them the stakeholders least likely to be left out of the MDI process. But it can happen and often does. Whatever the reason—managers' reluctance to take on additional responsibilities or the MDI team's desire to keep them from interfering in the process—the consequences can be fatal to the project.[16] Senior management is often the only source for the mother's milk of successful innovation: resources, legitimacy, and influence. No project can succeed without them. (As we noted in chapter 3, senior managers are more likely to serve on the steering committee than directly on the MDI team, unless the project involves the development of information technology applications for the senior management team.)

Probably the single most important conclusion to be drawn from this and the preceding chapter is applicable to all stakeholder groups, and that is that all participants must be able to work effectively with people of different functional backgrounds, work experiences, knowledge bases, and skills. *Laterality* is the term we use from here on to describe this ability to cut across functional boundaries and relate to others from different areas. People with this capability:

- can act as a bridge and interpreter between different functional areas;
- can rapidly learn the basic language and conceptual framework of their collaborators from other areas;
- are confident, but not egotistical, about what they know; and
- are not defensive about their lack of knowledge in other areas and are willing to learn.

This quality will come in handy when the MDI team begins to deal with the consequences of change. Some stakeholders may lose more than others, no matter how much "win-win" rhetoric surrounds the project. Only by facing these issues of gains and loses from technological and organizational change can MDI team participants expect to deal with them effectively. And only if the participants possess the qualities previously described can the MDI team expect to deal creatively with the tension and conflict these issues will inevitably engender.[17]

A little over a decade ago, the systems development process was primarily driven by information technology expertise. User involvement was typically limited to a one-shot opportunity to fill out an "information needs" survey or react to more-or-less finished designs. Other influences were negligible. Through this decade and beyond, the process will evolve into something quite different—an ongoing, proactive, open-ended collaboration among diverse stakeholder groups. In this and preceding chapters we have discussed who these stakeholders are and how to select their representatives to serve on the MDI team. Now the challenge is to continue this team design process by molding the members into a team and creating the conditions for their successful collaboration.

◆ ◆ ◆

Early December, SICIM project conference room . . .

The members of the newly expanded SICIM project team slowly drift into the room as the scheduled time for the weekly project team meeting approaches. Chris is the last to enter. *After a few minutes of schmoozing with several team members, he moves to the front of the room and waits patiently as the murmur of separate conversations dies down.*

He begins. "I would like to welcome everybody to the first meeting of the new SICIM development project team. Before I brief the new members about the project and the reason they are here and bring the rest of you up to date, I want to go around the room and have everyone introduce themselves. Tell us your name, where you work, and briefly describe two of your most notable characteristics—one that you consider positive, the other, negative. You should pick those characteristics we are most likely to experience as we work with you on the project.

"To illustrate what I mean, I'll begin. I'm Chris DeManconi, director of special projects for the manufacturing division, Paws & Claws, Inc. Until you or someone else decides otherwise, I will lead the team. Those of you who have worked with me in the past know I can be a bull-headed, demanding, and arrogant SOB. I hope you also think I am a helluva a lot of fun to work with. So much for me. Steve, why don't you go next?"

For the next few minutes the introductions continue around the room. The new members include representatives from MIS, cost accounting, and human resources, the last added in response to Mark's parting recommendation that an internal HR representative should take his place on the project team. This person would help facilitate team meetings and provide substantive expertise on user team design and the human resources impacts of the new system and other work-related changes.

Chris follows the introductions with a brief but inspiring project overview for the new members. His presentation has the rhythm and feel of an evangelical preacher addressing his congregation. As he reaches his dramatic climax, he shifts from preacher to football coach, metaphorically slapping the fannies of his charged-up minions rushing out of the locker room on to the playing field. By the end of the presentation, the believers are revitalized and the skeptics have been converted.

6

Designing the
MDI Team

Two months later, the SICIM project conference room . . .

The SICIM project team members straggle sullenly into the conference room for their weekly meeting. In recent weeks they have begun to refer to this meeting as the B³ meeting—for "briefing, bitching, and b.s.'ing." This note of good-natured irony is turning increasingly strident, however, as they continue to fall behind schedule with few visible signs of progress to show for their considerable efforts.

Most everyone believes that the problems can be traced back to Chris's leadership style, though no one seems willing to state this belief out loud. While his leadership style is great for getting everyone juiced up and raring to go, it's essentially useless for managing the day-to-day details of such a complex project. Objectives are vague, resources are overlooked, critical tasks remain undone, deadlines are missed, and no one seems to know what's going on from one moment to the next. "Once you get past the vision," one brave team member muttered in Chris's absence at one meeting, "he doesn't seem to have the vaguest notion about how to get things done."

To make matters even worse, the intended users in the plant are growing increasingly skeptical about the project. Despite Bill's addition to the project team, they still feel left out. They are only marginally better informed about the project and no more involved than they were before he joined the team. The source of the problem seems to be Bill himself. By all appearances, he has lost touch with the very people he is supposed to represent.

Ironically, one indication of this is how well he now seems to fit into the project team. For one thing, he is beginning to look almost comfortable in the new suits he purchased for the project. Losing a few pounds no doubt helped. According to Bill the weight loss was completely unintentional since he no longer joined his former coworkers at the plant for their weekly evenings of bowling and beer. Instead, he was now meeting with Chris and Steve two nights a week to discuss the project over snifters of single-malt whiskey.

Perhaps the best indication of how out of touch he is with the production workers is his continued reluctance to meet with them at the plant to tell them about the project, answer questions, and get their input. Every time Chris and Steve suggest that he do, his response is essentially the same. "I'm not so sure that's a good idea," he would say. "They don't understand the project, and they don't know much about computers, either. If we give them the chance, they'll just ask for stuff they don't need or we can't give them. Besides, I know what they want. That's what I'm here for, right?" The last was more a statement of irrefutable fact than a question.

"When I have the time," he would say, "I'll let the users back at the plant know what's going on and get their feedback." But he rarely does.

Chris opens up the meeting with a plea. "Will someone please tell me what's wrong. Why can't we move off square one on this project? Does anyone know . . . or maybe you're afraid to tell me? Come on, level with me, I won't bite . . . hard." A ripple of embarrassed laughter followed by a long awkward silence. Finally, a tentative voice from the back of the room, "Chris, I think that before we design the system, we need to design ourselves. And the first design task is the management of the project. In other words, Chris, I'm afraid part of the problem is you. . . ."

◆ ◆ ◆

IN THIS CHAPTER we discuss the design of the team that is central to the entire MDI process: the MDI team. In at least one respect, the MDI team is like all other teams. It is not enough to just throw people together (even the right people), provide them with a facilitator, and tell them to go to work. As we argued in chapter 2, teams need to be designed for effectiveness, and different types of teams need to be designed differently.

The MDI team is a project team. But not just any project team. Like all project teams, functional diversity is a given. But the potentially wide and contentious differences between users and information technology experts can make this an especially difficult and critical issue for the MDI team. Furthermore, while maintaining connections with stakeholders is important for all project teams, effective linkages with intended user teams are absolutely essential for successful MDI projects. These are the core issues affecting the design of the MDI team.

Chapter 2 described the general principles of effective team design. In this chapter we narrow our focus, examining first what each step of the process means for project teams, then for a particular kind of project team, the MDI team.[1] By the end of the chapter we will have a good idea as to how the MDI team should be structured, how it should be managed and linked with the rest of the organization, and what can be done to enhance its performance. Once designed, the MDI team will be ready to take on its real work: the mutual design and implementation of teams, technology, and organizational change. But first, it needs to design itself.

DEFINING PROJECT TEAM COMPOSITION

At the risk of stating the obvious, the rule of thumb for project teams is that individual team members should be especially knowledgeable in their specialties; the team as a whole should contain most of the skills and competencies needed to fulfill its mission and goals. While this is true for all types of teams, the particular nature of project teams adds layers of complexity to this apparently straightforward statement. Since project team members are typically drawn from different units and departments, they have different functional backgrounds and different kinds of training and experience. These differences can lead either to destructive conflict and tension or to synergy, creativity, and innovation. Therefore, project team members should possess the ability to communicate with and relate to others with different backgrounds, skills, values, and perspectives. Team members with this quality are adaptable, possess good interpersonal skills, and are able to transcend the parochial concerns and perspectives of their disciplines (we refer to this as *laterality* in chapter 5).

Given the temporary nature of projects, project team membership is also temporary. But during the life cycle of the project, members may work on it full- or part-time depending on their role and the requirements of the project. As the project moves forward, the membership can change to include the particular skills and knowledge required at different points in the project. Nonetheless, some core members—in the case of the MDI team, the user team and IT delegates (see chapters 4 and 5)—should remain on the team from beginning to end to ensure continuity. Finally, the size of the team should be limited to the smallest number required to do the work effectively.

DEFINING THE PROJECT TEAM LEADER'S ROLE

Two questions are relevant to the leadership of project teams. The first is "Who should lead project teams?" The second is "How should this leader lead?" The answer to the first can be quite complicated. If the project is critical to the organization, if credibility within the organization is dependent on rank, and if the team has the authority to make key project decisions, the project leader should hold a relatively high-level position in the organization. Otherwise, the project can be led by someone of lesser rank. In some cases, a leader can be selected from within the team, and leadership can change depending on the task or stage of the project (for a new product development team, the leader might be from R&D during design and from manufacturing later on). In general, what matters is not position per se but whether the leader can obtain support from key stakeholders and manage the complexities of the project and the team's diverse membership.

The answer to the second question is easier to state—there are fewer contingencies and caveats—but can be particularly difficult to implement. In general, project team leadership should facilitate, not direct. Since each member is on the team at least partly because of her or his knowledge and expertise, a leader would be ill-advised to try to tell team members what they should do and how they should do it. Instead, the leader's role is to create conditions and circumstances that enable the team to decide these issues on its own in an effective and informed manner.

An important part of this facilitative role is to create a supportive, unobtrusive, and focused environment within which project team members can concentrate on their primary, substantive tasks with minimal distraction. Project leaders should, for example, take on responsibility for project management—tracking progress, budgets, workloads, and schedules. They should also be responsible for boundary management—managing the relations between the team, individuals and units external to the team, and the overall organization. This involves many tasks. One of the most important is helping the team understand its mission and align its efforts with the organization's goals and objectives. Other tasks include coordinating, acting as a liaison, acquiring resources, bringing in outside expertise when needed, tracking performance, and maintaining accountability.

Team leaders should also help facilitate the internal functioning of the team. One aspect of this role is to manage the project team's life cycle. Timing is as important for project team leaders as it is for stand-up comics. When and how particular issues are addressed, events planned, and interventions introduced can dramatically affect team progress. Some points in the project team life cycle are more critical than others. Not surprisingly, the beginning is one. Problems in the early stages can significantly inhibit progress throughout the entire project. The mid-point is another. Project teams often get bogged down midway through their work. They may lose focus, go back to earlier work, and begin to reexamine their initial assumptions. Project team leaders need to be sensitive to these important junctures and transitions. Rather than barreling blindly ahead, astute leaders will treat them as opportunities and will time events and interventions to help the team manage its passage through the critical stages of the project life cycle.[2]

The project team leader can also facilitate the internal functioning of the team by helping members use objective, structured decision-making techniques to resolve differences. These methodologies can be critical to a project team's success.[3] Most everyone has been on teams in which highly assertive members dominated meetings and influenced decisions by the force of their personality or the volume of their voice rather than by reasoned argument, data, or other evidence. Other factors, such as professional status, personal appearance, and the like, can also unfairly influence decisions. Numerous techniques are available to help teams reduce the influence of such factors and create fairer and more objective decision-making processes.[4] As early in the team's life cycle as possible, the project team leader should help the team identify techniques it can use and when to use them. Leaders should also be responsible for monitoring the group process so that they can introduce these techniques as needed.

At least as important and far more difficult is the task of facilitating the internal dynamics of the team, particularly dealing with tension and conflict. Whenever individuals with different values, goals, backgrounds, and political agendas work together on projects that can dramatically alter their work lives, conflict and tension are inevitable. The leader's task is to manage this conflict productively—not to eliminate it, on the one hand, or to allow it to undermine the team's work, on the other. Sometimes the conflict arises from particular personalities on the team or from other personal differences among members. At least as often, though, it occurs because the various parties to the conflict have legitimate but diverse and often contradictory concerns and interests. No one will get everything he or she wants, and some may get less than what they feel they need or deserve. The challenge is to get all parties to work together and use their differences to inspire compromises, trade-offs, and creative solutions that they all can commit to and support.[5]

The differences and potential tensions between user delegates and information technology experts make *MDI team leadership* an especially critical and difficult issue. The primary challenge is resisting the temptation to do too much. Throughout the process, particularly in the early stages, the team will struggle with basic issues and questions, especially the potential conflict between user needs and IT experts' commitment to particular technological solutions. Language differences (technical versus substantive, for instance) can exacerbate the conflict. At these times, the leader must resist resolving the issues for the team and providing "the answers." This muddling through is an important part of the process. As the MDI team struggles with these issues, it will be creating and learning a process for resolving not just current issues but the ones that may come up later.

The MDI team leader can prime the members for this learning-by-muddling-through process by telling them about it before it happens. And when it does, the leader can help them understand the reason why they seem to be having so much difficulty resolving even the most straightforward issues—that is, the differing needs and concerns of the stakeholder groups they represent. Project leaders can pose the key questions, clarify the differences, and then give team members the room to figure it all out.

When the team experiences difficulty in moving toward solutions and compromises, the leader can help by reminding the members of the general direction in which they are headed, the parameters of their work, and their shared goals. The leader can also act as a translator between user team delegates and IT experts, especially in the early stages of the project, before the delegates have had time to learn each other's language. In addition, effective MDI team leaders will know when to introduce critical information into the debates. They will be able to interject relevant ideas and to reframe, refocus, and redefine the issues as needed. They are sensitive to critical transitions and junctures in the project that can be used for holding special events, taking stock, communicating with stakeholders, and reflecting on—and if necessary, reformulating—strategies.[6]

In sum, the purpose of the MDI team leader is not to push and pull the MDI team in particular directions or toward specific designs and solutions. It is more akin to group therapy. The leader asks the right questions, reassures the team members that they are on the right track, and helps them deal with tension and anxiety. Most important, the leader gives the team members the space, assistance, and resources they need. But the leader also knows when to intervene and take a more directive role. The point of all of this should be to help the teams move beyond potentially contentious debates to shared understandings and solutions of the MDI team's own design.

DEVELOPING EXTERNAL CONNECTIONS

Keeping connected to stakeholders outside of the project team is one of the keys to designing an effective project team. Throughout the project, the team must create and maintain linkages with stakeholders and other key individuals, units, and systems. Because of the intensity of their focus on the work to be done, an intensity often exacerbated by tight schedules and budgets, project teams may pay little attention to anyone on whom they are not immediately dependent. Keeping sponsors, stakeholders, and managers informed and involved may not seem important in the face of looming deadlines, but the failure to do so can come back to haunt the project once the dust has settled.

The project team needs to function within the constraints imposed by the organization and the team's customers. Although project teams need considerable latitude and autonomy in how they do their work, their authority has its limits. If the team's goals and objectives are not aligned with those of its customers and the overall organization, the project will not succeed. Project teams must balance their need for independent thinking with responsiveness to key stakeholders. Therefore, the project team should develop linkages with its stakeholders to keep them informed, solicit their input, and develop oversight mechanisms to ensure that the team stays on track.[7]

Individual project team members also need to maintain connections outside the team, particularly with their functional work units. Most organizations still base pay increases and promotions exclusively on performance reviews conducted within functional units. Therefore, project team members cannot afford to neglect their functional roots. If they are doing their job well, they will often feel as if they are walking a tightrope between their functional responsibilities on one end and the needs of the project on the other. Keeping these functional ties while building new, cross-functional ties via the project team will be one of the most difficult challenges facing organizations as they make the transition to more team-based structures and cultures.

Communication systems are essential for creating and maintaining these external links. Project teams need to be aware of what systems are available for their use (E-mail, for instance). They can then carefully plan how they will use these systems to keep their stakeholders informed, solicit their input as needed, and keep in touch with their functional units. As strategic alliances among multiple, geographically dispersed organizations lead to increasingly complex projects, the need for these connections and systems will grow. Keeping project teams connected with external stakeholders will then become even more critical—and even more difficult to effect. This is yet another reason for organizations to develop these systems and create a culture that will support their use. The kind of dynamic cross-functional and cross-organizational team structure these projects require may be impossible without them.

Connecting the MDI Team with Intended Users

In chapter 4 we noted how easy it is for user delegates to lose the user's perspective as they work closely with other stakeholder delegates, particularly technical experts. We therefore recommended the selection of delegates who are empathetic with those they represent, sensitive enough to recognize how important this issue is, and motivated to try to do something about it. But even the most sensitive and best-intentioned delegates can become absorbed in the challenges posed by their new tasks and responsibilities and lose touch with their "roots." Activities and methods that are consciously designed to keep user delegates in sync with their constituents must also be in place.

To understand the kinds of activities and methods that may best serve this purpose, we need to return to the discussion in chapter 4 on the role of user delegate as user team representative and to examine this role more closely. User delegates can approach their role in two different ways—as the user expert or as the facilitator of this expertise. In the story installment that opened this chapter, Bill views himself as the resident expert on what "his users" need and want. He figures that he knows everything there is to know about their work—how tasks should be performed, what information is critical to effective performance, who needs to work with whom, and so on. His primary job, he feels, is to employ this knowledge as he participates in the systems development process and serves as the source of this knowledge for the SICIM project team. Although he frequently promises to involve other users, he rarely does. In spite of his claims to the contrary, his actions—or lack thereof—belie his words. Apparently, this is not a high priority for him, and the project has suffered as a result.

Clearly, he needs to pay more attention to linking the project team with the intended users of the system. But merely acting as a passive conduit of information between the two—by keeping the users informed and passing on their feedback to the design team—is not enough. A better approach would be for Bill to work with the other members of the project team and the production workers not on the team to create links that *actively* involve a broad spectrum of intended users. There are a number of specific activities and methods he could use to forge these links.

Meetings, Memos, and Newsletters The most frequently used linking methods are meetings, memos, and newsletters. If they are used judiciously they can also be quite effective. Formal meetings involving the MDI team, user teams, and other key constituents are valuable for both substantive and symbolic reasons and should be employed at key junctures and milestones during the project. Specifically, the MDI team should be introduced to the user teams via a formal presentation or meeting as early in the project as possible. This is an important step that can help cut off rumors before they begin. The issues addressed should include what the purpose of the project is, who the MDI team members are, what will happen during the course of the project, and when and how they, the users, will be involved.

Similar events should be held later in the project, when the design approach has been chosen, even later when the designs are ready for implementation, and at other critical junctures identified by the MDI team. All such events should feature progress reports, information on what is being planned, and the implications, if any, for user teams. Furthermore, the structure of the meetings should provide users in attendance with ample opportunity to ask questions and provide input.

The input they provide must be taken seriously. One of the most serious mistakes the MDI team can make at these events is to convey the impression that all of the important decisions have already been made. If so, users will believe that the real purpose of these events is to convey only the illusion of involvement. Such events, they may conclude, do not represent a sincere commitment to their participation.[8] The guiding principle is to schedule these meetings before key decisions are made but after detailed information relevant to these decisions is available. This way users will be able to make informed and meaningful contributions to these decisions. Newsletters and memos can be used between formal meetings to keep users informed about progress, upcoming events, meeting schedules, and other issues. If it is available, E-mail can be an effective medium for these newsletters and memos, especially if it provides users with an opportunity to respond and react to specific items.

Surveys, Interviews, and Focus Groups The methods described above are most effective for conveying information in one direction, from the MDI team to the user teams. While they do provide some opportunity for information to flow back to the MDI team, the flow can be sporadic and unsystematic. For example, user input during formal meetings is usually provided by the most vocal and assertive users, not necessarily by the most representative. To obtain more comprehensive information more systematically, the MDI team should use surveys, interviews, and focus groups.

Surveys are especially useful for gathering highly structured and well-defined information from a large number of people. But many issues require information that is richer, more complex, and more in-depth than what can typically be uncovered by a single question or survey item—for example, user team needs, their response to various design alternatives, and the potential work-related impact of these alternatives. More intensive, interactive methods such as interviews and focus groups are better suited to gathering information of this sort. The questions posed can produce discussions and lead in turn to follow-up questions, like a searching spotlight narrowing its focus to probe farther into the darkness. Ideas and information can ricochet from one person to another, building on previous responses and triggering ideas and insights that would otherwise remain concealed. Surveys can be used to supplement these methods, especially as the impetus to get the initial discussion started.

Colocation The MDI team should move its work to the user teams' site as early in the project as possible.[9] The development team at Paws & Claws did not follow this advice. Because of the noise, dirt, and commuting distance, it set up operations at corporate headquarters rather than at the plant. The team then compounded its mistake by moving the user delegate, Bill, to its offices at corporate headquarters. As a result, the production workers correctly perceived the team as being out of touch with their needs and the day-to-day experience of their work. Even worse, their representative was no longer one of them. He had become "a suit," just like the others at headquarters.

If the intended user teams are located in several different sites, the MDI team should move to where the system will ultimately be piloted. If moving the entire project is not feasible, a project office can be established at or near the users' workplace; this office should be used often by the MDI team. MDI team members should walk around and "hang out" at the work site whenever they can. The point is for the MDI team to be as visible and close to the users as possible to create opportunities for spontaneous, informal conversations and observations as well as to learn informally about the users' culture, work methods, interaction style, and so on. Just as important, they will also demonstrate the MDI team's commitment to serving its "customers."

Technology Links Technology-based communication systems— ranging in complexity from voice mail to E-mail to more advanced "groupware" applications[10]—can be the medium for a number of the methods described above. They work especially well for memos and newsletters and can even be used for surveys and interviews. Under certain circumstances, internal and external communication networks can substitute for the MDI team's physical presence at or near the user teams' workplace, offering virtual proximity in the place of actual proximity. This capability is particularly important when the members of the MDI team or user teams work in different locations or for different organizations. In these cases, there may be no other reasonable alternative but to use these communication links.

The critical factor is whether there exists a communication network with which the MDI team and user team members are already comfortable and satisfied. If so, technology-based networking may compensate effectively for physical proximity, especially in the later stages of the project, when the issues to be addressed are fairly well structured and defined.[11] If such a system does not already exist, developing one can be the first order of business for the MDI team. This would be impractical in most cases, however, unless the network can also be used for other purposes—for the user teams, for example, in the course of their normal daily work. The MDI team's use of the network can then serve as a prototype or pilot for these future applications. Whatever the case, occasional in-person meetings on-site are strongly recommended, especially at the beginning of the project and at critical junctures along the way. These personal connections can help guide the project through the compromises and trade-offs that may threaten it along the way.

Prototypes One of the most effective methods for linking the MDI team with user teams is to put a preliminary version of the information technology system under development in the hands of potential users. Systems developers have long recognized the advantages of prototypes. According to MIS expert Raymond McLeod, "A prototype provides the developers and the potential users with an idea of how the system in its completed form will function. . . . [I]t is best suited for those situations where the user is not completely certain what he or she wants. By providing a prototype, the user is better able to see what the possibilities are, and this better understanding can trigger more exact specifications."[12]

It is easy to see from this description how prototypes can help involve user teams in the MDI process. For example, Bill could have tried out a prototype of the SICIM system with the intended users to get their feedback and suggest modifications for later versions. His role, then, would have been to plan this experiment in mutual learning by working with both the users and the development team to collaborate on the

Figure 6–1   MDI Team Linkage with User Teams

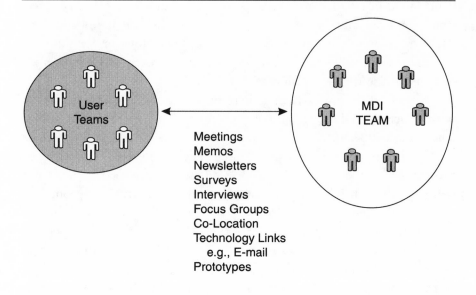

evaluation and redesign of the system. In effect, Bill would have served as a facilitator of user knowledge rather than trying to act—unsuccessfully, as it turned out—as a proxy for it. Since we talk about prototypes in more detail in chapter 8, we will defer further discussion until then.

Many Means to a Common End   The linking methods and activities described in the last several pages are summarized in figure 6–1. These are not the only ways to link the MDI team with user teams. The range of possible linking activities and methods is limited only by the collective imagination of the MDI team and the user teams and by the resources available to them. In any case, what is important is not so much the specific activities themselves as the ways in which they are employed. The methods we have described are flexible and can be adapted to specific situations and circumstances.

While the particular adaptation, mix, and timing of activities will depend on the project, the end result should be a dynamic, integrated program that engages a broad spectrum of users in intensive, ongoing interactions with the MDI team. This program should include a clear plan for incorporating the user feedback generated by the various linking methods and activities and for letting users know how the ideas and advice they offered were put to use. Only then will the project benefit fully from their knowledge and insights; only then will they genuinely feel that they are an essential part of the MDI process.

Connecting the MDI Team with the Internal IT Department

Regardless of which source of technical expertise the MDI team uses to develop the new system, the corporate information technology department may be responsible for maintaining and supporting it, or at least for integrating it into the organization's IT infrastructure. Therefore, this department should also be linked with the MDI team. Establishing a connection can sometimes be problematic when other sources of information technology expertise are used.

When local, team-based experts are the primary source of expertise, the source of the problem is the historically thorny relationship between internal information technology departments and the user teams they serve. The principal tensions arise from their frequently conflicting objectives—business users want the tools that best fit their needs, while IT departments want systems that are compatible with each other and that serve the needs of many units. When the IT department prevails, users may feel that their needs have been compromised. When users prevail, the IT department may resent being asked to provide support for systems it had no role in purchasing or developing and with which it has little experience and expertise. In addition, each may undervalue the other's expertise and attribute too much significance to what they may lack—technological sophistication on the part of the user, and knowledge of the users' business and information needs by the IT department.

Most projects require both. To develop applications that can meet business needs as well as be integrated into the IT infrastructure, the two sources of expertise must collaborate. Our example from SWP&L (see chapter 5) illustrates some of the forms this collaboration can take. The systems consultant from the information services department helped create a dotted-line relationship between ISD and the field service technician who served as the project team's local information technology expert. More important than the fact of the connection itself was the nature of that connection. The local expert, the systems consultant, and ISD established a complementary, noncompetitive, collaborative relationship in which the different kinds of expertise and responsibilities of the two individuals were acknowledged, respected, and used to good effect.

The underlying issue is somewhat different when an external contractor is used as the MDI team's principal source of information technology expertise. The problem arises from what actually happens when systems development is "outsourced." In spite of what this expression implies, the work is rarely shipped out to offices, locations, or personnel outside the organization. Instead, as our Paws & Claws story illustrates, external participants often take up residence in the organization as if they themselves were at least part-time employees for the duration of the project. And as our story also suggests, the close proximity of external contractors can create significant tensions with corporate IT departments and personnel, especially if they have been passed over for the project because of perceived or actual inadequacies. These circumstances can make it difficult to forge collaborative links—and even more important to do so. In time, the external contractor will be gone, and the information technology department may end up supporting and maintaining the system. Clearly, the IT department needs to be involved, at least in collaboration with the external contractors.

External communication networks offer a technology-based approach to creating these linkages. Electronic links between the external experts and the corporate IT department as well as the user teams will become easier to establish and will have far more to offer than they do at present. Currently, many organizations are moving from project-by-project outsourcing to long-term alliances with "preferred suppliers"—large companies that offer a full range of information services, including facilities, equipment, software, and personnel. We need not stretch our imaginations far to envision technology-enabled metaorganizations of external IT experts and internal IT departments located far apart but working closely together. Using the same technology, they will be able to serve user team clients in locations just as distant to establish similar virtual relationships and connections.

Ultimately, the best solution, regardless of the source of project-specific IT expertise, may be to add a representative from the internal IT department to the MDI team. In this capacity, corporate IT experts can help the team understand the implications of various design options on systems integration and identify the trade-offs associated with each option. Their technical sophistication may also come in handy in the development of the applications themselves. Finally, with their broad-based knowledge of IT applications throughout the organization, they can fulfill an important internal "benchmarking" function for the project. By helping the MDI team identify and adapt systems and tools used successfully by others in the organization, the project can save considerable time, money, and aggravation.[13]

Connecting with Other Stakeholder Groups

Representatives of the other stakeholder groups in the MDI process—supervisors and managers, human resource professionals, customers and suppliers, and other key functional groups—also need to maintain connections with their constituents. The methods for establishing and maintaining these connections are the same as those described earlier in the chapter. But the impact of the new technology and team designs on these other stakeholder groups will in most cases not be as great as it is on the user teams. Therefore, they generally do not need to be as closely linked to the MDI process.

This is a general conclusion that can vary depending on the particular stakeholder group or project stage. Specifically, supervisors and managers to whom user teams directly report need to be more closely linked to the project than senior management. But the latter should be more closely involved in the process when it comes time to address the broad organizational implications of team and technology designs.

Similarly, human resource representatives on the MDI team do not need to be as closely connected to their department in the early stages of the project, when their responsibilities are primarily MDI team design and facilitation. But as the process begins to focus on user team design and related human resource practice, the representatives would be well advised to draw on the expertise of their colleagues in the HR department to help them deal with these complex and far-ranging issues. Human resource representatives on the MDI team will also need to keep their department informed of developments that may have implications for organization-wide policies on performance appraisal, compensation, training, career development, and the like.

PROVIDING ACCESS TO INFORMATION RESOURCES

All teams need information about task requirements and constraints, performance standards, available resources, relevant technical data, and the strategic context of their work. But the time-bound, cross-functional, nonroutine nature of project teams imposes additional complexity and unique requirements. The functional diversity of the membership means that the strategic context for its work is more dynamic and multidimensional. The nonroutine nature of the work makes it more difficult to coordinate and manage schedules, timelines, and tasks. In addition, the sources for project data vary more and are less predictable (for instance, marketing data on customers for new product development). And the external communications—to stakeholders, project sponsors, and other project teams—are more complex. Therefore, project teams also need the following:

- *In the early, formative stages of the project:* systems and tools that will enable them to scan and browse beyond their usual information sources.

- *Later in the project:* analytical tools to weigh the costs and benefits of alternative products and designs.

- *Even later:* problem-solving and decision-making tools to provide them with a structured process for resolving difficult issues and negotiating the trade-offs that will enable them to converge on a particular approach.

- *Throughout:* (1) project management tools to pull all of their tasks together to produce the desired result, on schedule and within budget; (2) integrated data bases and tools that can operate on data from different functions and sources; (3) communication systems that link all team members and stakeholder groups, regardless of location and schedule; and (4) organization-wide human resource information systems to identify potential team members and experts with skills relevant to the project.

Since developing information resources is one of the MDI team's primary objectives, discussion of the tools and resources needed to fulfill this objective is inseparable from the technology development process itself. Therefore, we will defer discussion of information resources for the MDI team to chapter 8, where we describe this process in detail.

PROVIDING TRAINING

Because project team members are drawn from different functional units, they often require training to familiarize themselves with the language, conceptual frameworks, and fundamentals of one another's specialties. Functional differences have other consequences as well. As noted in earlier chapters, members with different backgrounds, skills, kinds of experience, and knowledge bases may also differ in terms of their perspectives, values, and goals.[14] One of the most important truths organizations have learned in recent years is that diversity breeds conflict. Perhaps less well known, but equally important, is the corollary that diversity can be a source of creativity. Project team members need to learn how to appreciate their differences, communicate in spite of these differences, and creatively manage, not suppress, the conflict that inevitably emerges from them. This means that training programs in conflict resolution, group process, and diversity can be highly beneficial for project teams, especially if the diversity programs are adapted to include issues related to *functional* diversity.[15] Training in the structured decision-making techniques described earlier can also help project teams transcend their functional differences.

The training approach is another important issue for project teams. Learning by doing should be the guiding principle and timing the key. When possible, training should be successively layered on prior project training and experience. Initially, training should be designed to provide team members with enough knowledge to at least get started on the tasks that immediately face them. They can then learn as they do their work. As they work their way up the learning curve, their tasks will become more complex. More advanced training should be available to help them deal with these challenges as they arise. In addition, case studies based on other, similar cross-functional projects should be used when possible. These studies can accomplish what training in the separate specialties cannot—they demonstrate how all of the specialties can be integrated and used to develop new products, systems, and organizational designs.

In the MDI team, knowledge and skill differences between users and IT experts shape training needs. Training in problem-solving, conflict resolution, group process, and decision-making techniques is thus especially helpful in dealing with the tensions and conflicts that can emerge from these differences. The two groups also differ in their work-related languages, concepts, and frames of reference. Since a significant portion of the MDI team's mission involves systems development, user delegates and others on the team may need special training in this area. The training does not have to be highly technical in nature; user delegates will probably not spend a great deal of time on tasks related to systems architecture, programming, and the like. But they do need to be familiar with basic applications such as word processing, data base management, and, increasingly, electronic mail. They should also know enough about the technology to understand the implications of various options on such issues as ease of use and the functionality of the system from the user's point of view.

Furthermore, since they will be heavily involved in applications development, they will have to know how to translate work needs into system capabilities. The converse is also true—the IT experts may need to develop their knowledge of the functional areas, disciplines, and tasks related to the user teams' work. The language and concepts of functional area specialties can be just arcane to IT experts as theirs are to users.

In addition, almost all team members, regardless of their functional specialties or experience, should learn more about team design and the processes of organizational change. The latter can be particularly useful in countering the all-to-common perception that change comes easily. It's *not* like the old Judy Garland, Mickey Rooney movie in which the pair exuberantly exclaim, "Let's put on a show!" in one scene and mount a fully staged, elaborately costumed production in the next. Too many people see workplace change in the same, almost magical light. They think that stating intention—as in "from now on we will be a team"—is enough. Only when their efforts fail do they realize that the process of implementing change involves a series of painstaking, calculated, complicated, and almost hopelessly intertwined tasks. If they are prepared for this difficult process, they can avoid many mistakes and be less discouraged by those they cannot avoid.

Training for the MDI team is not a one-time event. The timing of particular training opportunities should coincide with the steps and stages of the MDI process. IT training, for example, should be available at the beginning of the project. Throughout the entire project the MDI team and its leader need to be sensitive to the points at which certain kinds of training might be needed.

CONCLUSION

The purpose of this chapter was to describe how to design project teams, the MDI team in particular (see table 6–1 for a summary of the design

Table 6–1 Design of Project Teams

Design Feature	Characteristics
Defining team composition: The team . . .	• has members from different backgrounds and organizational units • has specialized expertise • has necessary competencies • demonstrates "laterality" • is temporary • is full- or part-time • may have different members over life cycle • has some core members
Defining the leader's role: The leader . . .	• is credible • may rotate * facilitates, coaches, and consults • undertakes project management • undertakes boundary management • manages team life cycle • encourages structured decision making
Developing external connections: The team . . .	• maintains ongoing linkages with key stakeholders • employs communication systems
Providing access to information resources: The team . . .	• has access to scanning systems • has access to analytical tools • has access to problem-solving and decision-making tools • has access to project management tools • has access to integrated data bases and tools • has access to communication systems • has access to human resources information systems
Providing training: The team . . .	• develops "laterality" • learns to manage conflict • learns to use group process • learns to deal with diversity • learns to use structured decision-making techniques • is given just-in-time training

criteria for project teams). Once the MDI team has designed itself, it can turn its attentions to its primary mission—the design of user teams, new technologies, and, eventually, new organizational structures and policies. We have already touched on some of the properties of this process in this and the preceding chapters. Now we examine this process more closely and look at how these properties manifest themselves in the specific stages, steps, and activities the MDI team must follow to produce successful project outcomes.

◆ ◆ ◆

EARLY SPRING, the SICIM pilot site offices in the plant . . .

The movers have just finished setting up the last of the partitions in what will soon be the on-site offices for the SICIM project team. Bill has been using the space for a few weeks already, ever since the decision was made to create an office on-site. Joining him during much of this time were several systems people who had recently been added to the project team—some were from Storm & Drang and others from the Paws & Claws MIS department. A production worker from the plant has also been added to the project team because of her knowledge of the plant's existing information systems, knowledge gained primarily by her own initiative and on her own time. They set up makeshift offices in this space to be closer to, in their words, "their customers." Now that the offices are ready, Bill is planning a series of focus groups and other events with the production teams to get them even more involved in the process.

Several other major developments have occurred in the last few weeks. A steering committee made up of several senior managers has been created to oversee the project and ensure that the teams have all the resources and support they need. Just as important are the changes to the project team itself. The S & D consultants are working closely with the Paws & Claws MIS people on the most technically challenging aspects of the project. Because of its complexity, both the S & D and Paws & Claws people are pleased to have each other's help. In addition, Chris has passed on day-to-day management of the project to Steve and is now spending more time on managing the boundaries of the project, especially on building relations between the project team and the rest of the organization. This will come in handy as implementation approaches. Steve, in his new capacity as project leader, is working with the HR delegate to help the project team become more self-directed.

For the first time since the project began everyone seems happy—particularly Chris, Steve, Bill, and, most important, Chris's boss. Things seem to have finally fallen into place, and the project team now appears ready to tackle the mission it was assigned several months earlier: to design and implement a team-based, technology-enabled manufacturing organization.

Part Three

Designing and Implementing Teams and Technology

The chapters in Part III describe how the MDI process unfolds. As we noted in chapter 1, the flow from one chapter to the next suggests a process that is far more linear in description than it is in practice. The progression of actual projects reflects the complex, multidimensional nature of the real world, not the orderly, sequential structure of the printed page. This said, we are nonetheless faced with the necessity in Part III of breaking down the MDI process into various stages and steps, pointing out the critical issues that will emerge as the project moves forward.★

The overall process can be roughly partitioned into three stages. In the first stage, described in chapter 7, the MDI team begins by addressing broad, general issues, such as where the project fits into the organization's strategy and structure and what is the project's overall mission and objectives. From there, the MDI team members progressively narrow their focus until they decide on the particular design strategy they will pursue.

★ The activities and steps described in part III do not need to wait until all of the steps described in part II have concluded. The groundwork should at least be laid—i.e., composition, leadership, and external connections—before moving too far ahead. But information resources and training can be acquired as needed throughout the process, depending on the specific needs of particular steps.

This marks the transition to the design stage of the project, which consists of two streams of activities. The first, described in chapter 8, involves designing and developing the technology. The other stream is team design (chapter 9). These streams are interrelated. That is, decisions made in one area (teams or technology) should influence, be informed by, and complement decisions made in the other. The process should involve mutual design of both, not separate design of each.

While the end product of technology design is a physical system or software application, the end product of team design is more intangible—usually a plan for reconfiguring (or "reengineering") the tasks and working arrangements that go along with the new system. The team designs (or redesigns) are not converted into actual teams—with their new arrangements, tasks, understandings, work flows, and processes—until the final stage of the MDI process, implementation. In this stage, described in chapter 10, the new technologies and team designs are actually incorporated into the ongoing work flow of the organization, usually one "piece" at a time. The activities of this stage focus on the changeover from the old systems and ways of working to the new systems and designs.

Part III is the heart of the book; it is where the mutual design and implementation process is put into action and begins to create organizational change.

7

Stage One: Positioning, Exploring, and Focusing

6:00 A.M., early April, Los Angeles . . .

The rain fell all night. It was one of those intense rainstorms that seem to come only in early April, just as the residents of the hillsides and canyons are ready to breathe a sigh of relief, believing their homes have survived yet another rainy season. Mark tosses fitfully in his bed as he listens to his house creak, flexing with the shifting ground underneath.

The phone rings. It's Steve. "Yeah, I know its 6 A.M. I figured you were probably awake waiting for your house to slide into the canyon."

"Very funny. What's up?"

Steve explains. "I'm calling about the project, of course. We need your help again." For the next 15 minutes he summarizes where the project stands. All of the right people and all of the key stakeholder groups are represented on the project team. For the first time the team is confident of top management's unequivocal support. The team has access to all of the resources it needs and the authority to carry out its mission. The groundwork has been laid and the members are ready to move aggressively ahead with the real "meat" of the project, building the system and creating the production teams that will use it.

But Chris, uncharacteristically, is urging caution. At the last meeting, he suggested that the project team take stock before moving too far ahead. He was concerned that in all of the turmoil and changes of the past year they may have forgotten much of what they had learned, the understandings they reached, and even some important decisions. He felt—and everyone ultimately agreed—that they should document what they have done to date, along with the areas of agreement and disagreement, so that everyone involved would have a clear picture of what they are trying to do and why.

In his words, as Steve remembered it: "If we don't do it now, what lies ahead will make this past year look like a stroll in the park." Besides, he wants the steering committee and the production workers to sign off on what they have agreed on so far. Then the project team can be sure they are on the right track before they go too much further. Bill had suggested that they ask Mark to come back for a couple of weeks to talk to a number of people, go over project memos and documents, and prepare a report on the project to this point.

"So what do you think?" Steve asks.

"What kind of report does Chris want?" Mark says. "Is he just interested in documenting agreements and understandings on what the system and production teams should do?"

"What else is there?"

"How about a comprehensive, no-holds-barred, in-progress case history of the project, including an analysis of what was done well, where mistakes were made, and what should have been done differently? There's a lot to be learned that could be applied to other projects. We could do this 'for project team eyes only' if people are nervous about what a report like this might reveal. How about it?"

"I'll check with Chris, but I think he'll buy it. Anything else?"

"It's not raining there, is it?"

"No, it's a perfect spring day."

"Are crabs in season?"

"Soon."

"If I get there by the weekend can you get tickets to an Orioles game?"

"No problem."

"Tell Chris that as soon as he gives the word, I'm on my way."

◆ ◆ ◆

THE FIRST STAGE of an MDI project is the most important. Activities during this stage lay the groundwork and set the tone for the rest of the project. Minor mistakes made early on can grow into major problems by the later stages. By then options are limited—either go back to square one or do the best with what's been done.

The activities of stage 1 are as difficult as they are important. The more complex the project, the harder it is to get started. Initially, the boundaries may seem sketchy, the mission vaguely defined and ephemeral, and the path long and daunting. No one is quite sure where to start or how to proceed. The temptation is either to rush through the early steps to get to the "real" work or to get bogged down in "navel gazing."

To avoid these pitfalls, it's best to take one step at a time. And, as it is in most situations, the first step is understanding where the project is starting from. In other words, what is the context for the project and where is the project positioned within that context?

DETERMINING THE PROJECT CONTEXT

Change efforts that disregard the strategic, political, and organizational context can be as much of a struggle as swimming against the tide and are as likely to be successful. Those who think they can ignore such elemental forces will end up back where they started if they are lucky, or be swept away to points unknown if they are not. Therefore, one of the first tasks for the MDI team is to understand the strategic, organizational, and technological context of the project and the limits this may place on what they can reasonably do.[1] This may involve addressing such issues as:

- ◆ What are the organization's strategic direction and performance goals?

- ◆ What role is the project expected to play in helping the organization vis-à-vis these directions and goals?

- ◆ What are the technological constraints—for example, the existing IT platform, corporate-wide standards for the acquisition and development of new systems?

- ◆ What are the organizational barriers? For example, does the culture of the organization support risk taking? Are there enough human and financial resources available to support the project, or should it be scaled back?

- ◆ Where does the MDI team fit within the organization, vertically and laterally?

- ◆ Who are the key players outside the team who can help or hinder their work? What can the project do to enlist their support? Should they be added to the team?

- What level of support and resources does the team need and what do they have?

- What is the timeline for the project?

- What approval process, if any, do they need for the changes and systems they will design?

Let us now look at three examples to illustrate this task and the ones that follow. Two of the examples are familiar; one consists of excerpts from Mark's progress report on the Paws & Claws SICIM project, and the other is based on the SouthWest Power & Light gas emergency response (GER) project. In both cases we retrace the earliest stages of the respective projects to see how they approached these critical first steps. One more example is from Vector Computers, a manufacturer of work stations used for computer-aided design and simulations. We will return to all three examples throughout the chapter and develop them further as we successively describe each step of stage 1.

Paws & Claws: One of the most important early steps a project team should take is to analyze the organizational context of the project and respond to this context accordingly. This step helps lay the foundation for the rest of the project. In at least one respect, the project team did carry out this step effectively. As we will see in a later section of this report, the organization's overall goal of increased profitability was reflected in the design of the system and of the management process.

But the project team did overlook, sometimes intentionally, much of the rest of the organizational context. One of the most glaring examples was the early attempt by the project leadership to isolate the project from other key players throughout the organization, particularly senior management and the MIS department. Little progress was made until this "oversight" was corrected later in the year.

SWP&L: At the time the project was initiated, the utility was in the process of implementing a large-scale "service excellence" program throughout the organization. The goal of the program was to improve service to internal and external customers. The overall mission of the project was consistent with that program and to a considerable degree was inspired by it.

At first the GER project involved only the gas distribution division (GDD). The GDD manager provided all resources and approved all changes. In the early stages of the project, however, it became clear that the response teams would either need to include or be closely linked with the customer service representatives who were taking the calls reporting possible gas leaks. As a result, the project team added representatives from the customer service department. They also asked their division manager to join the GDD manager in forming a steering committee to provide resources for the project and to oversee it.

The steering committee and project team also recognized that the mobile data terminal system they were developing would need to be compatible with the existing organization-wide IT platform and eventually supported by SWPL's IT department. The IT manager was then invited to join the steering committee and nominate an IT representative to serve on the project team.

Vector Computers: For several years Vector Computers had been having trouble meeting production schedules and filling customer orders in a timely fashion. To remedy this problem, the plant manager, with the support and authority of the VP of manufacturing, initiated a project to develop a production control system for tracking the progress of customer orders from the receipt of the initial order, through all stages of the production process, to final systems test, and then to shipping. Before beginning design of the system, the project team decided to reexamine the reasons for the frequent delays in meeting customer orders. This examination revealed that the real problem was not Vector's production process but the frequent delays and inconsistent quality of the incoming parts supplied by their external vendors.

With the support of the production control, incoming inspection, materials storage, and quality assurance departments, the project team asked the plant manager to reconceptualize the project to address what they believed was the real problem. What they really needed was a system that they and their suppliers could use to track inventory, order parts, and monitor delivery and quality of incoming parts. They also decided to create joint problem-solving teams with their major suppliers. These cross-organizational teams would use the system to track supplier performance and help identify and solve persistent problems in parts delivery and quality.

IDENTIFYING PROJECT VALUES AND OBJECTIVES

The challenge of the second step in this first stage of the project is to develop mission statements and objectives that go beyond the usual platitudes and clichés about quality and service. Fortunately, the statements and objectives themselves may not be the most important outcome of this step. Just as important is the process itself and what the project team learns about itself as it grapples with the difficult trade-offs that often underlie these statements. Quality is important, but how much and at what cost? Can customers actually perceive incremental increases in quality? How much are they willing to pay for these gains? How important is it for workers to be more productive on their jobs if, by achieving this goal, others lose their jobs? Is teamwork a value in and of itself, or is it important only when it leads to improved performance? Is it more important to improve performance by using new information systems to cut costs or to increase innovation?

By debating these issues, MDI team members will achieve a greater appreciation for the complexities that underlie many of the difficult decisions and trade-offs they will have to make during the course of the project. They will also be able to push beyond truisms to the next level of concreteness—that is, to project objectives that are meaningful and relevant to user team performance. The challenge here is to articulate objectives that are concrete and focused but not so specific that they prematurely create tunnel vision and preclude other, unanticipated outcomes and surprises.

After the MDI team has agreed on the objectives, it should consider reporting its work to the various stakeholder groups, perhaps in a series of formal presentations and question-and-answer sessions. The purpose of these presentations is to keep the stakeholders informed about the project—what the project is about, what's happening now, what will happen in the future, and who is involved. Another purpose is to compare the project objectives with the stakeholders' expectations and perceptions and resolve inconsistencies that might exist at this point.

Paws & Claws: The project's objective was to enable the production teams to contribute to the company's overall profitability. This was to be accomplished by giving them the information, tools, knowledge, and authority they needed to (1) devise cost-saving interventions and innovations in their production process and (2) make strategic production decisions. The latter objective was by far the most ambitious and controversial. The underlying belief was that with access to the right information and expertise, the production teams could maximize their revenues by adjusting their product mix in response to changing material costs and markets.

This was an easier objective to accept in theory than it was in potential practice. Early in the project a training exercise was developed to help the project team anticipate how the production teams might use the system. The exercise would simulate the kinds of decisions a production team could make with the information provided by the new system and the processes they might employ to make these decisions. It was also hoped that the simulation could be used as part of the training program to help production teams apply the new system to their work.

The simulation was more helpful than expected. It did enable the project team to simulate potential applications of the system and get a sense of how the system and team designs might affect the production teams' work. But it had an unanticipated effect as well. For several members of the project team, participation in the simulation helped clarify some concerns they had about one of the primary goals of the project. Although they were never comfortable with the idea of empowering production teams to make strategic production decisions, they were initially willing to go along with the other, more adventuresome members of the project team on this issue. But the simulation forced them to face the reality of what was actually being considered. Their vague, uneasy hesitance had been converted into real, palpable concerns about placing so much responsibility and authority in the hands of the production teams.

After much discussion of this issue plus substantial pressure from the project leader, the project team agreed to continue with its original mission. But the reservations expressed by the more conservative members were seriously considered. The project team agreed to keep these issues in mind as it proceeded with the design of the system and the production teams. Specifically, a primary focus of the project team's efforts would be to ensure that the production teams have the members, training, information, and other resources and support they would need to perform effectively in their new, more strategic roles.

SWP&L: The primary objective of the project was to reduce the amount of time between the receipt of a customer call reporting a possible gas leak and the arrival of a field service technician. A secondary objective was to give the field service technicians more control over decisions about who responds to each report and when.

Quantifying the primary objective proved to be far more difficult than the project team anticipated. The attempt was invaluable, however, for what it revealed about the kinds of trade-offs that would have to be made to achieve the most ambitious outcomes. Incremental reductions in response time could be achieved by making modest improvements in technology and work procedures. But significant gains beyond that could probably be realized only at considerable cost—by increasing the number of technicians in the field, for example.

The project team finally decided that it was enough to agree on decreased response time as the overriding objective of the project without getting too specific at this point. They also recognized the trade-offs and costs associated with trying to push this objective too far. Armed with this knowledge, they were ready to move on to the next step.

Vector Computers: The project team added a representative from the company that supplied most of the parts used in the manufacture of Vector products. As a result, the team decided to temporarily switch its priorities. The team members felt that before they could begin the process of systems development, they should concentrate on establishing a good working relationship with suppliers. And the best way to accomplish that purpose, they decided, was to focus on jointly resolving the parts availability problems that had soured those relationships in recent years. By doing so, team members hoped to learn more about the overall process of parts procurement and to improve Vector's working relationship with its suppliers. This would make it easier to create the kind of system that would ultimately support collaboration among all parties involved.

IDENTIFYING TECHNOLOGY/TEAM FUNCTIONS

The next step for the MDI team is to convert the project objectives into system and user team functions—that is, what the systems and work designs will enable user teams to do and how those functions will contribute to the overall goals of the organization. Once these functions have been identified, the MDI team can begin to develop evaluation criteria for the project. These criteria can then be used to measure progress as the project unfolds and will ultimately determine just how successful the project has been in meeting its objectives. During this step, the MDI team may experience pressures from management stakeholders and others to express these criteria in cost/benefit terms. The members should try their best to resist these pressures. By focusing narrowly on easy-to-measure outcomes (labor savings, for instance), they may overlook less tangible results that could have far greater impact in the long run (process innovations and new products and services).

Before proceeding further, the MDI team may need to check in again with the stakeholder groups to clarify priorities and constraints, possibly in another series of meetings. The MDI team should work with the user teams to distinguish the functions the teams would *like* to have from those they believe they *must* have. With the help of management and the corporate IT department, the MDI team should identify the "givens," both technological and organizational, that may constrain the designs they can consider. This step is a continuation of the one addressing the project context, but it is more focused and specifically referenced to the functions the designs are intended to fulfill.

Paws & Claws: The SICIM project team identified the following functions to be performed by the SICIM system and production team designs:

- break down information about costs of production by source and product;
- make projections of sales, revenue, and profitability for different product mixes;
- create opportunity for input from marketing and other units about what to produce and how much; and
- make it possible to communicate with similar production teams at other plants so that they can share information and ideas about cost-saving interventions and innovations.

SWP&L: To provide faster response to customer calls by the gas emergency response teams, the project team identified a number of functions that should be fulfilled by the new mobile data terminal system and team designs. They included:

- direct communication between customer service representatives and field service technicians about possible gas leaks;
- complete information about the location of these leaks; and
- direct communication between all field service technicians so that they can allocate job orders among themselves while in the field.

Vector Computers: The project team spent several months analyzing the parts-ordering and -delivery process and working on interim solutions to some of the problems that for years have strained relations between Vector and its main supplier. This task-focused work helped them develop a better working relationship and facilitated joint problem solving. With this foundation established, the project team decided that it was ready to proceed with the development of a materials management system. This system would be used by the cross-organizational team of Vector employees and supplier representatives. They identified the following functions to be served by the system and team design:

- the ability to track projected delivery and production schedules, inventory, part orders, and incoming part quality; and

- joint problem analysis and solution with suppliers, particularly quick, effective resolution of quality and delivery problems.

GENERATING ALTERNATIVE APPROACHES TO FULFILL FUNCTIONS

At this point the MDI team has enough information to start exploring alternative ways to fulfill the functions that have been clarified and refined throughout much of stage 1. The inclination will be to focus primarily on technological alternatives—on different system architectures, hardware options, and software. But this is not enough. The alternatives should blend technological options with task, team, and organizational designs. The quality of the ultimate design will be enhanced by having a broad set of alternatives from which to choose.

Internal and external scans of new technologies and workplace and organizational innovations are an important part of this step. Internally, the MDI team should look for what has been implemented elsewhere in the organization that might be useful for the project. Externally, it should look at technologies available on the market and at benchmarking studies of what other organizations have done under similar circumstances.

Paws & Claws: The SICIM project team developed two principal design alternatives. The two alternatives offered very different approaches to fulfilling two of the functions defined in the previous step—projecting sales, revenue, and profitability, and getting input from marketing on production decisions.

In the first alternative, the production teams would include only production workers, supervisors, and managers. The system would provide them with cost breakdowns on the products they make. The teams could then use these cost breakdowns to identify potential targets of opportunity for cost reductions. The marketing department would have access to an additional module, a "what-if" module it could use to project the profitability of different product mixes. It would use the system to perform the analyses and then pass on its recommendations to the production teams, which would be responsible for actually deciding what mix of products they would produce.

A second alternative was generated to allay some of the misgivings of the more conservative members of the team. Someone from marketing would be assigned to each production team, and the "what-if" module would be included in the production floor system. This would enhance the production teams' capability for making the kind of strategic production decisions that were being so strongly advocated by the less conservative members of the project team.

SWP&L: The GER project team also came up with two alternative designs. The first involved putting the field service technicians in direct voice contact with the customer service representatives via the radio phones the technicians used to communicate with each other. With this additional link, technicians responding to calls could keep the CSRs informed about where they were and when they would get to the site of the reported leak. This information could then be passed on to the customers anxiously waiting for the technicians to arrive.

The second alternative would expand the capabilities of the mobile data terminal to include electronic messaging so that CSRs could call up information on their desktop terminals about the position and estimated time of arrival of the technicians who were responding to the calls. The link between CSR and technician would be "asynchronous" rather than real-time. That is, instead of responding immediately to calls from the service technicians in the field, the CSRs could call up the information they needed when they had the time.

Vector Computers: One strategy considered by the project team was primarily technology based. It involved creating a materials management system to be used by both companies to project production schedules, track inventory, order supplies, track incoming quality, and automatically invoice and issue payments for parts. With this system, Vector's materials department would work directly with the supplier to project anticipated orders for new parts and resolve problems.

The second, team-based strategy was to extend the form and focus of the work the team had been engaged in for the last several months. Since the members of the combined Vector/supplier team seemed to work so well together and consistently demonstrated the ability to resolve difficult issues, they proposed transforming themselves into an ongoing cross-organizational-planning and problem-solving team. The team would meet regularly and use existing communication technologies and information resources rather than develop a new system. This included the fax, the phone, and the weekly reports and daily updates generated by Vector's materials resource planning system.

SELECTING A DESIGN STRATEGY

The MDI team evaluates the various alternatives by assessing how effectively each fits both the functional requirements and constraints identified earlier (under the heading "Identifying Technology/Team Functions"). During this process, some alternatives will be eliminated and others will be adjusted and modified. Features of some will be combined with features of others to produce new alternatives. Different trade-offs between technological, team, and organizational approaches may be considered, discarded, or modified. The set of alternatives changes and narrows until the MDI team finally focuses on the design strategy that seems to offer the most promise. The rationale for choosing the particular strategy, as well as the criteria for evaluating the systems and work designs, will also emerge from this iterative process.

Choice of design strategy marks the last substantive step of stage 1 and is a good time for another series of meetings with the various stakeholder groups. In these meetings, the MDI team should describe the design strategy it has chosen, the process by which the decision was made, and the rationale for its choice. The purpose of the meetings is to get the stakeholders to sign off on the design strategy and gain their explicit acceptance of and commitment to the MDI team's recommendations to this point.

Paws & Claws: With some reservations on the part of several of the members, the project team decided to go with the more ambitious design—place representatives from marketing on the production teams, provide the teams with access to the "what-if" module, and give them responsibility for making production decisions. The rationale was that this alternative offered greater flexibility and faster response to fluctuating material costs and market conditions.

SWP&L: The project team decided that an asynchronous E-mail link between the field service technicians and the customer service representatives was preferable to the real-time voice link, even though the former would take more time and expense to develop. The rationale for the decision was that the CSRs were already severely overloaded by incoming customer calls. The project team was afraid that without increasing the number of CSRs, calls from technicians in the field would place an additional and probably intolerable burden on the already stressed representatives. With an E-mail system, they could call up the information as needed to respond to particular follow-up calls from worried customers.

Vector Computers: After going back and forth between the two alternatives, the project team decided to go ahead with both—to create the cross-organizational team *and* develop a materials management system to be used by the team. The alternatives, the members felt, were synergistic and offered unique advantages that could be realized only by jointly developing and integrating both. The system would work best if used by Vector and its suppliers to collaborate on planning and problem solving. The cross-organizational team could do its work most effectively if it had access to a system that provided up-to-date information on orders, inventory, and production schedules.

With the completion of this step, the MDI team is almost ready to move on to the design stage of the process. Before making that transition, the team needs to organize the design effort. And to carry out the design tasks, the MDI team may need to redesign itself.

ORGANIZING THE DESIGN EFFORT

Organizing the design effort means partitioning it into smaller tasks. These tasks represent particular "domains" of work that are internally coherent and externally distinct—that is, everything within a given domain fits together, and each domain is logically and functionally different from the others. For example, software development can be defined as one domain that is distinct from hardware acquisition, another domain, and user training, yet another.

The MDI team then organizes itself around these domain tasks. If the scope of the project warrants, a separate subteam can be created for each task. Since design tasks typically require more work and, therefore, more people than the previous activities in the MDI process; the MDI team might be expanded at this point. Each MDI team member is assigned to at least one domain subteam, based on his or her particular expertise and interests. Care should be taken to ensure that each domain subteam includes members from a variety of functional backgrounds. Because these subteams are relatively small and specialized, it is not necessary to replicate the cross-functionality of the MDI team. The point is to guard against placing all software experts on one team, user team representatives on another, cost accountants on another, and so on.

Integrating the work of these subteams may be one of the most important challenges the MDI team faces. An overlapping team composed of representatives from each subteam—an integrating team—can be created for this purpose.

Paws & Claws: The SICIM project team is now too large to accomplish its goal with its present structure. This situation presents an opportunity for the team to consider restructuring itself to better fit the growing complexity of its task. The overall project task should be divided into five subtasks with at least one team for each task. For example, there could be subteams for software development, hardware acquisition, integration with existing systems, interface design, and design of the user teams. This last team could also be responsible for developing training programs and other user supports for the system. A team of representatives from each subteam should also be created to keep the subteam efforts integrated and coordinated.

Other people should be added to the project as needed to staff the subteams. Team assignments can be based on the member's particular expertise, the concerns of the stakeholder groups being represented, and the nature of each subteam's task. Having each team member serve on more than one subteam when possible will also help integrate the work of the different subteams.

The integrating team should meet every week. At these meetings, each team's representative will review his or her subteam's progress and identify the issues and problems it is dealing with at the moment or anticipates in the near future. Other representatives can offer suggestions as to how the subteam might approach these problems and issues, as well as identify the issues that might affect the work of their own subteams. These overlapping issues can be addressed during the meeting via joint problem-solving and planning sessions, involving all of the members of the integrating team. The integrating team can serve as the mechanism by which the project restructures itself to adapt to different phases and circumstances, creating new teams and disbanding old teams as needed.

Other, less complex approaches to project structure are illustrated in the examples from SWP&L and Vector Computers.

SWP&L: Since the overall design task was relatively uncomplicated, it was possible to keep the project team small and the design tasks simple. As small as the team was, it contained all of the people needed to fulfill its mission: the local IT expert and his liaison with SWP&L's IT department and delegates representing customer service, the field service technicians, and their supervisors. As a result, they were able to address most of the design tasks without dividing into smaller subteams.

Vector Computers: The complexity of Vector's project was somewhere between those of Paws & Claws and SWP&L. The project team divided the overall design effort into system design and team design and created two subteams with partially overlapping membership. The team was thus able to accomplish most of its integration and project management tasks without creating additional structures and roles.

CONCLUSION

With the conclusion of stage 1, the large set of vague ideas and notions with which the MDI team started has been focused and narrowed down into a single, concrete design strategy and an organized design effort, not unlike being run through a funnel, defined by the steps described in this chapter (figure 7–1). The foundation has now been laid for the rest of the MDI project. The objectives and functions have been identified, the design strategy chosen, the design task structured, and the MDI team restructured around these design tasks. The MDI team is now ready to move on to the next stage of the project, carrying out the design strategy it has selected.

◆ ◆ ◆

From Mark's confidential report, *An Interim Case History of the SICIM Project* . . .

. . . To conclude, progress has been anything but smooth and steady. Rather, it is more accurately described as two steps forward, one or more steps back, or even off into an entirely different direction. Given the complexity and scope of the project, much of this erratic path was unavoidable. Nonetheless, several of the decisions made and directions taken made this an even more challenging project

Figure 7–1   Stage One of the MDI Process

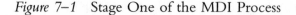

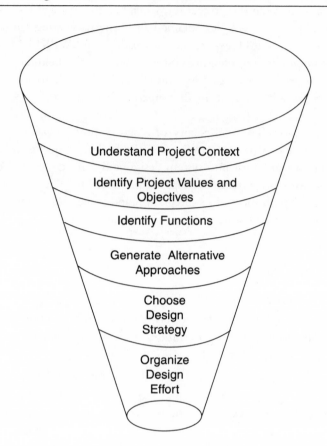

than it had to be. Given the wisdom of hindsight, some decisions and directions now appear to have been ill considered. They include:

1. *Deciding what the system would do and how the project would be structured very early on without consulting the individuals and groups who would be most affected.*

2. *Failing to include representatives of these key stakeholders on the project team until the project was well under way. In particular, representatives from the production teams and from the sales and marketing, cost accounting, and MIS departments should have been added to the team as early as possible. The project team might also have made more rapid progress if it had brought in human resources sooner.*

3. *Ignoring probably the most important stakeholder of all, the senior VP of manufacturing. The project leader made little effort early on to enlist his VP's unequivocal support for the project. His explicit, enthusiastic, and highly visible support from the beginning would have made the first year of the project run much more smoothly than it did.*

4. *Isolating the project from the rest of the organization. This issue, as well as the one preceding, reflects the project leader's initial attitude with respect to anyone he feared might stand in the way of his vision—SICIM (read "sic 'em"). His approach was to exclude rather than include, pointedly ignore rather than build coalitions and collaborate.*

5. *Viewing the potential system users, the production teams, as obstacles rather than as partners. Initially, the idea was to impose the systems and work changes on them and then try to coerce and convince these teams of their value.*

6. *Bringing in the production teams for the wrong reason. Once the importance of their role in the development process was finally acknowledged, the rationale for including them was to get their "buy-in" rather than to solicit their valuable knowledge and expertise.*

7. *Moving the user representative from the plant to project headquarters rather than moving the project team to the plant. As a result, he lost touch with the stakeholders he was supposed to represent—the production workers. In fact, the entire project suffered by the distance—both physical and psychological—between the project team and the intended users in the plant.*

8. *Waiting too long to establish linkages between the project team and the users. The user representative was for the first few months of his involvement too closely aligned with the technical experts on the team and apparently lost sight of the users' concerns. This tended to disperse the creative tension between the perspectives of the production teams and the IT experts, a tension that might have infused the project with more vitality and moved it forward at a faster pace.*

9. *Assuming that the considerable group facilitation and team-building skills of the project leader were all that was needed to help the project team work together effectively. As a result, the project team seemed disorganized and adrift for much of the first year of the project.*

Fortunately, all of these problem areas were identified and addressed early enough to keep the project moving forward. In fact, the project team's ability to respond to the evolving nature of the project was one of its strengths. Throughout the first year of the project, the leader and team members have been able to recognize problems, opportunities, and changing circumstances; to remain flexible and open to these changes; and to adapt their goals and structure as needed.

In conclusion, the first year of the project has been marked by both successes and disappointments. The project team is now ready to make the transition into a new and markedly different stage. This report should help the project make this important transition smoothly and effectively. It documents what has been accomplished so far and what choices have been made concerning what the system and team designs should accomplish and what particular design strategies will be pursued. It also documents how these decisions were made, how the project has moved—albeit erratically at times—from its beginnings to the present. As such, those responsible for preparing this report hope that it will serve as a learning document to guide the rest of this project—as well as future projects of a similar sort—to a successful and productive end.

8

Stage Two: Designing the Technology

NINE MONTHS LATER, a joint meeting of the software development and interface design subteams . . .

Once again, the project seems to be slogging knee-deep through mud. After several months of steady progress, intense bickering has brought the project to a grinding halt. The members of the interface design subteam feel particularly overwhelmed by the details of their work. They seem to be arguing over everything. What information should the system present to the users? How should it be arrayed on the screens? How will users navigate through the data? Should the navigation process be point-and-click or should the interface be designed so that users can customize it as they learn the system? These are just a few of the nontrivial issues at the focal point of their constant arguments.

Two quarreling camps have consistently emerged on opposite sides in the debate over each issue. One camp is unofficially led by Bill. As a born-again advocate of user involvement, Bill wants to get a simple prototype into the hands of the production teams as soon as possible and work with them to resolve the issues that come up as they try out the prototype. His idea is that the project team would look over the users' shoulders, literally and figuratively, as they try out the prototype and simulate the kind of decision-making processes they might employ with the actual system. He believes that a prototype would also help the subteam focusing on user team design.

"Besides," as Bill argues in this, the latest in a growing series of contentious meetings, "we don't know what they might come up with unless we give them a chance to use the system and play with it a bit to see what it can do. Without

this information we can't predict how they will use the system, so we can't plan for those uses. Its hard to develop training programs if we don't know what functions to train for."

Cindy Bransom, a manager from the Paws & Claws MIS department who had joined the project just a few weeks earlier, is the unofficial leader of the other camp. Its position is straightforward. As Cindy presents it, "We can't afford to take the chance of releasing something that we're not completely comfortable with. We've had enough problems with credibility in this project. What if the prototype doesn't work the way it's supposed to, what if the users don't like it, what if they decide they can't use it? What do we do then?"

A related issue dividing the teams is the planned life cycle for the system. Cindy's camp wants to develop a system that will endure without significant modification for a long time. "The costs of the project, including disruption and lost productivity when the system is implemented, will be huge," she argues. "We want to make sure that it's a long time before we need go through this again."

"Bull—," Bill begins, then catches himself. He tries again, trying to be more diplomatic. "We have no idea what uses will evolve for the system, what new technologies will come along in the next few years that we might want to integrate with the new system. We need to design the system for change, even if that means we don't get it completely right the first time.

"Listen, Cindy, I know where you're coming from, but we need to take the risk. No pain, no gain. You can't make an omelet without breaking some eggs. . . ." Bill's voice trails off distractedly as he remembers the prodigious breakfasts he used to eat before joining the project team.

"Spare me the clichés," Cindy retorts wryly. "What do you propose we do? How do we do it? What specifically do you have in mind?"

Bill shakes his head to dispel the images of breakfasts past. "Well, this is what I'm thinking about . . ."

◆ ◆ ◆

THE SECOND STAGE of the MDI process involves the execution of the design tasks. The success of this stage depends heavily on how effectively the MDI team has addressed the activities of the first stage. If those activities have been carried out well, the next stage of the project will proceed much more smoothly than would otherwise be possible. But even then, the MDI team members will need to deal with a number of difficult and challenging issues as they work on technology and team design. In this chapter we focus on technology design.[1] We first describe the general principles and criteria that should guide the design of the technology. We then apply these principles to "groupware"—systems and applications specifically designed to support teamwork. The remainder of the chapter describes how the technology is actually designed and built.

THE PRINCIPLES OF TECHNOLOGY DESIGN

The real value of technology lies not in its sophistication but in how effectively it supports the business objectives of the organization and helps collaborating users achieve them. Therefore, the purpose of technology development is to ensure that the resulting information systems serve organizational and user needs, whether individually or in teams. The principles discussed here are intended to help guide the design of new information systems and applications so that they can serve these needs.

We have grouped these principles into three categories. The first includes those principles linked directly to the organizational context and user functions identified in stage 1. They define the minimally necessary conditions for making sure that the technology will *serve organizational, team, and individual needs*. The second category is related to the technology's ability to *provide access to the information resources*—data, tools, and people—needed to fulfill these needs. Whether the technology can *continue to serve these needs and provide access to these resources over time* is the focus of the principles in the third category. We should note that the categories do not necessarily reflect intrinsically fundamental distinctions. They overlap and in some cases may be somewhat arbitrary. But they do provide a useful way of organizing the principles that can help guide technology development and evaluation.

Fulfill Business Objectives and User Functions

Technology design should be driven by business objectives and needs, the problems to be solved, and the opportunities to be grasped. Focusing on the properties of the technology independent of their responsiveness to identified needs is a prescription for failure. Therefore, new information systems should be *mission focused*. At XYZ, Inc., a mid-sized manufacturer of consumer goods (a real company; the name has been changed), this principle is reflected in the organizational culture and structure, in development and implementation processes, and ultimately in the systems themselves. In the following quote, we see what "mission-focused" means for them. "XYZ has a clear picture of the role of information in its business activities. As one high level manager, when talking about XYZ's Business Systems Department—the name they use for the IS [Information Systems] function—put it, 'That's why *business* always comes before *systems* in *business systems*.'"[2]

New systems should also be *user-driven*. Because the people who use them will be critical to their success, new systems need to be responsive to user needs. Users should be able to guide system operations so that the technology can be flexibly applied to their work. XYZ's information system meets this criterion as well.

> While [the system] is highly complex, its operations can be guided, modified, and manipulated by end users who had no prior experience with computer systems. Knowledge about how to exploit the system's capabilities can be acquired in stages, as needed, so that the technology affords a powerful and flexible tool kit. Frequently, organizations opt instead for systems that are "idiot-proof"—easy to use, impossible to interfere with, and require little learning. Such systems, however, are typically "competency proof," allowing little room for the exercise of users' skills. The choice of user-driven technology permits XYZ to take advantage of the full potential of interactive systems and substantively knowledgeable users.[3]

Users also need tools that enable them to create filters and partial views of data so that they will not be overwhelmed by all the people and information that are literally brought to their fingertips by new communications networks. As Benjamin and Blount note: "Today, instead of being starved of information, managers and workers are in danger of dying from a surfeit of communication. The average information content of 'information' is rapidly falling. When the number of electronic messages per day exceeds two hundred, they cease to attract attention."[4]

Design for Integration

Peter Keen defines integration as "making the separate components of a technology base or business service work together and share resources."[5] This is one of the most talked about and challenging technical issues of our times, with profound implications for team-based work. Indeed, the collaboration imperative is clearly one of the primary factors driving the rapidly growing interest in this important technical area. The vision of communication networks that can connect employees, teams, organizations, and ever more powerful information resources has transformed the landscape and raised the ante. It is no longer a parochial concern for businesses and technologists but a critical factor in the future economic competitiveness of entire nations.

The goal is to avoid creating "technology islands," systems that cannot directly communicate with each other. For example, to get information from users on one "island" to users on another may require printing out a copy and sending it via another, less efficient channel—fax, mail, or courier. A similar problem can also occur at the level of individual systems or workstations. Applications that are not integrated—"application islands"—require users to execute extra, time-consuming steps, which also increase the possibility of errors. For example, to create reports and documents users often need to rekey data from formatted text files into spreadsheets, and vice versa.

The information technology design selected should enable users of one system to communicate and work with users of other systems—directly, seamlessly, and transparently. Ideally, individuals and teams should:

- have access to and be able to work with information resources, people, and other units throughout the organization and beyond;

- be able to integrate their own data and tools with each other as well as to integrate them with those of the people with whom they work.

- be free of constraints on communication by virtue of their location or the location of the resources and people they are working with, the particular hardware and software they use, or the vendors that produced them.

Ideally, technology should pose no limits on who users (individuals or teams) work with, what they work on, or what information and tools they use. Instead, the limits should be policy based and managerial, reflecting such considerations as work needs and tasks, data integrity, security, and efficiency. The closer systems are to this ideal, the easier it is for users to collaborate.

The key to integration is open, nonproprietary standards. *Standards* are defined as "agreements on formats, procedures, and interfaces that permit designers of hardware, software, data bases, and telecommunications facilities to develop products and systems independent of one another with the assurance that they will be compatible with any other product or system that adheres to the same standards." According to Keen, the author of this definition, nonproprietary, or open, standards are "the single most important element in achieving integration of the corporate information and communications resource."[6] To support effective, technology-enabled, boundary-spanning collaboration and teams, these cannot be just corporate or industry standards. Rather, the agreements noted above must be widely shared and, ultimately, international in their reach.

A number of standards now compete for dominance. The Open Systems Interconnection (OSI) reference model is perhaps the most promising source for these standards. The goal of the OSI movement is to replace manufacturers' proprietary standards with "open" interfaces, architectures, and protocols. The objective is to facilitate integration between different organizations and between different parts of the same organization even if the organizations or their parts have different information technologies. In Keen's words, it is a "framework for creating vendor- and equipment-independent systems that can work together."[7]

For a number of reasons, full integration is at this time unattainable. Some open standards have not yet been fully defined and ratified. In other cases, open but ostensibly conflicting standards compete for acceptance among actual and potential adopters.[8] Even when standards are well defined and no competing nonproprietary standards exist, software producers are not falling all over each other in a rush to get products on the market that do comply with these standards. While there is general agreement on the need for openness, there is little implementation of open systems standards at the application level. Market forces, however, are impelling vendors to make at least some of their applications interoperable with those of other vendors.

These obstacles to integration are likely to be overcome in one way or another as systems evolve. The MDI team, IT managers, and others need to pay attention to open standards as they are defined and developed. When possible, they should choose technologies consistent with such standards so that they can interact as widely and as fully as possible with existing technologies and potential collaborators in other organizations. And as we will see in the next section, choosing open systems technologies today will make it easier to integrate new technologies tomorrow.

Design for the Future

One thing organizations can count on is that technology will change. The state-of-the-art systems being implemented today could be outdated before they have had a chance to produce their expected returns on investment. Therefore, systems should be *designed for change* so that they can incorporate new technology as it comes on the market. Successful organizations continually scan for new technological developments in their core business areas and assess their usefulness relative to their needs. They are prepared to upgrade and alter their designs and implementation plans in light of the technical advances they identify. Such an approach is especially important for long-term development efforts, so that new systems will not be obsolete by the time they are implemented. Clearly, this criterion is related to the previous one. If a system is relatively open, it is likely to be more compatible not just with contemporary systems but also with future, open systems products as well.

Systems should also be *user-modifiable*. In our earlier discussion of user-driven systems, we noted that the technology should offer users "a powerful and flexible tool kit" that they can apply to their work as needed. We now extend this principle into the future. If the tools *in* this kit are flexible, users will be able to adapt them to match their skill levels and needs as they change over time. The tool kit should be flexible enough to allow users to modify the tools as they become more familiar with their functionality and as they learn how to apply them to their work. In time, many users will identify applications and adaptations that even the most visionary systems designers could not have anticipated. Therefore, users should be able to modify functions, menus, applications, and tools to keep up with their changing needs and increasing knowledge of the system.

The last principle is represented by the concepts of *modularity and extensibility*. Building in *modularity* means designing systems, tools, and applications as relatively self-contained sets of functions that are relatively independent of and yet compatible with other modules. In effect, modularity is a prerequisite for the kind of flexible tool kit referred to earlier. If applications are designed as modules, users can pick and choose among them to address particular tasks. *Extensibility* refers to the ability to successively add or upgrade modules—in other words, to incorporate new applications into the tool kit and adapt it to changing needs.

From this description, we can see the relationship between modularity and the design for integration. Modules should be designed in accordance with these criteria so they can fit together and interoperate as a larger system of integrated functions. We will return to this issue later in the chapter, when we talk about the role of modularization in the technology design process.

Applying the Principles to Groupware

The principles outlined above should be useful for evaluating all technologies, whether they are purchased off-the-shelf, built to order by outside vendors, developed in-house, or instituted in some combination of these options (for example, an off-the-shelf package customized for particular users). In this section we apply these criteria to *groupware*. This term is used to refer to a broad category of computer applications designed to support cooperative work. These technologies have attracted considerable attention from both technology developers and a small but growing number of social and behavioral scientists in recent years.[9] As is the case with any new development, there is no widely accepted definition of groupware (or of "coordination technologies," a less used, alternative expression), but nearly all definitions include several common elements. A composite might describe groupware as (1) computers and communications technology intended to support (2) multiple users with different roles doing (3) shared, information-based work, sometimes with (4) specialized applications. Lotus Notes™ and Ventana GroupSystems™ are two examples of commercially available groupware.

The reason for this rapidly growing interest seems to be a combination of "technology push" and "workplace pull." Networks, client-server architectures, and distributed information systems are increasingly replacing both the centralized and the stand-alone computing environments of years past. At the same time, organizations have moved aggressively to introduce team-based work because they need quicker responses to changing conditions and markets. Many see an opportunity for innovative deployment of group-oriented technologies. Therefore, the growing need for teams is pulling groupware into the workplace, while advances in computers and network architecture are pushing old technologies out.

It would be premature to try to inventory or otherwise categorize the different types of groupware. While the number of groupware products is expected to grow rapidly, only a few have actually emerged in the marketplace. And those that have emerged vary greatly. Existing applications include:

- enhanced communication and conferencing systems, including multimedia systems;

- networked tools for shared editing or drawing, or for group document management;

- workflow systems that help organize group tasks;

- group decision support systems;

- meeting-support systems (aka *roomware*) that feature conference rooms with networked computers at each seat to help structure and facilitate task-focused interaction during face-to-face meetings.

If the research and trade literatures are any indication, future products will be even more varied.[10]

Perhaps it is best to characterize groupware not as a product class but as a new way of thinking about information systems and work, as a strategy for building technologies that take the needs of teams into account from the very beginning. The MDI team can thus apply the principles described in the last several pages to help it identify what to look for, and what to look *out* for, when putting together a new groupware application. These principles can help the team make wise decisions about what to buy, what to develop, and how to develop it.

The risk involved in jumping on the groupware bandwagon is perhaps best demonstrated by the principle of creating *mission-focused* systems. News that a new groupware application is the "wave of the future" and is the hot trend pursued by nearly everyone else is not a good reason to expend time, money, and effort on it. Will it serve the needs of the teams and the organization? Is it the most cost-effective way to meet these needs, or is there a cheaper, simpler, and quicker approach?

Even if the application has the potential to serve organizational needs, the way in which users interact with it may limit its functionality. In other words, is the groupware technology *user-driven,* or does it force users to do particular things, in certain ways, in predetermined sequences? Some meeting-support and first-generation workflow applications fall into this latter category. They do not allow users to develop the richer, more spontaneous processes that might better match their needs. In effect, they inhibit one property that seems to characterize all successful collaborations—that property that gives the unexpected the opportunity to occur and be exploited.

The relevance of the principles of *integration* should be readily apparent. The fundamental idea behind groupware is helping people work together more effectively. But unless groupware applications can communicate with other applications in use, they are more likely to inhibit than to promote effective collaboration. Therefore, the MDI team should make sure that any new systems effectively link collaborators, data bases, and tools. The groupware tools they build or acquire will have to be integrated into existing networked hardware and software.

Groupware should of course also be *designed for change*—that is, compatible with possible future collaborators, including those in other organizations, such as customers and suppliers. And the best way to do that is to design groupware applications in accordance with open, nonproprietary standards. Indeed, the growth in network-enabled groupware applications and the open systems movement go hand in hand. Together they expand the universe of possible collaborators by diminishing the boundaries between different organizations, locations, and equipment.

Just about everything said earlier about user-driven groupware tools could be repeated here regarding *user-modifiability.* Teams need applications that they can adapt on-the-fly to capture the spontaneous, creative flow that is the raw material of the collaborative process. The spontaneous nature of group behavior also suggests that groupware tools should be designed as *modules.* Groupware developers can not anticipate the specific requirements of teams involved in nonroutine work. The best they can do is provide these teams with the aforementioned flexible tool kit, a kit comprising modularized tools. Team members will then be able to select and combine these modules to match the unpredictable conditions and tasks that will inevitably emerge in the everyday conduct of their work.[11]

In conclusion, the more goal-driven, flexible, adaptable, and inclusive groupware tools are, the more effective they will be in supporting team-based work. Even then, the groupware approach to team performance is inherently limited and cannot by itself unleash the full potential of collaborative work. As we have argued throughout this book, new information systems need to be coupled with complementary changes in teams and organizations. In other words, good groupware is not enough.[12] What is needed is an approach that integrates the development of this technology with the design of teams and the overall organization. Groupware can then be more than just a tool for efficient coordination; it can become, as Ciborra argues, a tool for organizational transformation.[13]

Popular accounts of how groupware products are being used suggest a growing awareness of the value of this integrated approach. The increased use of cross-functional teams operating out of different locations provides an opportunity for unprecedented synergies between organizational and technological change. Consider the following example of the use of Lotus Notes by one of the Big Six consulting firms, Coopers and Lybrand.

> Last year, big client Texaco asked for a business proposal at 4 P.M., demanding it by 10 the next morning. Employees in five cities and from three departments worked through the night—calling up data from databases, creating tables and charts, editing text, all through Notes.™ In Dallas, the proposal was electronically assembled. Then it was e-mailed to New York, and presented to the client. Result: the firm won a multimillion-dollar consulting contract.[14]

This is an excellent demonstration of what can happen when new technologies are combined with new team and organizational designs. We will be talking much more about this issue in the next chapter. But first we need to examine the processes by which new collaboration technologies can be designed and created.

THE PROCESS OF TECHNOLOGY DESIGN

"Paradigm shift" and "sea change" may be the most overused expressions in business today, referring as they do to the latest ideas and practices that promise to revolutionize what organizations do and how they do it. But when applied to the processes[15] by which new technologies are developed, they accurately describe not just the degree of change but the impact of the change as well. According to technology guru Patricia Seybold, the "waterfall method of application development"—the traditional approach of choice in most organizations—"doesn't work anymore."[16] In this section, we begin by describing this traditional approach to technology development. We then describe a more dynamic alternative that Seybold and a growing number of others advocate based on the successful experience of major companies in all sectors of the economy. Finally, we compare and contrast this emerging model with its more traditional counterpart.

The "Waterfall" Model of Systems Development

Information technology professionals use a variety of expressions to refer to the traditional technology design process, including "system life cycle," "system development life cycle," and "systems development process." While descriptions vary widely—each one describing different steps and using different names for these steps—a look below the surface reveals similar characterizations of the same basic process.[17] Most characterizations divide the systems development process into three broadly defined and roughly sequential steps: (1) establish functional requirements, (2) design and build, and (3) test and evaluate. We discuss each of these steps in turn.

Establish Functional Requirements This step is frequently described as an information requirements analysis—a "detailed statement of the information needs that a new system must satisfy." It "identifies who needs what information, and when, where, and how the information is needed." An information requirements analysis defines "the objectives of the new or modified system and develops a detailed description of the functions that the new system must perform."[18] Since this step should identify not only user requirements for information but also user requirements for applications or tools to work on the information, we prefer the broader expression "functional requirements" to describe it. These functions follow from the team-technology functions identified in stage 1 of the MDI process (see chapter 7). The functions identified in this step differ from those earlier functions in two ways: (1) as a second pass, they are more detailed, and (2) they are referenced primarily to the information and technology, particularly to system capabilities and operations.

Design and Build Systems design lays out in detail how a system will meet the functional requirements identified by the analyses described above. Kenneth Laudon and Jane Laudon describe the design as an overall plan or model for that system. They liken it to the blueprint for a building or house that provides all of the detail and "specifications that give the system its form and structure."[19]

The first step in developing this blueprint is to construct a high-level logical design model that lays out the components of the system and illustrates their functional relationships with each other. The model will describe the inputs, outputs, and functions of each component from the user's point of view. This abstract logical model is then mapped onto the physical design for the system—that is, the general hardware, software, platforms, and architecture for the system. Systems that are especially complex are broken down into subsystems, which are then designed "in a *top-down* manner by first specifying the processes and data in general terms and gradually increasing the detail."[20] Various structured design techniques and tools are often used to help create these detailed designs. Before the design is finalized, system designers need to consider a number of alternative configurations, evaluate them based on their relative costs and benefits, strengths and weaknesses, and then select the best one.

The next step is to literally build the system by either developing or purchasing its components. While hardware—computers and peripherals (input/output devices)—is usually purchased off the shelf, software development can follow a number of different routes. Information technology experts can develop specific applications essentially from scratch. Or, as is being done in an increasing number of cases, commercial software can be purchased and modified to meet the organization's specific application needs. In either case, documentation is critical to software development. Documentation is defined by Donna Hussain and K. M. Hussain as "a written description of choices and decisions during the development process . . . needed for operation and use of the system . . . [and] for auditing and evaluating the project."[21] Documentation is important for training users, for modifying and updating the system, and for making sure that knowledge of the system is not lost when those involved in its creation leave the organization or move on to other jobs.

Test and Evaluate Just about every discussion of the systems development process includes a section on testing. These tests are primarily technical in nature; that is, they are designed to ensure that the programs and system function as they are supposed to. These tests include: *unit tests,* which involve separate tests of each program in the system to locate and correct errors, and *system tests,* which help evaluate the functioning of the system as a whole "to determine if discrete modules will function together as planned."[22] After the technical properties of the system have been checked out, the system is ready to be tested in the context of its intended use, that is, by a limited set of potential users applying the system to actual work situations. This *pilot test* marks the beginning of implementation. We will return to this topic in chapter 10 when we discuss implementation of the team-technology designs.

Problems with This Model From this discussion of the waterfall model of systems development and from figure 8–1, we can see why the expression "waterfall" is used to describe it. The process flows downstream, one waterfall spilling over to another in a one–way series of sequential steps. And therein lies some of the problems with this model: "The development process doesn't move from one . . . [step] to the next until the prior one is complete," and "none of the earlier phases can benefit from the knowledge gained in the performance of the later [ones]."[23]

Other problems with this approach include the amount of up-front planning time it requires and the relative lack of flexibility it offers. In addition, approximations of the final system are typically not available for user reaction and feedback until it is too late for them to have much impact. The system that results is likely to be costly, overdue, and possibly obsolete by the time it is finally ready for use. Furthermore, it will have benefited little from serendipity and unexpected opportunities. The most damning problem is perhaps best summed up by these frequently voiced conflicting complaints: while the users claim that "[the system developers] didn't give us what we asked for," the systems developers counter that "[the users] didn't know what they wanted."[24]

Horror stories about such projects abound. It should not be surprising, then, that organizations are desperately seeking alternatives to the

Figure 8–1   The Waterfall Model of Systems Development

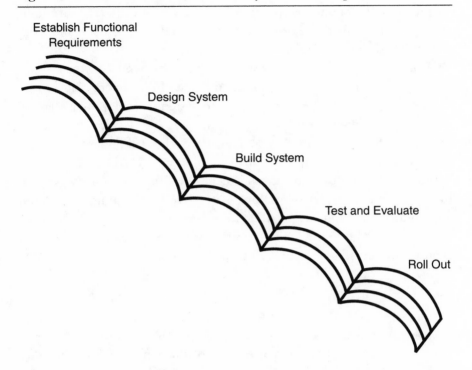

Establish Functional
Requirements

Design System

Build System

Test and Evaluate

Roll Out

traditional systems development model. And what they are finding is an alternative that is, to mix a metaphor or two, as different from a waterfall as rugby is from a relay race.

Rapid Application Development

In one of the few cases where a sports metaphor actually leads to better understanding of a business process, Hirotaka Takeuchi and Ikujiro Nonaka urge organizations to "stop running the relay race and take up rugby."[25] Although they are talking about new product development, they could just as well be talking about new approaches to systems development. The game of systems development should be played less like a relay race, in which runners pass a baton to one another in a series of legs, than like rugby, in which players move down the field as a unit while passing the ball back and forth. The path is rarely straight ahead; a player carries the ball a few steps forward, passes it sideways or backward to another runner, all the time probing for an opportunity to break through and score a "try" (the rugby counterpart of a touchdown). In the case of systems development, the players on the team are users and developers, passing information, ideas, and designs back and forth as they head toward implementation.

While the metaphor has expository limits (what would be the systems development counterpart of the scrum?), it does convey the critical elements most of the new approaches to systems development share— iteration, dynamic coordination between users and developers, and opportunities for serendipity. These new approaches fall under the generic category called "rapid application development" (RAD). The various approaches, methods, models, and techniques within this category go by such names as "spiral workflow," "iterative prototyping," and "joint application development" (JAD), to mention just a few of the most widely used. The following description of the spiral workflow method captures the critical elements of this new approach to systems development.

> You combine process definition, functional design, interface design and application development into a series of overlapping spirals, each one including the involvement and sign-off of the application's end-users. You cycle through each spiral in overlapping parallel, rather than serial, steps. And you don't iterate once: you run through the process at least three or four times. The resulting applications are designed faster, deployed sooner, map directly to the business process, deliver immediate business benefits, and are simpler to improve and less costly to maintain.[26]

The spiral workflow model is illustrated in figure 8–2.

Iterative Prototyping The concept of iterative prototyping is critical to this entire process of systems development and perhaps captures the defining nature of all of the alternative approaches. Prototypes provide potential users with an opportunity to actually experience the work in progress—to "see, feel, and touch"[27] aspects of the systems and tools they will eventually use in their work.

This is especially important when the purpose of the system is not just to automate users' preexisting tasks but to enable them to do new things. The possibilities offered by new systems will be little more than abstractions to users in the early stages of the project. What better way then to get a handle on just what the new system has to offer than to

Figure 8–2 The Spiral Workflow Model of Systems Development

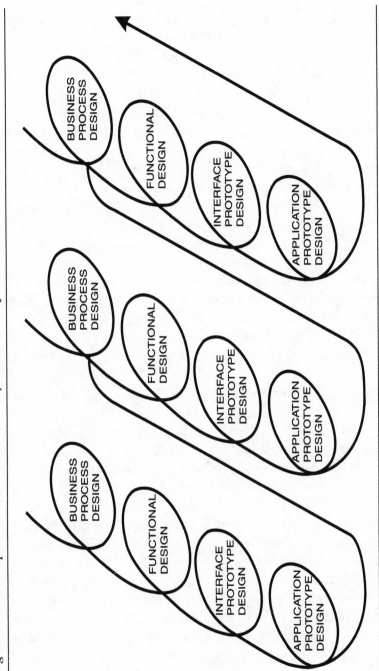

Adapted from P. Seybold, "How to Leapfrog Your Organization into the Twenty-first Century: Highlights from Patricia Seybold's 1994 Technology Forum," Patricia Seybold Group, 1994, 2.

try out a preliminary version to see what it can do—and what users can do when they apply it to their work?

Prototypes can help users expand their horizons beyond immediate needs and existing technologies. In effect, prototypes "concretize the abstract." A prototype provides users with the opportunity to explore the system's potential, give feedback based on actual use, and make suggestions as to how it might be modified to better fulfill its potential. It also gives designers a way to gauge how well they have understood users' verbally expressed needs and requirements and how well they have interpreted them in terms of the technology.

This information can then be used by the MDI team to revise and refine its designs. Prototype trials with intended users provide the first real test of the MDI team's ideas and its ability to convert these ideas into workable designs. Does the system offer users what they think they need? Does it offer these functions in a way that is accessible, useful, and "friendly"? What problems remain? What unanticipated opportunities might it offer? Until trials with the prototype have been conducted, answers to these questions will be little more than speculations. In the process of trying out successive approximations of the final system, user teams and the MDI team can work together to identify problems, deficiencies, and opportunities that neither could have anticipated alone.

As noted above, prototypes should be created as early in the design process as possible. To shorten the time needed to develop and release the prototype, initial versions can be limited and rely on simulated data. But the MDI team needs to be careful about going too far in this direction by releasing a prototype too soon, before it can include a minimally acceptable level of functionality. Prototyping trivial functions and cosmetic features will reveal little of worth to the MDI team and potential users. The latter may even resent the time spent with a premature prototype and resist later trials with more useful versions.

To be effective, the MDI team needs not only a prototype of the system but a prototype of the ways in which the user teams can apply the system to their work. Having users try out a fixed set of operations and functions is appropriate early in the development process but will not be adequate later on. At some point, users should also have the opportunity to explore novel applications of the system to actual work situations or to realistic simulations. User delegates can play a critical role in designing this prototype "experience"—the application exercise, the feedback and evaluation methods, and the means by which users and

MDI team members collaborate on system redesign. As the spiral workflow imagery suggests, prototyping may require several iterations before the system is ready for implementation; the larger and more complex the project, the more iterations that may be required.

One last word before we leave this important topic. Prototyping can be one of the most contentious issues in the technology design process. Information technology developers—like Cindy Bransom in the story installment that opened this chapter—may sometimes resist releasing incomplete, interim designs for review and feedback from stakeholders, particularly from the user teams. They often want to keep their designs close to the vest until the technology feels "right." Because of organizational politics, investment of ego in their work, and fear of taking risks, to mention just a few reasons, developers may be reluctant to expose the imperfections of their work to others. "It's not ready yet," is an all-too-familiar reason to delay release of a prototype. Trial and error, design and redesign, iteration and feedback are an integral part of the MDI process. It is far better to receive critical input early in the process when modifications can be made relatively painlessly than to wait until it's so late that the implications of such changes might sink the entire project. Although this can be a difficult and unnerving process for the MDI team, it is critical to the project's success.

Modular, Concurrent Development In many of the new, alternative approaches to systems development, the planned system is partitioned into modules that can then be developed concurrently. For example, most systems can be partitioned into core versus application functions. The core functions, often referred to as the "back-end," include the systems architecture and generic capabilities that will serve all users. Applications are the "front-end," the specific tools the team members will use.

Core and applications modules can often be developed in tandem by different but overlapping subteams. The subteams responsible for developing the core modules may require little if any user involvement early in the design stage. As far as the users are concerned, the core functions operate behind the scenes; different back-end solutions make little difference from the user's point of view. Applications and tools, on the other hand, directly affect users' work. Like mechanics and their tools, system users have an immediate, hands–on relationship with their electronic counterparts. Users interact directly with them and literally apply them to their work tasks. Therefore, as we have argued in earlier chapters, users should be an integral part of the subteams responsible for developing applications and tools. They can even be the primary developers, adapting off-the-shelf tools when possible or using any of the end-user application development tools coming on the market at ever increasing rates.[28]

Individual modules—for example, the interface and an application—can be developed independently and concurrently. Not all modules need to be developed at once. The MDI team can focus initially on the development of only a couple—using iterative prototyping, of course. The functionality of these initial modules is critical; they should be key modules within the overall system and they should fit together. When implemented as a set, these new modules should add enough capability to give users a good reason for switching over to their new tools. Other modules can be added as the project takes on additional staff, and as both the project and user teams move up the new technology learning curve. Throughout much of the midway to later portions of this stage, the MDI team will be implementing some modules at the same time it is developing others.[29] The development process itself should be guided by agreed-upon, overall standards so that all system modules can be successfully integrated over time and remain open-ended for future extensions.

Documentation should be generated as the subteams proceed, preferably online. Most tools for user-developed applications include prompts and routines to guide user-developers through the documentation process. Many also include mechanisms for automatically gathering the user-developers' running documentation notes into text files. These files can be edited and structured into manuals and other forms of documentation at some later point in the project.[30]

The following example, based on an actual project for a large international nonprofit organization, illustrates this new approach to systems development and many of the principles discussed in the last several pages.

The project involved the development of a new, integrated system for acquiring, processing, and disseminating data on economic and social conditions in various regions of the world. The data serve many purposes, including planning, research, problem identification, and policy development. The data sources included both questionnaires and electronic data bases provided by other organizations and agencies. The intended users were statisticians, researchers, and policy analysts.

The new system was designed to replace an existing system that had evolved during a period of rapid technological change. As a result, the existing system included a wide range of frequently incompatible computer products, data-base systems, communications media, and data-processing techniques that varied in age and flexibility. The systems' relative lack of interconnectivity made it very difficult for the highly interdependent, worldwide network of researchers, statisticians, policy analysts, and administrators to share data, collaborate on analyses, and generally work together on common tasks and joint projects. In contrast, the new system was to be fully integrated. It was also planned as a modular, user-driven system that would enable users to choose the applications and tools that best suited their tasks, to modify the way these applications and tools functioned, and to integrate compatible external products—existing and future—into their work.

The new system was designed as a collection of information resources and services that could be accessed by users via desktop client programs residing on their workstation computers. All desktop computers and resource servers were to be networked via local and wide area networks, and the new system was to be available throughout the organization worldwide.

The development strategy involved two converging tracks, referred to by the development team as the "technology" track and the "substantive" track. The technology track included all of those activities concerned chiefly with the development of the system's core components. These activities were independent of specific end-user applications, which were the main focus of the activities in the substantive track. User representatives worked closely with the systems experts in the substantive track but were less involved in the activities within the technology track.

Each track involved three stages. In general, the first two stages in each track would proceed independently, although high-level decision making and consultation would be conducted across tracks throughout the entire effort, particularly during the first stage. The teams and the products of the two tracks would be merged in stage 3 to produce a prototype of the system for pilot testing.

In this example we can see all of the critical elements of the rapid application development approach. The system is divided into separate core and application modules that are then developed concurrently. Users are intensively involved in the process, especially in application development. And, perhaps most important, prototypes are used throughout—to test designs, to elicit user feedback, and to generate new ideas and uses for the system.

Clearly, the MDI team will need special information tools to develop the modules and prototypes discussed in the last several pages. In chapter 6 we described the information resources required by all project teams. But the technological nature of the MDI team's task means that it will require much more than the generic tools described in that chapter. To be specific, the MDI team will need tools to produce the prototypes and modules described in the last several pages. These tools are similar to the tools the MDI team might develop for the user teams—modular programming, application development, documentation, and other prototyping tools. This continuity and flow between development tools and end-user tools should be no surprise given the iterative, open, seamless, and user-involved nature of the MDI framework. In effect, the MDI team will be transferring the technological capability it developed to do its own work to the user teams who are the focus of its efforts.

Comparing the Waterfall and the RAD Models

There are some superficial similarities between the waterfall and the rapid application development models of systems development. The RAD model can be subdivided into phases that correspond roughly to the steps described earlier for the waterfall model: (1) establish functional requirements, (2) design and build, (3) test and evaluate. Despite this apparent similarity the two models are quite different. The different connotation of step and phase is one of the best indications of how different they are. That is, it is clear where one step ends and the next begins, while the same cannot be said for phases, which often overlap. There are also critical differences in how each step or phase is conducted.

To *establish functional requirements* in the traditional approach, would-be users are interviewed and surveyed to find out what they want and need from the system to be developed. After this initial effort, specifications are developed from the data, and the system is designed to meet these specifications. Users are not likely to be involved again until an interface for the completed design is tested. The process is quite different when joint application development, or JAD, is used to help establish these requirements.

Part of the rapid application development . . . tool kit, JAD is a series of highly structured interview sessions aimed at reaching consensus on a project's goals and scope. From the moment participants belly up to the conference table, the JAD professionals in the room begin to create data models, build process-flow diagrams and shape prototypes that express users' needs and desires.

What's more, the experts say such near-instantaneous feedback must never stop—continuing in the form of new screens, progress updates, and status reports. That's where JAD segues into RAD to provide a constant new cut at the application under development.[31]

We have already described many of the differences between the two approaches to *designing and building* systems. There is also an apparent similarity between the two approaches that on closer inspection reveals once again just how different they can be. Both approaches employ prototypes, but when you look closely at the system components that are included in the prototype, the differences become clear. Prototypes of user interfaces are typically employed by traditional system developers to elicit user input on the look and feel of the computer screens and data displays. But basic issues concerning what functions the system will perform, how users will navigate through the system, and the like are rarely subject to prototyping or otherwise open for user input. In RAD, on the other hand, basic functional issues are often open to user input from the very beginning and are the main focus, along with screen design, of the prototyping process.

With respect to *testing and evaluation,* the critical difference is that in the traditional approach this is typically a well-defined step that is formally distinct from designing and building. In RAD these "final tests" are replaced by successive iterations designed to provide the MDI team with feedback that can be used to redesign and modify the system. As such, they overlap the prototyping and design activities of the preceding phase.

The real test of the system comes within the context of its intended use—the pilot test. The pilot test should also include the new team designs that are being developed at the same time as the technology. Therefore, before we can discuss the pilot test, we need to turn our attention to user team design and the issues and factors critical to its success.

◆ ◆ ◆

Four months later, a joint meeting of the software development and interface design subteams . . .

Prototype trials have been run and the system has been tested with the actual monthly cost breakdowns by product, brand, and source. Everyone is pleased with the results. The system has been modified to reflect what was learned from the trials, and it is finally ready for implementation. The technology design teams are meeting to plan the implementation, which will start with a comprehensive pilot test in the plant. The subteams are only a few minutes into the meeting when the focus shifts to the subteam of user team designers.

Bill, who has been serving on both the technology and user team design subteams, is the first to voice what the others are beginning to think. "We can't plan this pilot without the user team designers. The pilot has got to include the new team designs they've been working on or this will be just another system test. We need to see how the system does in actual work situations before we move too far ahead, and we need to get together with them to plan the pilot."

"You're on that team, aren't you?" Cindy asks. "You know what they've been doing. Can't you speak for them? We can't afford to delay this any further. We're way behind schedule already."

Bill squirms in his seat. "Well, I hate to admit it," as his face turns red and the telltale blotches of perspiration begin to dampen his shirt collar, "but I haven't been paying too much attention. I've been preoccupied with the prototype trials and missed a lot of meetings. To be honest, I wasn't even paying close attention in the meetings I was at. Sorry." He perceptibly blushes.

Cindy tries to put him at ease. "Hey, no sweat." ("Easy for her to say," Bill thinks as he wipes his rapidly dampening brow.) "Why don't you schedule a meeting between us and them for next week. What the hell, another week or so isn't going to matter all that much at this point."

Bill, temporarily off the hook, looks relieved. But his relief is short-lived as the vague memories of recent user team design meetings seep back into his consciousness. Cindy brings the meeting to a close. Bill rises from his seat and moves distractedly toward the door.

9

Stage Two (Continued): Designing User Teams

THE FOLLOWING WEEK, a joint meeting between the software development, interface design, and user team design subteams . . .

As the team members slowly drift into the room, chatting about what they did over the weekend or about last night's football game, Bill stands nervously at the front of the room. In the week preceding, he has learned that his worst fears were true. He already knew that the user team designers had been working in almost total isolation from the software development and interface design subteams for the last several months. Now he realizes that their independent paths are reflected in the incompatible designs they have generated. The feeling in the pit of his stomach has nothing to do with what he ate for lunch.

In the original design strategy, which was chosen in the early stages of the project, representatives from marketing would be added to the production teams. Then the teams could be given responsibility for making decisions about what, when, and how much to produce. But, as Bill now realizes, the user team designers began to deviate from this strategy some time ago.

Several months earlier they had decided that adding representatives from marketing to the production teams would be too difficult and could have potentially disastrous political consequences. For one thing, the subteam of user team designers did not have the authority to restructure the marketing and production functions. Besides, marketing staff members did not respond favorably to trial balloons about moving them to the plants and adding them to the production teams. So the design subteam figured that a communications link between marketing and the production teams would be an acceptable alternative. With shared data views and analytical tools they could work together on key tasks. While marketing would not be formally represented on the production teams, it would be at least available to help the teams when needed.

The user team designers thought that Bill had communicated their decision to the other subteams, but this was apparently one of the items that had slipped through the cracks during the transition into the design stage of the project. The software development and interface design subteams continued to follow the original design strategy, not realizing that their user team counterparts had gone off in an entirely different direction. Assuming that representatives from marketing would be on the production teams and physically located in the plant, these subteams never considered communications links with the marketing department to be a particularly high priority.

Bill felt awful. It was now his responsibility to inform them that their incompatible designs made it impossible to fulfill one of the most important objectives of the entire project. And the fault rested primarily with him. Sure, Chris and the other project sponsors had put too much responsibility on his admittedly broad shoulders. No one person, regardless of how capable, could have done everything they and the others have asked of him. Still . . .

Finally, everyone was seated and looking at him expectantly. "How to begin?" he thought. "You all know the purpose of this meeting. In the words of that revered and beloved sportscaster, the late Howard Cosell, the man who has inspired me throughout the years, I'm going to 'tell it like it is.'"

◆ ◆ ◆

IDEALLY, THE MDI TEAM should be working on the design of the user teams at the same time it is designing and building the technology. But in real life, work on one usually precedes the other, depending on whether the project is either IT- or team-driven (see chapter 3). The sequencing of team and technology design, however, is beside the point. The *mutual design* of both is not. Decisions and designs concerning one must be integrated with decisions and designs concerning the other throughout the MDI process, even though different emphases (technology versus teams) may prevail at different times. Now that we have covered the principles and techniques of technology design (in chapter 8), it is time to turn our attention to the other side of the MDI coin, team design.

In chapter 2 we introduced the concept of team design, discussed the five types of teams, and briefly described the steps involved in the team design process. In chapter 6 we applied the concept to the design of the MDI team, which is a project team. In this chapter we apply the same concepts to the process of user team design.[1] In effect, as we move through this chapter we will fill in the cells of the matrix depicted in table 9–1. (We have started by incorporating a summary of the characteristics from table 6–1 under the column for project teams.) Since team/technology integration is at the core of the MDI framework, this chapter concludes with a discussion of team/technology design trade-offs and the ways in which decisions in one area can affect those in the other.

The end result of the team design process is somewhat different from that of the technology design process. Technology design results in a tangible object—a software application or a computer system. Team designs exist primarily on paper; that is, they will consist largely of plans and proposals to be implemented as actual working arrangements and structures in the final stage of the MDI process.

DESIGNING WORK TEAMS

As described in chapter 2, work teams are responsible for producing products or providing services. Unlike the other team types, they perform regular, ongoing work. The continuing, predictable, and well-defined nature of their work is their most important characteristic and the one that most strongly influences their design.

Composition

Individual members should possess not only the skills they need to fill their assigned roles on the team but also some of the skills of other members so that they can cover for other members when they are absent or can help them when they are overloaded. Team members need cognitive skills as well, for problem solving, troubleshooting, and equipment repair. These cognitive skills will also come in handy as they tinker with and modify their new technology to fit their tasks and modify their tasks to take advantage of the unanticipated opportunities offered by the technology (more on this in chapter 10).

Because of the ongoing nature of the team's work, membership is usually fixed and permanent. The size of the team should be limited to the smallest number required to do the work effectively. Depending on

Table 9–1 Matrix of Key Characteristics for the Design of User Teams

| | Design Sequence | Team Type | | | | |
	Identify Team Type	Work Team (SMWT)	Project Team	Parallel Team	Management Team	Ad Hoc Network
Design Team Structure	Composition		Different backgrounds and organizational units Specialized expertise "Laterality" Full- or part-time Members may change over life cycle Some core members			
	Leadership		Credibility is key May rotate Facilitate, coach, and consult Project management Boundary management			
	External Connections		Ongoing linkages to key stakeholders Communication systems			
Develop Team Capabilities	Information Resources		Tools for scanning, analysis, problem solving, project management Integrated data bases Communication systems			
	Training Programs		Conflict management Just-in-time training Develop "laterality"			

the nature of the tasks and purpose, team members may be full- or part-time, working in the same location at approximately the same time (colocated) or not. For example, production team members typically need to be colocated, full-time members of the team. On the other hand, the customer service representatives at SWP&L were only on the gas emergency response team when they were handling calls reporting suspected gas leaks. When fulfilling other responsibilities, they either worked independently (for example, responding to customer calls to schedule routine service or to answer questions about bills) or on other teams (for example, the quality improvement team for their department). The CSRs were also in different locations from the field technicians, and the technicians themselves covered separate, albeit overlapping territories.

Leadership

As work teams become more self-managed, the role of the immediate supervisor can change dramatically. In some cases it may be eliminated entirely, with the team reporting directly to the next level of management. Within the team, the supervisor is replaced by the team leader, a position that can be permanently assigned to a particular team member or rotated among some or all. Leadership can also be shared by several team members, with each providing leadership for different aspects of a team's work—technical, administrative, and so forth.

The leader of a self-managed team has a role very different from that of an immediate supervisor. The leader does not tell members what to do or how to do it and does not look over their shoulders to make sure they are doing it right. But self-management does not mean that the leader abdicates responsibility entirely. The appropriate position and approach lies somewhere in between. Leaders of self-managed teams should neither direct nor withdraw; they need to facilitate. Team leaders can foster self-management in three ways:

- ◆ *Task management* helps team members determine how they will complete their tasks; the leader provides coaching, consultation, and resources as needed.

- ◆ *Boundary management* helps members identify who they need to coordinate and communicate with outside the team; the leader acts as a liaison when necessary.

♦ *Performance management* ensures that the team is involved in goal setting and that the goals are aligned with overall business objectives. The leader also sees that the team monitors its performance and steps in when it does not.[2]

Whatever he or she does, the person serving in the team leader role should *not* perform traditional supervisory functions that can be handled by the team. This would defeat the purpose of the self-managed team and offset one of its most reliable benefits—helping reduce unnecessary layers of management and supervision. In many cases, special training will be needed to help team leaders adjust to their new roles as coaches, facilitators, and liaisons.[3]

External Connections

The external connections that are critical to work teams are those with others immediately "upstream" and "downstream" from them in the overall work process, whether they work for the same organization or not. This connection means more than receiving materials, subassemblies, or reports from their "suppliers," transforming or otherwise adding value to what they receive and sending it on to their "customers." It also means information about the work in process—where it is in the process, scheduled completion, and so on—so that the team can coordinate activities and collaborate to solve problems. Work teams also need to maintain connections with those who support their work, such as technical people who fix their equipment, statistical experts who help them analyze data, graphic designers who help them prepare reports, human resources personnel who help them hire new team members, and others with specialized expertise and knowledge.

Information Resources

The more self-managed a team is, the more information and information tools it needs. Self-managed work teams require information about:

♦ task requirements and constraints;
♦ general and specific knowledge relevant to the nature and domain of their work (at Paws & Claws, for instance, production cost breakdowns for different products);
♦ performance standards and customer requirements;

- the responsibilities of each team member for certain tasks, the status of the work on each task, and the ways in which variances will affect other tasks;

- the strategic context of their work (for example, where their work fits into the overall process, business forecasts, information about their competitors); and

- experts and other resources that may be available to them—both inside and outside the organization.

Information systems can also include tools for analyzing data and solving problems, and a means of online feedback so that individual team members can monitor their individual performance and the performance of the team. New information systems can serve other team needs as well, including communicating with team members and linking the team with customers, suppliers, and those with needed expertise. Applications can also be developed to simulate the consequences of different strategies and actions (like the "what-if" module in the Paws & Claws SICIM system) so that they can make better-informed decisions about their work. All of this added capability can push decision making down or out to all members of the team, ultimately enabling the team to manage itself.

Training

Members of the self-managed work team rarely possess all of the skills they need at the time the team is created (or converted from a more traditional form). Therefore, they almost always require some training. This can include:

- training in the skills team members need to perform their tasks;

- training in problem solving, group interaction, and conflict management to help members work more effectively in groups;

- cross-training to provide members with the variety of skills required for team flexibility;

- training in quality analysis or statistical process control to help teams monitor and improve their performance; and

- business and economic education to help teams understand their activities in the context of overall business goals and strategy.

Table 9–2 Design of Work Teams

Design Step	Characteristics
Composition	Necessary competencies in team Multiskilled; cognitive skills important Fixed and permanent membership Full- or part-time Colocated or not
Leadership	Leader may or may not be an immediate supervisor Team leader role: permanently assigned or rotated Members may share leadership functions Foster self-management by encouraging team task management, boundary management, performance management Function as coach, facilitator, liaison
External Connections	"Upstream" and "downstream" in work process: suppliers and customers Staff support
Information Resources	Task requirements and constraints Domain of work Performance standards and customer requirements Team responsibilities and work status Strategic context Resources Analytical tools Problem-solving and decision-making tools Communication systems
Training Programs	Technical skills Problem solving Group process Conflict management Cross-training Quality analysis and statistical process control Business and economic education

The design features of self-managed work teams are summarized in table 9–2.

DESIGNING PARALLEL TEAMS

Parallel teams supplement the formal hierarchy and structure of the organization. They literally exist in parallel with the rest of the organization, pulling together people from different work units or performing different functions that can not be accomplished within the existing structures, such as coordination, problem-solving, and improvement-oriented tasks. The dual responsibilities of the team members—as part of the parallel team in addition to their regular, formal job—and the nature of the team's tasks are the factors that exert the most influence on the design of parallel teams.

Composition

Unlike work teams and project teams, whose work is ongoing, parallel teams tend to have work that is episodic. Much of the work takes place in meetings that may or may not be frequently and regularly scheduled. But these meetings should not be the only venues in which work is conducted. The effectiveness of parallel teams is often determined by how much effort members, individually or in small groups, are willing to expend outside of formally scheduled team meetings. Between meetings members may need to conduct research, consult with stakeholders, read notes and minutes from previous meetings, and write reports. With this "extracurricular" work, team members will be better prepared for meetings, and the time allotted will be used much more effectively.

The team's composition should be representative of the units that will be affected by the team's work. Members usually devote only part of their time to the team; the rest of the time they will be engaged in fulfilling their formally designated job responsibilities. They do not need to be colocated except during team meetings, and perhaps not even then if they have access to compatible communications systems. Like project team members, their assignment to the team may be temporary if the team's mission has an end or if members' terms are temporary (for example, a task force versus a grievance committee).

As with all other team types, parallel teams should be made up of people whose expertise is relevant to its focus, but this is not always possible. Members may be volunteers, or they may be nominated by a supervisor or manager for reasons other than relevant expertise (to achieve demographic balance, to serve political ends, to provide representation and opportunities to as many employees or units as possible). Training and access to outside expertise is thus especially critical. These teams need to be flexible in terms of how they define their membership and keep their boundaries somewhat permeable so that expertise can be pulled into the team as needed. Because of political considerations and the need to minimize "in-group"/"out-group" tensions, the size of the team may have to be larger than the smallest number needed for optimal performance.

Leadership

Leaders of parallel teams should facilitate meetings, coach team members, help them to use problem-solving techniques, link up with management and other stakeholders, and obtain training and outside resources. Experienced facilitators are frequently used to fulfill these roles, though managers and supervisors can also serve this function.

Parallel teams responsible for decisions and recommendations that will affect others (improvement teams, coordination teams, task forces, and reengineering teams) pose special challenges to team leaders. Parallel teams need legitimacy to implement (or even recommend) significant and potentially unpopular changes. The status and personal characteristics of the leader can go a long way toward establishing the legitimacy of the team and its task. Negotiation skills and political savvy are also important for leaders of parallel teams with controversial missions. In some cases an external consultant or third party may be the best choice to lead the team, especially for particularly significant and controversial tasks. They are more likely to be seen as objective by all stakeholders and can take the heat and leave when the team's work is done.

External Connections

As the work of the team heats up, members may divert more and more of their time away from their formal, functional-area responsibilities and may neglect to inform their functional supervisors about their team assignments and responsibilities. Individual members should therefore make a special effort to keep these lines of communication open. Furthermore, since parallel teams are less likely to include within their boundaries all of the expertise they need, they should establish connections with possible external sources of expertise. They may not be able to anticipate the specific expertise they will require until the need is immediately upon them, but they can at least alert the manager of the functional unit where this expertise resides so that it will be available when the time comes.

Information Resources

Because parallel teams are typically part-time teams that meet regularly for relatively short periods, they need internal communications to keep team members informed about important developments that occur between meetings. They also need ongoing documentation and records of each meeting's deliberations and agreements (in the form of minutes, agendas, and action items); memory fades quickly in the face of pressing day-to-day work demands. Additional needs include communication of progress to sponsors and other interested stakeholders, access to business information concerning the issues that are central to the team's mission, and information about the units the team represents and the availability of potential members and experts.

Training

Training needs for parallel teams can include problem-solving and group process skills, quality improvement concepts and tools (for instance, total quality management) and general education about the organization so that the team can generate recommendations that make good business sense. One alternative to investing in training programs for teams that will be in existence for only a relatively short while, such as a temporary task force, is to bring in external professional and staff personnel as needed to act as expert resources.

The design features of parallel teams are summarized in table 9–3.

DESIGNING MANAGEMENT TEAMS

Management teams are responsible for the overall performance of a business unit. They provide direction and resources to the individual units that make up the business unit and coordinate their activities. The high-level position of the individual members within the organization and the team's integrative, strategic responsibilities are the factors that most influence management team design.

Composition

The function of management teams significantly limits the size of the pool from which members can be drawn. Since they direct, monitor, and integrate the work of different business units, management team members are typically the managers to whom these business units report.

Table 9–3 Design of Parallel Teams

Design Step	Characteristics
Composition	Members represent units affected by teams' work Part-time Usually temporary Members may volunteer or be nominated by supervisor
Leadership	Facilitate meetings Participative and coaching skills Link to managers and other stakeholders Obtain training and outside resources Needs organizational legitimacy Negotiation skills and political savvy
External Connections	Ongoing linkages to key stakeholders, such as: sponsors; customers; supervisors; managers of functional work units; other potential sources of expertise
Information Resources	Internal and external communications Regular meeting records and documentation Business information Organizational information Availability of potential members and experts
Training Programs	Problem solving Group process Quality improvement concepts and tools Consultants and staff can provide needed expertise

For example, the senior management team consists of all the managers of the company's major divisions. The members are typically vice presidents or higher. Similarly, the management team for a division will include all of the managers of the highest-level units that make up the division. As these examples illustrate, selection of members is not an issue for most management teams. Whoever serves in the appropriate role or level is on the team.

Aside from this important distinction, the recommendations we made concerning the composition of parallel teams apply to management teams as well. That is, while much of the work takes place in regularly scheduled meetings, individual work outside of these meetings plays a critical role in team effectiveness. Management teams are usually ongoing and last as long as does the business unit for which they are collectively responsible.

Leadership

Management teams are usually led by the senior executive to whom the members of the team formally report. Senior management teams are led by the CEO, division management teams are led by the division manager (in large companies, a senior VP), and so on. Management teams can be subject to two different tendencies, both of which can present formidable challenges to the leader. One is that management teams often function in decidedly "unteamlike" ways. To reach the uppermost levels of the organizational hierarchy requires a strong ego. The problem is that this characteristic can get in the way of collaboration and teamwork, especially when management team members compete for authority, resources, and the opportunity to succeed the CEO when he or she moves on.

Leaders can do a number of things to foster collaboration and build teamwork in their management teams. One of the most important is to create a shared understanding among team members that transcends their competing interests. The leader needs to provide a clear vision of the team's purpose. The significance of this purpose should be readily apparent to members—in most cases, mere symbolism will not be enough. The leader can also align cross-functional interests within the team by identifying the areas and tasks for which the members are collectively responsible and how they can individually contribute to this effort. Finally, the leader needs to provide feedback on members' performance as a team and find ways to reward their collective efforts.

Like project teams, management teams often exhibit a diversity of functions and interests that can lead to fragmentation. By keeping the team focused on its overarching strategic concerns, collective responsibilities, and shared rewards, leaders can help members transcend their differences and the centrifugal forces that might otherwise tear the team apart.

On the other hand, management teams can be subject to centripetal forces that bind them together too closely, usually around what they believe is the team leader's position.[4] This is more likely to occur in highly bureaucratic organizations where "yes men" and "yes women" find it easier to climb the path toward upper management than the strong personalities who constantly question the status quo. The challenge for management team leaders in this situation is to recognize "groupthink" and encourage, even provoke, dissent while resisting the temptation to move prematurely toward convergence.

External Connections

Chance meetings with new people make life interesting. They enrich our lives in unexpected ways, they provide us with new ideas and different perspectives, they create new opportunities. These serendipitous occasions can take individuals, units, and organizations off into entirely new and exciting directions. The problem is that those people who have the greatest impact on the future direction of the organization—senior managers—are the least likely to have the time and opportunity to make these connections. They are typically so focused on the here and now demands of their work, their boards, their peers, and direct reports that the opportunities for serendipitous meetings with new people are few and far between. As a consequence, their opportunities for exposure to fresh, new ideas are just as constrained.

Like all teams, management teams need to build and maintain connections with parties external to the team. There are two key differences, however. One is that *external* often means external to the organization. According to Deborah Ancona and David Nadler, these external "actors," as they call them, can include "financial markets, the media, key customers, competitors, and governments."[5] External connections with potential partners in new business ventures are particularly important these days. They can provide the strategic flexibility that organizations need to compete in today's rapidly changing, intensely competitive business environment.

A second difference is that the specific people, groups, or organizations the management team needs to connect with are frequently unknown. If the team knows who to contact, it already knows something about what these contacts think, do, and know. The serendipitous encounters with those who they don't know are the ones that can often make the biggest difference. Therefore, perhaps more than any other group, the senior management team needs access to communication systems that span organizational boundaries and expose them to a wide range of new ideas and potential collaborators—perhaps via Internet interest groups.[6]

Information Resources

Senior managers have other critical information needs as well. The senior management team is the strategic focal point for the organization, the point where everything comes together, where internal operations are linked to external factors, and where strategy is formed and redirected. The principal challenge for high-level management teams is formulating strategy in the face of an increasingly complex and turbulent environment. In effect, management teams need to steer the organization across stormy and unpredictable seas, rapidly changing direction as they scan the horizon for early warnings of trouble ahead.

To do this effectively, they need tools that can pull together all of the information the team needs to make rapid shifts in strategic direction. This requires easy access to up-to-date information on the internal operations and performance of the organization and on the changing conditions in the external environment. They need tools for scanning information from many diverse sources concerning a wide range of factors, and they need to be able to aggregate these data quickly in meaningful ways to arrive at high-level views of results and trends.[7] They also need analytical tools to generate alternative scenarios so that they can test the implications of their strategic options. In sum, the information needs of management teams include comprehensive sensing devices, efficient triggers for change, and tools for integrating and analyzing this information and for testing alternative courses of action.[8]

As the above description suggests, the information needs of management teams are highly complex and sophisticated—rivaled only, perhaps, by the information needs of project teams. The irony is that management team members are often the least accepting of new information technology and the most ill-prepared to take advantage of what it has to offer. Furthermore, the problem seems to get worse as one goes higher up in the organizational hierarchy, with senior management teams being the worst offenders. The reason of course is experience and background—most senior managers were not exposed to information technology when they were in school or as they moved up the ranks. It is not surprising that they are uneasy about relying on a technology with which they have little hands-on experience. As lower-level managers who are familiar with computers and cognizant of their value move up through the ranks, management teams will increasingly recognize information technology for what it is—a work tool that is as indispensable for them as it is for every other individual, team, and unit in the organization.

Training

Management teams have a need for broader and more strategic knowledge and skills than other team types—for example, knowledge of emerging social and business trends, business strategy, new approaches to management, and organizational design. But they also have some training needs in common with other team types. Training in group dynamics and problem-solving techniques is an example. That members of management teams tend to be even more resistant to such training than other teams suggests that their need is at least as great. In fact, resistance to training in general is likely to be one of the more daunting issues designers of management teams are likely to face. Managers have more difficulty than most acknowledging that they do not know everything, especially in front of their peers. But they have to get over their reticence and serve as models for the rest of the organization—to "walk their talk," as it were—if they expect those reporting to them to follow suit.

The design features of management teams are summarized in table 9–4.

DESIGNING AD HOC NETWORKS

In chapter 2 we described ad hoc networks as informal collections of individuals and groups connected by shared interests, purposes, or goals. They typically emerge spontaneously within organizations and, increasingly, across them as well. We also noted in chapter 2 that ad hoc networks are particularly important for team-based organizations since they can serve as the "primordial soup" from which other types of teams can be formed.

Because ad hoc networks tend to be spontaneous and informal, their design is rarely planned.[9] The only appropriate "design" strategy is to create the conditions, practices, and policies that will enable these networks to emerge and flourish. The core principle is to provide opportunities for individuals and groups to connect across functional, physical, and temporal boundaries. The task, therefore, according to organization designer Jay Galbraith, is to "increase the odds that voluntary contacts

Table 9–4 Design of Management Teams

Design Step	Characteristics
Composition	Managers of subunits that make up larger organizational unit Membership depends on position Fixed and permanent membership
Leadership	Senior executive to whom the members of the team report Foster collaboration and build teamwork; create shared understanding; define collective responsibilities; provide team performance feedback; reward collective efforts
External Connections	Connections often external to organization: financial markets; media; customers; competitors; governments; potential partners for new business ventures
Information Resources	Strategy formulation and change Internal operations and performance Changing conditions in marketplace Scanning systems and tools Analytical tools Integrated data bases and tools Problem-solving and decision-making tools
Training Programs	Emerging social and business trends Business strategy New approaches to management Organization design Group process Problem solving and decision making

will occur and that they will occur in pursuit of organizational goals."[10] He goes on to explain how voluntary contacts can lead to networked relationships:

> Informal networks occur naturally, randomly, spontaneously, and voluntarily throughout organizations. Whenever two people with some affinity meet, a relationship is formed. The design of the informal network is simply to eliminate some of the randomness in its creation. The purpose is to increase the probability that important relationships are created and used. The organization designer acts as a relationship broker and makes the introductions. Spontaneity and voluntarism reign from then on.[11]

The *composition* of the ad hoc network is defined by the networked relationships that emerge from these voluntary contacts. The nature of these relationships—spontaneous and emergent—belie traditional notions of *leadership*. Leaders are not designated but emerge spontaneously as the focus and purpose of the network shifts and evolves. Different "leaders" emerge at different times to serve different purposes, depending on their expertise and their relationships with others in the network. They are then replaced by new, ascendant leaders as the network redirects its attention.

The relationships that define ad hoc networks are a by-product of other actions taken to accomplish other purposes. The process of team design suggests several such actions. For example, enlightened organizations encourage their employees to join professional associations and attend conferences. They do this in the hope that employees will keep up with the latest developments in their field and, thereby, enhance the knowledge and skills they bring to the job. But the *external connections* that are created may be just as important. Through these associations and at these conferences employees of one organization can meet employees with similar interests from other organizations. They develop contacts. From these connections cross-organizational ad hoc networks may emerge, leading in turn to the kind of strategically important partnerships and project teams that can create new products, services, and markets.

Over the years, physical colocation has been one of the most important factors in the formation of ad hoc networks. Buildings and spaces have been intentionally designed to "facilitate communication between people and groups."[12] New *information resources* have made physical colocation and shared space somewhat less important. New communications systems reduce the barriers of time, space, hierarchy, and function, thereby greatly enhancing the opportunity for ad hoc networks to form. With electronic mail and conferencing systems, people in distant locations can communicate with one another and work together. These systems enable ad hoc networks to form rapidly as "virtual organizations" with minimal investments in physical space and administrative support. They can also facilitate coordination among the members of the network without creating new reporting relationships. By now the process is familiar. As Galbraith describes it: "It is very easy for someone to broadcast (via e-mail), 'Anyone interested in XXX, please contact sender. Next steps will follow.' When people respond, a network is born."[13]

Training is another factor that can lead to the formation of ad hoc networks. Training programs offer trainees an opportunity to meet and to network. Programs that bring together individuals from different departments and divisions who would otherwise have little opportunity to meet can be particularly helpful in spawning ad hoc networks. Rotating managers through different jobs in different departments, a popular management development tool, is another excellent way to spur the formation of ad hoc networks:

> [S]ome companies rotate managers across functions to train them to become general managers. As a by-product, the rotations help those managers build networks of contacts and communications channels that they can use in their day-to-day work. Today, the by-product, voluntary communication, is becoming as desirable as the primary product, personal development. If a company can achieve both results from the same experience, it can get effectively two for the price of one.[14]

Organizations have begun to realize just how important ad hoc networks can be. No collaborative form better conveys the essence of what the flexible, lateral organization is all about. In time, these networks may become as commonplace as work teams are today. We will return to this topic in the final chapter of the book when we talk about evolving organizational forms. (The conditions for ad hoc networks are summarized in table 9–5.)

With the discussion of ad hoc networks, we can now fill in the cells of the matrix presented at the beginning of this chapter. Table 9–6 depicts the completed matrix and summarizes the key design criteria for all of the different team types.

INTEGRATING TEAM DESIGN WITH TECHNOLOGY DESIGN

As we have noted throughout this book, team technology integration is central to the MDI framework. One cannot be examined in isolation from the other. What impact will technology design decisions have on team design, and vice versa? Can design choices in one domain be counterbalanced by or compensate for design choices in the other? In this section we address these issues by examining the possible trade-offs between team and technology design and the ways one can influence the other.

At each step of the process, technology design decisions and team

Table 9–5 Creating Conditions for Ad Hoc Networks

Conditions	Characteristics
Composition	Emerges spontaneously Based on relationships and shared interests Voluntary connections Builds on informal organization
Leadership	Emerges spontaneously Based on expertise and affinity Is distributed
External Connections	Within and across organizations Supported by participation in: professional and trade associations; conferences
Information Resources	New communications systems reduce barriers of: time; space; hierarchy; function; "Virtual organizations" that cross organizational boundaries Physical Colocation helps, but not necessary
Training Programs	Programs with participants from different functions, divisions, geographies Career rotation

design decisions can affect each other. Consider, for example, the possible interrelationships between technology and the composition of the user team.

> Initially, Vector Computer's materials management team met only once a week at a regularly scheduled time to track inventory levels, parts orders, and production schedules. Since its primary supplier was located only a few miles away, the supplier representative was able to attend most of the team meetings. This worked well at first. Business was slow, so it was easy to forecast upcoming production schedules and inventory needs. But as business began to pick up, and as work on the new materials management system linking Vector with its principal supplier intensified, meetings were scheduled more frequently and on shorter notice. As a result, the team decided it needed to accelerate development of the E-mail module so that the supplier representative could continue to participate even when she was not able to attend meetings in person.

As the example illustrates, technology choices can be made to enable individuals not on-site to participate fully in team activities. In general, technology designs can compensate for geographical distance or a limited pool of potential team members. Technology and team composition can influence each other in other ways as well. For example, certain technology designs may preclude the inclusion of team members who lack the technical skills or aptitude required by the new systems unless training is available that can remedy these deficiencies (this will be discussed in more detail shortly).

Technology decisions can also affect team *leadership*. New information systems are powerful enablers of team self-management. They enable all team members to participate in making decisions formerly made only by managers and supervisors. Contemporary communication systems enable team members to collaborate more effectively in planning and executing their work. These same systems allow peripheral members in distant locations and on other shifts to participate more fully in team deliberations and activities. And, perhaps most important, these systems place the means for tracking and monitoring the team's performance in the team's own hands.

> Dynatronics, a computer manufacturer, recently reorganized its printed circuit board (PCB) production facilities around self-managed work teams. In conjunction with the team redesign, it also modified the quality tracking system so that timely reports on manufacturing defects would be directly reported to the production teams. Any member of the team was able to use terminals conveniently placed throughout the production area to gain immediate access to the latest quality reports on the boards being produced. The teams used this data as needed, as well as in their weekly quality improvement meetings, to identify and remedy production problems and to continually improve production processes.[15]

In sum, new information systems can decentralize decision making and facilitate the emergence of de facto, shared leadership. They provide the opportunity as well as the means for team self-management.

But this outcome is by no means a given. Although the technology does make it easier to control behavior and performance, the decision as to who exercises this control and over whom they exercise it—managers and supervisors over employees or employees over themselves—is a policy decision. In other words, essentially the same technology can be used to reinforce either type of oversight.[16] What will the technology do, for whom, and for what purposes—these are some of the technology

Table 9–6 Completed Matrix of Key Characteristics for the Design of User Teams

Design Sequence		Team Type				
		Work Team (SMWT)	Project Team	Parallel Team	Management Team	Ad Hoc Network
Identify Team Type						
Composition		Necessary competencies in team Multiskilled Fixed and permanent membership	Different backgrounds and organizational units Specialized expertise "Laterality" Full- or part-time Members may change over life cycle Some core members	Represent work units Part-time Usually temporary Volunteer or nominated	Managers of subunits of organization Membership depends on position Fixed and permanent membership	Emerges spontaneously Based on relationships and shared interests Voluntary Builds on informal organization
Leadership		May or may not be immediate supervisor Team leader role Shared leadership Coach, facilitator, and liaison	Credibility is key May rotate Facilitate, coach, and consult Project management Boundary management	Facilitate meetings Link to stakeholders Obtain training Coaching skills Negotiation skills	Senior executive Foster collaboration and build teamwork	Emerges spontaneously Based on expertise and affinity Leadership is distributed
External Connections		"Upstream" and "downstream" in work process Staff support	Ongoing linkages to key stakeholders Communication systems	Ongoing linkages to key stakeholders	Stakeholders often outside organization	Within and across organizations Participation in professional associations

Design Team Structure

Develop Team Capabilities	Information Resources	Task requirements Performance standards and customer requirements Work status Tools for problem solving and analysis Communication systems	Tools for scanning, analysis, problem-solving, project management Integrated data bases Communication systems	Internal and external communications Regular meeting records Availability of experts	Strategy formulation and change Tools for scanning and analysis Integrated data bases	New communications systems reduce organizational barriers "Virtual organizations" Physical colocation helps
	Training Programs	Technical skills Problem solving Group process Conflict management Cross training Quality analysis Economic education	Conflict management Just-in-time training Develop "laterality"	Problem solving Group process Quality improvement	Emerging social and business trends Business strategy Organization design Group process	Participants from different units Career rotation

and team design decisions that can shape the outcomes. This is why we describe technology as an enabler, not a determinant. The integration of team design and information technology is nowhere more dramatically illustrated than it is in the issues of leadership and self-management.

Technology can also facilitate *external connections,* raising a number of design possibilities and trade-offs. Should the systems and applications include special technology-mediated links with other teams, units, and individuals, or will existing communications media—such as E-mail, phone, fax, and memos—suffice? If special links are to be included, what kinds of links will they be—for example, work flow systems or richer and significantly more expensive links such as video conferencing? This is an area where systems integration issues are critical. To ensure that user teams will be able to communicate with key external units and individuals, these external stakeholders may at some point have to be represented on the MDI team.

Of all of our team design factors, *training* is the one most likely to pop into people's mind when considering the impact of technology on teams. The critical relationship between new technologies and the skills needed to use them effectively is obvious. As soon as the broad functional outlines of the system start to emerge from the "drawing board" (or, to use a more contemporary version of this cliché, from the computer screen), work should begin on identifying the behavioral objectives for the training programs to be created. As the system develops, so should the training program. Ideally, a prototype training program should be available at the same time the prototype system is in use. The training program might even be imbedded within the system—that is, in the form of computer-based, interactive tutorials available to users on demand, "just in time and at their fingertips."[17]

The relationship between technology and training should flow in the other direction as well. Technology design should reflect the skill potential of the people who will be using the system. Developing sophisticated systems with complex interfaces is not the way to introduce technophobic users to the brave new world of information technology. The converse is also true—"idiot-proof" systems that are "easy to use, impossible to interfere with, and require little learning . . . are typically 'competency proof,' allowing little room for the exercise of users' skills."[18] Such systems can constrain the creativity of users who might otherwise find innovative ways to apply their new tools to their work.

Before we leave this topic, we should note a team technology relationship of a substantively different sort. A potentially promising but still speculative line of research has recently emerged from the groupware literature that focuses on the development of software tools to help design organizations and teams.[19] The details differ from one system to another, but the basic idea underlying all of them is essentially the same. The tools help users think through the design process by explicitly prompting them to consider key design issues, various design options, and their consequences.

The outcomes of this research vary widely, from preliminary conceptual frameworks to actual working tools. Perhaps most interesting are the divergent approaches taken by the researchers. In one approach, an expert system automatically generates designs based on simple input parameters such as descriptions of organizational tasks and other factors. For example, a plant manager would input information on tasks, nature of the production technology, and skill levels of the employees. Based on these factors, the system generates a team design to be implemented as is. An alternative approach is "to provide conceptual frameworks and partly automated tools to help intelligent people organize and use a large amount of information . . . to provide a 'handbook' for use by human experts, not an 'automated expert' that tells humans what to do."[20]

It is still too soon to evaluate the utility of such tools and the relative effectiveness of the various approaches, but this is clearly an area that deserves close scrutiny in the coming years by anyone interested in team and organizational design.

CONCLUSION

With the technology built and the team designs at least sketched out on paper, the project is now ready to move on to implementation, the "final" stage of the MDI process.[21] As we will see in the next chapter, this can be the most important and difficult stage of the entire MDI process. This is when the best of intentions and most thoughtful designs confront the realities of everyday organizational life. How this implementation process is handled can make or break a project, regardless of how well managed and supported it has been until now.

◆ ◆ ◆

THREE HOURS LATER . . .

Bill is relieved. Instead of the anger, frustration, and blame he expected, the team members were sympathetic and supportive. Cindy was the first to speak up after Bill had finished his opening remarks. In her typically straightforward manner, she summed up their feelings in a brief statement.

"Bill, we all know you've been trying to do too much, and it's mostly our fault. We kept piling one thing after another on your shoulders, and, like the good soldier you are, you accepted it all without complaining. In any case, that's history. Let's roll up our sleeves and get to work." Bill smiled at Cindy's metaphorical flourish. It was midsummer, the air conditioning was shot, and there was not a long-sleeved shirt in the room.

By the end of the meeting, they had come up with a plan of action. They would put desks on the production floor so representatives from marketing could spend one or two days a week in the plant to work with their production teams. The marketing people would, in effect, have a dotted-line relationship with the production teams. In the meantime, the software development and interface design subteams were to work on a quick and dirty version of the communication links between the shop floor and marketing that the user team designers had requested several months earlier. When they were ready to bring this module online, they would take another look at the interim arrangement to see what modifications might be in order. They also decided to create an integrating team made up of members from all of the design subteams to prevent future inconsistencies between the design of the system and the design of the production teams. This recommendation was contained in Mark's interim report but was never fully implemented . . . until now.

"Not a bad day's work," Bill thinks as he gathers up his notes. "The integrating team is a good idea. We should have created one months ago. And the solution to our incompatible designs looks pretty good also." He finally begins to relax. "Maybe everything will work out after all. I sure hope so. I could get to enjoy this. I wonder if I can make a career out of this kind of project work? Nah . . . not in this company. Too radical. What a shame."

10

Stage Three: Implementing the Teams and the Technology

SIX MONTHS LATER, the Paws & Claws plant on the outskirts of Baltimore . . .

The first two modules have finally been implemented at the Baltimore plant. Four production teams have been created to pilot the modules for the next six months before more modules and teams are added. After the numerous delays and significant cost overruns, the project team and its champions in the plant are anxious for a quick score. They believe that they need to show immediate, nontrivial gains to justify continuing the project. Their anxiety is contagious. The pilot production teams are also feeling the pressure—from their managers, of course, but much of it is self-imposed. Everyone has a stake in the success of the project.

The pressure is most noticeable on the production floor. Everyone wants to show how productive they can be as empowered teams working with their new tools. But learning how to work with the new system in new ways has been challenging to say the least. The system itself is deceptively simple. The basic operations are straightforward—for example, navigating down through the layers of successively more detailed cost breakdowns is easy, though somewhat time-consuming and tedious. But what to do with the information once you get there is another story. Interpreting the information, learning how to use the advanced analytical features, and applying all of this to their work—these tasks are far more difficult. More difficult still is learning to work together as a team. Making the transition from hierarchical to collaborative problem solving has been much harder than anyone expected.

Several team members have risen to the occasion only to be shot down by the pressures for immediate performance. Calvin Williams, a packing machine operator for the dry dog food production team, is one of the most notable examples. A former "gang banger" from the mean streets of Baltimore, Calvin had recently earned his high school equivalency diploma and was now enrolled in an evening program in production technology at the local community college. When SICIM was first implemented, Calvin took every opportunity to explore its capabilities, even coming in on weekends to "play" with it to see what it could do. As he learned more and more, others began to turn to him for help, asking him to teach them the functions, shortcuts, and tricks he had figured out.

He enjoyed his new role and tried his best to accommodate all requests for help, but it wasn't long before he was spending more time training others than doing his regular job. The demands on his time increased as the pressure mounted to get work out. The tension between Calvin and his supervisor intensified, and their tempers were beginning to fray. It was clear that something had to be done.

◆ ◆ ◆

IMPLEMENTATION IS THE STAGE where the best of intentions and the most carefully designed systems and interventions can run aground on the shoals of naive neglect. Everyone associated with the project thinks that the hard work has been done, that all they need to do is install the system and restructure the work process. They couldn't be more wrong!

Studies show that most organizations think very little about the processes by which new designs are introduced into the ongoing work flow of an organization.[1] They rarely plan for decreased productivity while users learn how to operate the new system and work together in new ways. Aside from training, organizations almost never budget for such nontechnology costs as the time needed for meetings and the development of implementation plans. They assume that the intrinsic value of good innovations ensures their enthusiastic adoption and use, an assumption that is all too often shot down in the everyday battles of organizational life. Most of the time, implementation more closely resembles ad hoc fire fighting than a smooth transition from the old to the new.

Organizations do much better if they consciously plan their implementation strategies and explicitly assign staff and budget for these efforts rather than try to squeeze them into already overburdened budgets and workloads.[2] The few implementation success stories demonstrate just how long and difficult a road an organization must travel before its new technologies and workplace designs are effectively incorporated into its ongoing work. This chapter describes this road trip—the decisions, activities, and issues that make up what we refer to as the implementation stage of the MDI process.

To carry this metaphor a bit further,[3] implementation is where the off-road activities of project formation and team and technology design merge with the ongoing workflow of the organization. Project activities become less and less distinguishable from the larger, continuous flow of everyday work processes. Therefore, the process we describe in this chapter should not be viewed as a series of discrete steps. It is best thought of as a series of streams that may start at different times and places but flow throughout the implementation stage, sometimes running parallel, often converging. The order in which they are presented in this chapter reflects a logic that is more functional and conceptual than it is temporal.

The first section of this chapter describes the implementation plan in general terms—the overall approach and the guiding principles. The issues and elements to be addressed in the plan and the activities to be carried out in this final stage of the project are covered in the remaining sections. Specifically, the second section covers how to set the stage for implementation, the third how to get the process started. The fourth section describes how to keep the process moving forward as users acquire new skills and knowledge and learn how to apply their new tools in innovative ways. The focus of the fifth section is how the process ends—if only for the moment, until the next MDI project begins.

IMPLEMENT TO LEARN, LEARN TO IMPLEMENT[4]

The overriding principle of this chapter is that organizations should consciously plan and budget for the implementation of teams and technology. The development of this plan should begin before the design stage is concluded and continue into the early stages of implementation. But planning and budgeting alone are not enough. The MDI team's approach to the overall process is critical. Sue Mohrman and Tom Cummings characterize the implementation process as "action learning"—"a process where organizational members try out new behaviors, processes, and structures; assess them; and make necessary modifications."[5]

In essence, the action-learning approach treats the implementation of change as an experiment in which ideas, theories, hypotheses, and informed guesses are tested in the real world of organizational life. Therefore, the change should be implemented in a way that enables implementers to learn from the consequences of their actions. The results of these action-learning experiments are examined. If they diverge significantly from what was expected or desired, actions and plans can be modified, based on what was learned from these analyses, and tried again. If successful, the learnings can be applied to subsequent steps—steps that may increase in complexity and scope. This process continues until all the changes are implemented successfully.

The implications of the action-learning process extend the boundaries of particular projects. The experience of one implementation project conducted in this manner will make it easier for the next project, and so on. Eventually, the organization will develop the ability to implement increasingly complex innovations with less disruption and greater success. The end result, therefore, is not just improved designs and interventions resulting from specific projects but also enhanced knowledge and skills for implementing change in general, regardless of the particular changes being implemented.

The relevance of the action-learning approach to MDI should be apparent. The real test of new technology and team designs begins when user teams start to translate them into everyday practice. Using these designs under real-world conditions may reveal inadequacies in either the technology or the team designs—as well as incompatibilities between them—that were not apparent when the designs were initially developed. The implementation process should therefore allow for the likely redesign of either or both.

Furthermore, these redesigns will have to reflect the conditions that have changed since the previous design. The rapid pace of technological change and the long lead time needed to implement complex innovations can render state-of-the-art designs considerably less so by the time they are ready for implementation. Technological developments, changing business conditions, and/or emergence of new organizational practices may create new opportunities and imperatives that were not available during the initial design stage. Instead of viewing these changes as inconvenient and disruptive, the MDI team should be prepared to respond to them—or, better, to embrace them as opportunities to create more effective designs or even to move off into unanticipated but potentially productive new directions.

SETTING THE STAGE

After months, even years, of design, MDI teams will be tempted to rush forward with implementation. Their enthusiasm to present the fruits of their labor to those for whom they are intended can ultimately undercut their good work. Users, their managers, and other key players may resist new ways of working and new tools. Even if their interests have been represented in the design process, they may remain skeptical about the utility of the changes they now face. Perhaps most important, the crucible of everyday use will reveal unanticipated flaws and limitations in the most carefully developed designs. Therefore, the stage must be set before proceeding with full implementation.

Conduct the Pilot Test

One of the most important implications of the action-learning approach is that change should be implemented incrementally, a chunk at a time, especially when the scope of change is broad and many user teams will be affected. By *chunk* we mean a set of technology modules that fit together functionally and can be implemented as a whole. This set should be large enough to enable users to accomplish a real piece of work that is an improvement over what they could do before.

This chunk of technology should initially be implemented for a subset of the intended user teams. The teams in this subset should be closely related to each other but only loosely connected to other users and teams. This subset will participate in the pilot test. The pilot test is the first time the new system, or at least a subset of the system, is tried out in the context of its intended use. This is where the technology designs described in chapter 8 and the team designs described in chapter 9 are brought together and tested as a fully integrated, sociotechnical work process—that is, as a mutual design. The pilot test gives everyone involved an opportunity to evaluate the new designs as a whole. The designs and the plans for implementing them can then be modified, based on what is learned from the pilot, before proceeding further. The pilot test is a critical step that will help set the stage for the eventual full implementation of the new designs throughout the entire organization.

Before we move on, we need to say more about the scope of the pilot, specifically, how many newly designed user teams should be involved in the pilot test and what should be the relationships among them. As mentioned above, the pilot should include a subset of user teams that are closely related to each other but only loosely connected to other users and teams. For example, if the system is designed to support teams that work closely together—for example, a production team and a materials inventory team—the teams in the pilot test should represent this collaboration. How else to examine the impact of the new designs on the critical interdependencies between teams linked in an overall process?

On the other hand, the pilot test should not be too broad in scope. Otherwise, the implementation process will no longer be incremental. The MDI team needs to find the middle ground between a test that is too small to evaluate adequately the mutual designs and too large to be considered just a test. A minienterprise or business unit, if small enough, where all of the new team and technology designs can be evaluated as a total, fully integrated innovation are often ideal sites for pilot tests—for example, a separate plant or office site, a work area within a plant that can be bounded and segmented, or a set of new product development teams responsible for a single product line.[6]

The pilot test looks very different in the two approaches to systems development we described in chapter 8—differences that are vividly conveyed by the names we use to describe them. The imagery evoked by the waterfall model is linear and sequential. In this model, the pilot test is one in a series of steps that follow one upon another—the next to the last step, to be specific. If the pilot test is successfully concluded, it will be followed by system "rollout," the implementation of the final system for all intended users.

In the spiral workflow model one set of modules undergoes pilot testing with the first set of user teams while the next set of modules is being developed. The second set can be brought into the pilot test when it is ready, while the first is still being tested. When the pilot test of the first is finished, it is rolled out to the other user teams. The overall picture looks like a spiral of ongoing and overlapping development, testing, and rollout—implementing the first set of modules for all users, while pilot testing the later sets and developing the last set. *Rolling implementation* is perhaps the best way to describe this process.

Involve Managers and Create Champions

During the pilot, if not earlier, the MDI team and project sponsors should strengthen their ties with those who can help them roll out the new designs after the pilot has concluded. Line managers are particularly important in this regard. They and the people they manage will bear the brunt of the changes and will have to deal with their consequences most every minute of their work day. Their role in implementation, according to Mohrman and Cummings, is to "help organizational members recognize the need for change, create a vision of the desired future, and ensure that the changes are implemented and become part of the organization's normal functioning."[7] If line managers have not been involved in the MDI process to this point, their representatives should be added to the MDI team. At the very least, the MDI team should create strong links with line managers to ensure their active support and participation in the implementation efforts.

Senior managers—including but not limited to the project sponsors—also play an important role. Mohrman and Cummings describe this role as follows:

> Senior managers need to confer authority upon the change efforts and show active support for them. Because employees look to higher level management to determine the importance of the changes, executives must be visibly involved in the implementation process if it is to be taken seriously. They need to model the desired new behaviors and promote the new designs that are being created. They will need to show publicly that new behaviors are expected and will be rewarded.[8]

With respect to MDI, this means visibly using new information systems and collaborating with others throughout the organization—across functions and hierarchical levels. Senior managers generally show little interest in doing either, an inertia they will have to overcome if the change efforts they ostensibly support are to succeed.

Other key individuals throughout the organization who can champion the effort should also be involved in the project. A number of criteria are critical in identifying these potential "champions": they should be highly respected and influential, know how to get things done, or control critical resources (capital funds, technology, information, and so forth). It also helps if they have already demonstrated an initial interest in the project. To gain their further support, they "must be given the opportunity to contribute to the decisions, to achieve visibility, and to influence the design and implementation process in ways that help them achieve their goals."[9] As in the case of the line managers, this can be accomplished either by adding them to the MDI team or closely linking them to the team and the process.

This is also a good time to reconfirm the support of all stakeholders, unless this happened at the time the decision was made to proceed with the pilot. This can take the form of a formal report and presentation by the MDI team to the stakeholders on the results of the pilot test and the plans for implementation. These plans should be discussed with the stakeholders and modified when appropriate. If possible, the stakeholders should be included in the implementation effort. Stakeholder roles in the effort should be well defined, with respective responsibilities, expectations, and commitments carefully spelled out. If successful, this presentation and discussion should lead to a detailed implementation plan. But perhaps the most important result will be stakeholders' continued and unequivocal support for the remaining, final steps of the project.

Begin Rollout

If the pilot test reveals significant flaws in the team or technology designs or their integration, the project may have to recycle back to the design stage, or even earlier, for major rework. Fortunately, this will rarely be necessary if the MDI team has carefully worked through the various stages, steps, and activities described in the last several chapters. Of course, some repairs and alterations are sure to be needed in any case.

If major redesign is not required, the pilot test is concluded and desired modifications are made. The project can now move on to its next step, the wider release of the first set of modules to the next set of user teams.

GETTING STARTED

Early in the implementation stage, the MDI team will need to deal with a few additional issues.

Create Incentives for Change

The best incentive for implementing new technologies and work designs is performance improvement. Most people will work together, often enthusiastically, if they have reason to believe that by doing so they will work better as individuals and as teams. Most teams will gladly adopt and use new information systems if they feel that these systems will enable them to work smarter, perform their tasks faster and more effectively, and do things they have not been able to do before. To motivate users to change how they work, the MDI team must create designs that individuals and teams believe will enhance their performance.

The following example from XYZ, Inc., provides an excellent illustration of this point. The incentives for adopting the new work technology were consistent across all levels of the organization. The theme, expressed in myriad ways throughout the firm, was performance improvement.

> For all participating teams, decision support was emphasized. Whether for production planning, marketing, product development, or financial control, the installed information systems permitted them to carry out better analytic work than before, to make assumptions explicit, to experiment with the models underlying their judgments, to attain new task insights, and to base actions on wiser decisions. In addition, these groups found that online work allowed them to access more information, to integrate information from different sources, and to use information more flexibly. Further, they were all impelled toward system use by the timeliness and accuracy of data and by the savings in time and effort it promised.[10]

In general, the researchers found that the employees considered high performance to be intrinsically motivating. Furthermore, XYZ based pay increases in part on the performance improvements of business units. Since employees felt that the computers enhanced their performance, they had ample reason to value these new tools and to learn how to use them effectively.

As we argued in chapter 4, the best way to ensure that the technology will enhance users' performance is by involving them at the earliest stages of the MDI process, when the functions are being identified and critical design decisions made. If user teams are involved in the development of their new system and team designs, the result will be more effective designs that are, in and of themselves, the best possible incentives for their use!

Develop Adaptive Training Resources

Organizations adopting or developing new information systems can employ a wide variety of resources for training and technical assistance.[11] These resources range from highly structured, vendor-sponsored, off-site courses to informal peer training provided by local experts. The most successful training programs feature an eclectic mix of resources that can be adapted to employees' widely varying interests and skill levels. Adaptive training is also just-in-time training. It can accommodate the varying rates at which users' needs and skill levels change by providing training as close in time as possible to when the skill will actually be used. The opportunity to apply a new skill is the best motivation for learning it.

The following example from XYZ, as described by Mankin et al., illustrates the utility of adaptive training resources as well as one of the problems it can create.

> Company XYZ's learning resources are diverse and flexible and vary somewhat for different teams. Since the market research and planning departments use the same system, both make use of formal courses offered by the vendor. Basic courses are offered on-site. Advanced courses are offered off-site, and interested users can take them at company expense. In R&D, the tasks are so specialized that general purpose introductory and intermediate courses are of little help. So, individuals rely on local experts who are willing to train them on a particular task, when both are free.
>
> Informal peer training at XYZ is regarded as an inherent part of the way user teams operate. While there are no extrinsic incentives for de facto trainers, they appear to be motivated by the appreciation of their colleagues. Peer training is also widely believed to build cohesion and reciprocity in teams.

Formal job descriptions and official work schedules at XYZ do not reflect this role, however. Those assuming this role simply try to fit in user training, making trade-offs between what they have to do for themselves and what they believe they should do for others. While they enjoy the role, they say that learning support could be more effectively provided if some resources within the team were formally allocated for that purpose. On one team, demands on a particular expert's time were so great that his manager asked him to be less helpful and asked users to rely on him less.[12]

This example illustrates the critical role that job reinvention can play when new technologies are introduced into the workplace. In the next section, we take a closer look at this phenomenon—its varied forms, its potential consequences, and the ways organizations can take advantage of the significant opportunities it often presents.

MOVING FORWARD

Once the groundwork described in the preceding sections has been laid, the rest of the implementation process can unfold. As we will see in the next several pages, this process is primarily user driven; that is, within certain limits, the user teams should control what happens and how and when it happens. Nonetheless, the MDI team, managers, and others play an important role in this process. They should:

- ◆ provide direction and set limits;
- ◆ facilitate and monitor the process, provide resources, and let the user teams plan the details and execute their own implementation;
- ◆ allow the users to move forward at their own pace—within limits, of course—as they learn how to use their new tools, adapt to their new team designs, and apply this knowledge to enhance their work performance; and
- ◆ most important, and often most difficult, encourage and support users as they modify—reinvent—the designs to better fit their needs.

The concept of *reinvention* has only recently entered our daily lexicon. It is now almost commonplace to hear about rock stars, politicians, and celebrities periodically "reinventing" themselves to breathe some life into stalled careers. Therapists counsel their patients to reinvent their lives. Consultants urge organizations to reinvent their businesses.

The current popularity of this concept belies its more enduring origins in the early research on sociotechnical systems. The concept was initially used to describe how workers often change (reinvent) their work when new technologies are introduced to the workplace. The technology presents an opportunity—in some cases an imperative—to develop new processes, to identify new tasks and responsibilities, even to modify the technology itself. Many organizations, managers, and systems developers try to discourage reinvention because they fear that it will compromise the efficiency of the technology and the work process. Others recognize the vitality and potential of reinvention and try to find ways to encourage and channel it into productive directions.[13]

We align ourselves with the latter group. Specifically, we see reinvention as an essential element in the implementation of teams and technology. Organizations that support this process are more likely to succeed with their new designs than those that ignore it, or worse, spend considerable time and energy searching for ways to discourage and inhibit it.

Reinvention can take several forms: modifications of the technology ("tool" reinvention), of the task, of the job, and of the tasks, structure, and mission of the team. A team can experience all of these forms of reinvention. As we will see in the following, these different forms can evolve and build on each other to create dynamic, innovative workplaces and organizations.[14]

Tool, Task, and Job Reinvention

In chapter 8 we argued that new technologies should be user-modifiable—that is, designed so that users can adapt the technology to provide a better fit with the requirements of their jobs. This usually happens as they gain experience with the technology, begin to recognize its implications, and discover what it can and cannot do in its existing form. As Marci Tyre and Wanda Orlikowski note: "New technologies are almost never perfect upon initial introduction. Instead, users' efforts to apply technologies reveal problems and contingencies that were not apparent before introduction. . . . These problems, in turn, require adaptation of the technologies already in use."[15]

Tool reinvention often goes hand-in-hand with task reinvention, which goes hand-in-hand with job reinvention. One can lead to the other, which in turn can then reinforce the first. Given the close interrelationship between knowledge-based tasks and information technologies, the distinction is sometimes hard to make. The gas emergency response team project at SWP&L described in chapters 3 and 5 illustrates this process well.

As the reader will recall, the original function of the mobile data terminal (the new technology to be used by the field technicians) was to replace the cumbersome map books that helped them locate the position and possible source of reported gas leaks. It was the field service technician cum local expert, however, who recognized that a far more important purpose could be served by reinventing the technology. He modified the system to provide a direct data link between the customer service representatives and the field technicians. With the modified MDT technology, the field technicians were able to reinvent their tasks by taking over responsibility for job order assignment from the dispatchers (see chapter 3) and exercising more control over their work assignments. The field service technician who became the local expert is himself an example of job reinvention. In chapter 5 we defined local experts as highly motivated users with some technical aptitude who "reinvent" their jobs to include applications development and technical support for their coworkers. We used the field service technician as an example of that phenomenon. In effect, he reinvented his own job and career as he reinvented the MDT technology. His experience on the MDT project enhanced even further the technical aptitude and skills he initially brought to the project. As a result, he became the department's local IT expert and continued to serve in this capacity long after the project was concluded. Eventually, his job title, description, and level were changed to formally recognize his new responsibilities.

Still another form of job reinvention is related to the adaptive training resources discussed earlier in this chapter. We noted that peer training by local, team-based experts can be a team's most valuable learning resource. Where else can users turn to get such immediately relevant, hands-on help as they grapple with the system, trying to learn specific functions and features and apply them to their work? Help lines and user consultants? True, they can answer general technology-focused questions about system functions and operations. But only someone who knows the technology application *and* the work of the team can help users produce significant innovations, not just incremental improvements. As organizations become more collaborative and team based, users will naturally turn first to their more technically proficient team members when trying to master their new systems and tools.

In what is possibly the most familiar example of job reinvention, the secretaries of the 1970s and earlier have evolved into information assistants, coordinators, and managers. In the early 1980s, computers and word processors enabled managers and professionals to "type" their own letters, reports, and documents. Voice mail in the 1990s has enabled them to "take" their own messages. In response to these technological developments, innovative and resourceful secretaries have reinvented their jobs. Instead of typing and taking messages, they control documents, organize data bases, service printers and copiers, and teach others—including the managers and professionals for whom they used to type—how to use the new technology. This reinvention by the few in the 1980s has become the formal job description for most in the 1990s.[16]

Team Reinvention

If team members are highly interdependent, reinventions by one member can lead to reciprocal and complementary reinventions by others. Eventually, these individual reinventions may reach a critical mass. At that point the team can decide to redefine and reallocate tasks among its members and then redesign its structure to better accommodate and support these new tasks. This is what happened with the gas emergency response teams at SWP&L. They took advantage of the new technology and the task reinventions made possible by the technology to bypass the dispatchers and take reports of gas leaks directly from the customer service representatives. In essence, they redesigned their team tasks and structure, transforming themselves into self-managed work teams in the process.

New information tools also enabled several work groups at XYZ to take on new tasks and responsibilities and even widen or redefine their missions.

The industrial engineering department has redefined its mission to take in work "where the rubber meets the road." That is, making use of technical skills within its own staff, it is helping other work groups adapt PCs in unique ways to address specific XYZ objectives, filling a serious gap that could not have otherwise been closed by existing information support services.

This function was too small and short-term for the corporate IT department or for contracting to an external services vendor, so team members from industrial engineering stepped in to provide technical assistance. Nobody foresaw this need in the early stages of the project, and it would otherwise have gone unfulfilled if industrial engineering had not reinvented its mission and if management had not permitted this reinvention to occur.

The sales department also used the opportunities presented by new information tools to redefine its mission. By using portable computers, it was able to turn sales visits to customers, usually supermarkets, into data-based consultations. The sales representative would use the computers to download data about a range of relevant products (XYZ's and others) from commercial data bases to help customers analyze the potential profitability given different allocations of shelf space for various products. Instead of just selling a product, they saw themselves as "information teams," providing their customers with useful knowledge and reinforcing XYZ's ties to customers in the process.[17]

The Dilemma and the Challenge of Reinvention

Reinvention has its downside. Users can get so absorbed in exploring the potential of the technology and testing the boundaries of their jobs that they neglect their formal job responsibilities. This presents management with a dilemma, the resolution of which can strongly influence the ultimate success of the MDI process. Should job reinvention be discouraged and users be instructed to focus on their existing job responsibilities, or should it be encouraged and rewarded? The dilemma is illustrated in the following examples.

Melissa K., a secretary in the marketing department at Company DEF, initially viewed the new computers in her office with apprehension; it was rumored that they would eliminate at least two secretarial jobs within two years. Even though she was often bored at work and realized she was in a dead-end career, she did not want to lose her job to a machine. She was assured by her department head, however, that if any cuts were to be made, they would occur through attrition, and that she would be provided with all the training and time she needed to learn to use the new system effectively. She was encouraged to experiment with the system to see if she could come up with new, more productive ways to do her work.

She took little time to master the basics of the system and use it to improve her work performance. She developed her skills further through on-site training programs. With those skills, she developed several procedures to accomplish her tasks more effectively. Her coworkers increasingly turned to her to learn the advanced features of the system and to apply her routines to their own work.

Eventually, her manager noticed that Melissa was spending more and more time helping her coworkers and devising new ways to apply the system to her department's work. To reward her inventiveness and increased skill level, her manager formally requested that personnel reclassify Melissa's job and increase her salary accordingly. The request was turned down because it "was against company policy." Unhappy with the decision, Melissa began to look elsewhere for a position more appropriate for her growing technical skills. Within three months she was working for another company in a higher-level, better-paying job.[18]

This issue is not just for individual users. Team reinvention, as illustrated by the systems development project for the international nonprofit organization described in chapter 8, can pose a similar dilemma.

Before the new systems were introduced, the division of labor within the statistical analysis team was clear and unambiguous. The data managers were responsible for organizing, collating, and entering data. The analysts were responsible for analyzing the data and preparing reports based on these analyses. But the new system changed all of that by enabling the data managers to do some analyses as well as perform their usual functions. They began to work more closely with the analysts, and before long the division of labor between the two job categories started to crumble. It was replaced by increasing collaboration between all members of the team, regardless of their formal specialization.

Their supervisors were not happy about these unplanned developments. "We just wanted them to have new tools. We didn't expect them to change what they did and who they worked with," was the typical complaint. The supervisors finally decided to step in and take control. They reaffirmed the formal job descriptions for the two positions, making sure that everyone knew what they were supposed to do. They also made it clear that there would be consequences for those who persisted in stepping beyond the bounds of their job descriptions. Before long things were back to "normal." Everybody on the team was doing what they had done before, albeit with marginally greater efficiency, given their expensive, new tools. But a synergy had been lost, and the modest bottom-line improvements in performance were not nearly great enough to justify the costs, effort, and disruption associated with the development and implementation of the new system.

Of course, organizations can go down a path different from the one illustrated in these two examples. Enlightened managers are beginning to recognize what many kindergarten and elementary school teachers have long known: that the most successful learning often takes place in the context of play rather than work. Translated to the world of work, this insight implies that people best learn the capabilities and potential uses of their new tools when they are not under the gun to get work out. Successful implementation efforts will set aside some slack time for users to play with the tools without the immediate pressure of getting something done.[19]

The progressive and dynamic nature of reinvention is what keeps the implementation process moving forward. As users tinker, gain knowledge, and reinvent their technology, tasks, jobs, and teams, they will produce surprises that may transform entire organizations and industries.[20] To repeat a point made in chapter 1, "creative applications that have strategic impact will be invented, engineered, and tried out."[21] In the next chapter we will discuss how organizations can encourage, support, and leverage this dynamic, productive process by helping people move beyond the most obvious, limited, point-of-entry functions to new uses and reinvented tools.

CHANGEOVER

If the implementation has proceeded relatively smoothly and major redesign is not required, the project can move on to the last step of stage 3: *changeover*. This is when users stop using their former systems and work designs and change over completely to the new ones (*conversion* and *cutoff* are other expressions used to describe this process). The recommendations offered to this point will help produce a relatively seamless and timely changeover. Specifically, the changeover to the new ways of working should be relatively trouble-free if

- ◆ the team/technology designs reflect user needs;
- ◆ users have been provided with necessary training;
- ◆ the implementation process has been well planned; and

- users have been able to influence the designs and exercise some control over how they were implemented.

Even in the most thoughtfully planned and carefully conducted projects, however, some users will resist phasing out old ways of working. As they learn how to use their new tools and work in new ways with their coworkers, orders still need to be processed, goods produced, and products shipped. The desire to fall back on familiar systems and procedures will be hard to resist, especially when crunch time hits. In some instances these desires can be accommodated—if users operate fairly independently of each other and if the new technology has not dramatically altered work procedures. Under these circumstances, new systems and procedures can be implemented and used concurrently with the old, and users can work in the old ways when they need to while they learn the new ways.

But this is the exception, particularly for the kinds of projects described in this book. In teams, individual users do not function independently of other team members. And the technological innovations that can make a real difference do much more than automate or enhance old ways of working. They integrate tasks and processes to support coordinated efforts, they alter the very design of work and mesh intrinsically with it. If the projects are successful, the technology will be virtually indistinguishable from the tasks and procedures, and vice versa. Therefore, the more tightly linked the team members and the more dependent the work is on the technology, the more difficult it will be to let users fall back on their old tools and methods.

Ultimately, the MDI team and others in positions of authority need to make clear to the user teams their expectations about when changeover will occur, to be reasonably flexible about their performance expectations during the changeover period, and to provide as much help and support as possible. Given the task interdependencies within the team, most of the pressure on reluctant users will most likely come from their teammates. Whatever the source, in the final analysis there can be little question as to whether the changeover will happen and when.[22]

CONCLUSION

Let us now look back on the overall MDI process to summarize how projects flow from one stage to the next and to review the issues that

Figure 10–1 Stages of the MDI Process

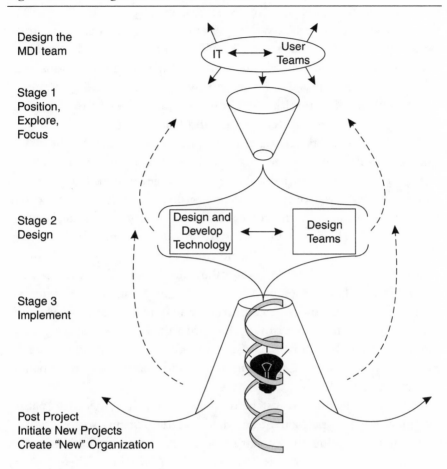

are key to the success of each stage. Figure 10–1 provides an impressionistic view of this process from beginning to end. Before the process can even begin, the MDI team must be created and designed. The MDI team is the change agent, the means by which the project will be carried out. Designing the MDI team means addressing two seemingly contrary issues: (1) facilitating internal collaboration among diverse team members, particularly between user team representatives and IT experts, and (2) creating external connections between the MDI team and the stakeholder groups represented on the team, among others.

Once the MDI team has designed itself, it is now ready to begin the design and implementation process. As shown by the dotted arrows in figure 10–1, this process is highly iterative. Although most iterations occur within each stage, decisions and lessons learned from one stage or step can lead the MDI team to revisit and modify previous work. The first stage of the process is well represented by the funnel shape in the figure. Early in this first stage the MDI team generates and explores many possibilities, literally opening up and expanding the options to be considered. Later on it will begin narrowing the set of design strategies under consideration until it settles on the one it plans to pursue in the next stage of the project, technology and team design.

The defining characteristic and the primary challenge of the design stage is the integration of technology design with team design. Design choices made in one area should be compatible with and complement choices made in the other. Iterative prototyping is another important feature of this stage. With prototypes, users can try out the technology and test its functionality while it is still possible to modify the designs with relative ease and minimal time and expense.

The team and technology designs are implemented in the last stage of the project. The implementation stage begins with a pilot test involving a small set of modules and user teams and continues as more modules are introduced and user teams included. In the process, the designs are often modified by individual users and user teams. If supported by managers and the organization, this reinvention process can be dynamic, creative, and productive.

At the conclusion of this stage the new designs have become "part of the more or less permanent standard practice of an organization."[23] While it is tempting to say at this point that implementation is now complete and the project is essentially done, we know better. New technologies will have created new opportunities; changing conditions will have created new challenges. The change process is ongoing. The end state defined at the beginning of the project, if it is ever reached as originally defined, is little more than a base camp for further exploration. There, the "explorers" can momentarily catch their breath as they identify new, uncharted destinations and begin to sketch out new plans for reaching them. It is now time to begin the process again.

This leads us to the final two chapters of the book. Ongoing technological and team-based change is now a fact of organizational life. Learning how to manage and support this change is rapidly becoming one of the most important challenges organizations face. MDI projects can help organizations recognize and confront these challenges.

$\blacklozenge \; \blacklozenge \; \blacklozenge$

THREE MONTHS LATER, the weekly meeting of the dry dog food production team . . .

Things have changed a great deal in the last several weeks. After almost coming to blows, Calvin and his supervisor decided that they needed some help. They joined with their counterparts from the other pilot teams to appeal directly to the production managers to "cut them a little slack and get off their backs" so that they could learn how to use the system more effectively. Chris and Ken's strong support helped turn the tide. As a result, the VP of manufacturing and the plant manager temporarily turned down the heat a notch or two on their performance expectations for the pilot teams. They also hired additional help so that Calvin and the "gurus" on the other teams could continue their exploration of the system's potential and officially provide technical support for their teams.

The meeting opens with Calvin demonstrating the modification to the data navigation system he has developed with the help of the technical liaison from the SICIM project team. With this modification, users could sidestep the menu and go directly to the data level and screen they wanted. As they became more familiar with the system and its application to their work, they could tell right away where they needed to go in the data without working their way through the idiot-proof but time-consuming menu options.

The team members then huddle around one of the computers just off the production floor to check out the new, improved navigation system. Using the latest cost breakdowns, they note a significant jump in material costs for one of the machines. "Yeh, that machine's really temperamental," Betty Armon, the machine operator notes. "If it's even the slightest bit out of calibration, it wastes a lot of ingredient." They begin discussing possible adjustments in the material mix to cut the costs of waste. The conversation then shifts to the implications of these adjustments for their end-customer, the pet dogs of North America.

"Would there be any impact on taste?" asks one team member. "Can dogs notice these differences, anyway?" says another. The speculation continues, increasing in intensity, involving everyone on the team. "Will dogs enjoy the modified mixtures?" "Does 'enjoy' even apply to dogs?" Without irony or self-consciousness, the discussion gets more esoteric, even beginning to border on the metaphysical.

"Hey, wait a second, what are we talking about here, anyway?" Calvin tries to bring the discussion back to earth. "The meaning of life, the ontological origins of the soul?" Calvin was taking a philosophy course this semester. "This is dog

food *we're talking about." His comment catches them short. They pause. Then a broad grin crosses his face. Chuckles turn into outright laughter. They shake their heads in amused self-deprecation. After a moment or two of reflection, the conversation picks up once again as they consider various solutions to the problem and its implications for customer satisfaction and, ultimately, the profitability of their team's work.*

Part Four

Creating New Organizations

In this concluding section of the book we examine the high-level organizational changes needed to support new team and technology designs, then speculate on the implications of these changes for the organization of the future. In time the impact of new teams and technologies will fade unless the overall organization changes as well. Organizations must adapt to their teams and technologies, just as these teams and technologies adapt to each other and to the constraints and culture of their organization. These organization-level changes may be initiated by proactive, forward-looking senior managers. Or they may be effected in response to recommendations from one or more MDI teams. Regardless of where the push comes from, policies, behaviors, and structures at the highest levels of the organization will eventually have to change to reinforce and support team and technology changes at all levels.

Chapter 11 describes the kind of human resource policies that are most appropriate for team-based organizations, especially performance assessment and reward systems and career development programs. The changing roles of human resource departments, corporate information technology departments, and senior management are also covered. Chapter 12 takes the notion of high-level organizational change a step further by presenting a speculative look at the team-based, technology-enabled organization of the future. Integrating themes from recent work on emerging organizational forms with the themes of this book, we present a vision of work freed from such traditional constraints as time, place, authority, function, and formal organizational boundaries. The book closes with the cautionary note that this vision does not come without a price—but that it is one worth paying.

11

The Team-based,
Technology-enabled
Organization

ONE YEAR LATER, the Paws & Claws pilot plant on the outskirts of Baltimore . . .

All of the modules of the SICIM system and the empowered teams concept have been implemented throughout the plant, and the results have already begun to show up in the quarterly reports. But this very success has created a new problem—resentment that the gains are not being shared by those who have made them possible: the members of the production teams.

In a recent team meeting, Calvin expressed a related concern. "What motivation do we have to act like a team? Our performance ratings, our pay, our promotions are still about what we do as individuals, not as team members." He felt particularly burned by the limitations of the company's performance appraisal and reward systems. Even though most everything else has changed in the plant, they have remained unchanged. He has busted his hump all year, going out of his way to learn about the system, try new things, and share what he has learned with his teammates. He has even taken extra courses in information systems in the evening at the community college to develop his skills.

But all of his efforts didn't seem to matter much when it came to his recent performance review. It wasn't bad, but the standard categories on the review didn't reflect his contribution to his team. All of the time he spent helping his teammates didn't seem to count for much on the same old form the company had been using for years. Calvin knew he wasn't the only one on his team who was unhappy.

It seemed as if the people he considered to be the best teammates, the ones who could always be counted on to help their coworkers, got the worst reviews.

Besides, he realized that he had probably reached the limits of his present position. He was beginning to look for new challenges, but there didn't seem to be anyplace for him to go with his new skills and interests. He would have to get a degree in systems engineering or something like that if he wanted to move into MIS. "That could take years," he thought. "What do I do till then?"

Just as he was working himself into a good funk, the phone rang. It was Kirby Steele, the director of human resources for the plant. "Calvin, I need your help. I'm putting together a task force to discuss what changes we need to make in our personnel policies to support our production teams and the people like you who really make them work. What do you think? What do I need to do to get you to serve on this task force?"

"Just ask, man, just ask."

◆ ◆ ◆

AT SOME POINT the organization itself must change so that it can better nurture, support, and integrate technology and teams. Without such high-level change, the impact of individual MDI projects will remain limited and local. Eventually, the impact may even be diluted by the inertia of business as usual. To repeat and extend the admonition from chapter 2: the ultimate goal is not *team* effectiveness but *organizational* effectiveness via teams. Therefore, organizations need to implement macrolevel changes to complement the microlevel changes we have described throughout this book. This chapter is about how organizations can take this last, important step.

In this chapter our principal focus is on human resource policies and practices that encourage people to work together, move forward, and innovate. We describe assessment, reward, and career development systems for team-based, technology-enabled work. We then address the implications of these new approaches and systems for the corporate human resource and information technology functions and for senior management. Each will have to adapt to these changes and evolve into new roles. Ultimately, the very organization itself—its structure, form, and culture—must adapt to, reinforce, and become one with the changes transpiring within and across its boundaries. As we will see in the last chapter, new organizational forms will emerge from these dynamic forces. But before we explore these new forms, let us first examine those changes that might at first glance appear mundane but that can be quite revolutionary in their own right.

ASSESSING AND REWARDING TEAM PERFORMANCE

In chapters 2, 6, and 9 we described the team design sequence. The last step in the sequence involves a major organization-level change: developing systems for assessing and rewarding team performance.[1] This is what ultimately motivates teams, what converts their potential into actual performance. By *assessing* we mean the processes used to define a team's objectives and to review its degree of success in achieving them. *Reward* systems are the means by which successful performance is encouraged, typically through pay increases, bonuses, promotions, and other forms of compensation. Traditional assessment and reward systems focus on individual performance in the belief that it is the key to organizational performance. Clearly, new systems are needed for team-based organizations. No other change will send as powerful a message to employees that the organization values teamwork.

Despite the intrinsic link between them, the process for changing assessment procedures differs in important ways from the process for changing reward systems. New assessment procedures can often be implemented at the level of individual teams, while new reward systems require changing the formal human resource policies for an entire business unit or organization. The former can happen without the latter, but not vice versa. Consequently, team-based performance assessment should precede the implementation of team-based reward systems. The following section reflects this temporal and functional logic. We first discuss the team-based assessment procedures that can be implemented by individual teams and managers; then we turn to new reward systems that can be implemented only by the larger organizations of which they are part.

Changing Assessment Practices at the Team Level

A critical first step in moving from competition between individual performers to collaboration among team members is to change performance assessment practices. The very process of assessing team performance, even in the absence of rewards tied to that performance, can have a significant impact. Indeed, recent research suggests that once team goals have been defined and performance assessed, rewards in and of themselves will result in only a small additional improvement in performance.[2]

What this means in terms of immediate practice is that teams and their managers should:

- identify and define team goals as well as methods for measuring progress toward these goals;
- add criteria to performance appraisals for individual team members that are related to their contribution to team performance;
- discard evaluation procedures that put individual team members in competition with each other—by ranking team members, for example, or making comparisons between them; and
- assess team performance and individual contributions to team performance systematically when possible. These assessments should incorporate input from managers, team members, and customers as well as other teams and individuals with whom the team collaborates to produce its goods or services.

It's not difficult to see how these practices can improve team performance. They help team members identify adjustments they need to make to improve their performance, develop more appropriate objectives, and address skill and resource deficiencies that may suppress performance.[3]

Creating New Reward Systems

Although adopting new team-based assessment practices may have the greatest impact, changes in existing reward systems should not be overlooked. Assessing team performance while continuing to reward only individual performance will be counterproductive in the long run. Eventually, reward systems must be brought in line with new team-based designs and assessment practices. Since these systems tend to be highly entrenched in organizational practices, they are not easy to change.

The answer lies in the "physics" of organizational change: mass + time = change. As successful projects accumulate, the number of teams will reach a critical mass. This mass will eventually push up against the constraints of existing policies and exert pressure on the organization to change its reward systems. Time is just as important when it comes to implementing team-based reward systems. These reward systems run counter to traditional notions of fairness that emphasize rewards for individual contributions. Therefore, people need experience working together on teams before they become comfortable with the idea of tying at least some of their rewards to the performance of others. It will take time before team members and their managers are ready to accept a new logic that emphasizes collective goals, team performance, and shared rewards. But as teams grow and endure, the next step will be easier to take. Moving from team-level modifications in how performance is assessed to organization-level changes in how it is rewarded should at that point be a small step from where the organization is, albeit a huge step from where it started.

Team-based Rewards Once team-based goals, measures, and appraisal systems become commonplace, salary increases, promotions and bonuses can be tied to actual team performance. In most cases this means that the team is rewarded as a unit and that all team members share equally in the rewards. For many, this may take some getting used to. Managers may be tempted, with the expressed or tacit support of the team members, to give out differential rewards for individual performance. "This is a mistake," Ed Lawler and Susan Cohen caution, because "[p]roviding different rewards to individual team members can undermine cooperation and collective effort."[4] There are circumstances under which differential rewards can work, however. For example, the members of a mature self-managing team in which the work is not highly interdependent may be able to use a peer evaluation system to differentially reward individual contributions to team performance. In this case, "some combination of group rewards and individually-based contingent rewards makes sense."[5]

New technology may render much of this moot. The kind of team and technology designs we have discussed throughout this book increase interdependencies between tasks and between people, making one person's tasks and contributions almost indistinguishable from those of the next person. As new technology creates a sense of shared work and purpose, as collaboration becomes intrinsic to their work, the logic of team-based rewards will become easier for team members to understand and, eventually, to accept.

Gainsharing One of the problems with team-based rewards is that the performance of one team is often dependent on the performance of other teams, units, or individuals. Production teams, for example, are highly dependent on others. Production schedules can be seriously disrupted if materials and parts are not available when needed or if machines break down. Therefore, the performance of production teams depends on the departments and individuals responsible for ordering and inspecting incoming parts and for maintaining and repairing equipment. Their success, as well as their failure, depends on the performance of others over whom they may have little or no authority.

Under these circumstances, profit-sharing or "gainsharing" plans in which every team and department shares in the successful financial performance of the larger business unit to which they belong may be more appropriate.[6] The key is the degree of interdependence. If the teams are relatively independent, their rewards can be separately based on their own, measurable performance, as described above. If they are highly interdependent, the most appropriate system is a gainsharing or profit-sharing plan that distributes the rewards among all of the teams, based on the performance of the higher-level unit of which they are part.

Gainsharing plans will become even more appropriate as new technologies bind individual teams closer together. The more integrated they become, the harder it will be to differentiate their performance from the teams with which they collaborate. Whether the interdependence comes into being by design or is an unanticipated consequence of a changing technology, organizations will increasingly need reward systems that treat all performers as interdependent contributors to the whole. The role of gainsharing in the team-based, technology-enabled organization will no doubt grow in the years to come.

Skill-based Pay Another system that has been successfully used to enhance team performance is that of skill-based pay. Under this system, team members are paid based on the skills they have rather than the jobs they hold. Skill-based pay systems can be used to motivate team members to acquire new skills deemed by the team to be critical to its effective performance. They are especially applicable in self-managed work teams, where they enhance team flexibility via cross-training, and self-management via the acquisition of traditional supervisory and management skills, such as budgeting, planning, and facilitation.[7]

Skill-based pay systems can also be helpful in upgrading team members' information technology skills as well as in encouraging the development of local gurus by rewarding them for the skills they acquire as they tinker with the new technologies. These systems can also work in the other direction—that is, provide incentives for corporate information technology staff to learn business skills. Of all of the reward systems discussed here, probably none has as much potential for developing the lateral skills we have advocated throughout this book.

Skill-based pay systems should be designed to produce outcomes that are aligned with team and organizational goals. Therefore, teams need to identify their priorities and create approval mechanisms to ensure that individual skill development is consistent with these goals. In effect, the skill-based system raises the overall skill level of the team, thereby increasing its potential for high performance. Performance-based systems can then be introduced to activate and guide this potential, to motivate team members to use their newly developed skills in the service of the team and the organization.

Adapting Assessment and Reward Issues for Different Team Types

Because assessment and reward systems are usually implemented for the organization as a whole, different systems cannot be developed for different team types. Fortunately, most of what has been said in the last several pages applies to all kinds of teams. Still, there are a number of issues that are especially relevant to particular team types.

A critical issue for *work teams* is computer-based monitoring and control. This is an extremely sensitive issue that conjures up Orwellian images of online Big Brothers, monitoring worker performance. Unfortunately, the heat generated by this controversy tends to cloud the real issue, the issue of control. In other words, who is in charge of the performance data? Specifically, who determines which data are gathered, how they are used, and what is the purpose of that use? Who designs and uses these systems? Is the purpose to help managers control the teams that report to them, or is it to help self-managed work teams track and manage their own performance (within the constraints of overall organizational goals, of course)? If it is the latter—the approach we strongly recommend—then user teams, directly or via their MDI team representatives, should be involved in defining what is to be measured, how it is to be measured, who will have access to it, and how it is to be used. Under these circumstances, well-designed tracking systems can be powerful tools for enhancing team performance.

The temporary nature of *project teams* can make it difficult to implement and administer team-based reward systems. One complicating factor is that team composition often changes during the project. When some individuals serve on the team for only a portion of the project and others from beginning to end, equal is not necessarily equitable when it comes to distribution of rewards among team members. Another complicating factor is that project life cycles rarely match corporate annual review calendars. Since the fruits of a project team's efforts may not be apparent until well after the project has ended (for example, after a new product has been on the market for a while), valid measures of the team's performance may not be available when performance reviews are conducted. Some ingenuity and tinkering with the review process may be needed to administer rewards when projects and activities are complete, not when the calendar says it's time.[8]

Skill-based pay is especially appropriate for project teams; it can provide incentives for team members to learn skills that match project needs. In the case of the MDI team, for example, skill-based pay can be used to develop the kind of lateral skills we discussed in earlier chapters: the ability to communicate and work effectively with people from different functional areas and to translate one's own concepts and issues in terms that others can understand. As we noted in those chapters, these skills are critical for all project teams, not just the MDI team. What better way to motivate people to develop their lateral skills than to reward them directly for doing so?

For *parallel teams,* a contemporary version of the classic individual suggestion system may be the best approach. For example, the potential cost savings that will result from implementing a team's suggestion are estimated, and a percentage of this amount is then given to the team to distribute among its members. There are a number of obvious problems with this approach, however. Often the estimated savings are not realized, or there may be some disagreement about who should be included among the recipients of the bonus. Also, most suggestions are implemented by other people. Shouldn't they also be rewarded?

Perhaps the best way to reward parallel teams is to implement the recommendations they make. Management should first make clear the criteria it will use to evaluate the recommendations, then follow through by implementing those recommendations that meet their criteria. It also needs to respond to those it does not accept in a thoughtful and productive way, suggesting how recommendations can be modified to make them more acceptable. The worst thing management can do is not respond. Ignoring the work of parallel teams will ensure that they will ultimately do no work at all. Furthermore, acknowledging good work is probably the easiest reward system to implement. It does not require high-level changes in human resource policy and can be implemented at all levels of the organization.

In comparison to the other team types, the *management team* can be rewarded in relatively straightforward fashion. Its rewards can be directly tied to the overall unit for which it is responsible—for a division management team, the performance of the division; for a senior management team, the performance of the overall organization; and so on. Appropriate measures are usually easy to identify at these levels, with profit and loss being the most common. Rewards for the management team based on the performance of the entire organization or unit for which it is responsible should not only encourage cooperation between the members of the team but also between the units that report to them. If managed well, team-based rewards can help managers overcome the obstacles that get in the way of their thinking and acting as members of a team (see chapter 9). Tying their fates together is the most powerful way to get them to work together.

As with all of the other team design factors, *ad hoc networks* are a special case when it comes to discussions of performance assessment and rewards. Assessing how well a team has fulfilled its objectives and goals makes little sense if its objectives and goals are neither well defined nor measurable. As preteam collaborative forms, ad hoc networks lack explicit goals until another team type is created or evolves from the network. At that point participants in the network become a team with an explicit and potentially measurable goal. Then performance can be assessed and rewarded. Nonetheless, organizations can do a number of things to motivate employees to acquire the skills necessary for functioning effectively within ad hoc networks. Skill-based pay, in particular, can motivate people to develop their lateral skills. It can also encourage them to develop their ability to use the very technology that makes ad hoc networks the promising vehicle for collaboration and innovation that it is.

CREATING LATERAL CAREER PATHS

Laterality is not just important for network building. It may soon become the model of choice for career planning and development. No longer can skillful, smart, conscientious, hard-working employees count on fast progress up the career ladder. After years of downsizing, not much remains of the traditional management hierarchy. What little has survived cannot accommodate the bulge of aging baby boomers trying to squeeze through a promotion bottleneck that grows narrower each year. Only a few will make it through and move into management careers. As a result, what may well be the most important reward system of all, career advancement, is no longer available in its traditional form. New, lateral models of career progression are needed to give these ambitious, highly educated employees opportunities for growth and new challenges to strive for. Team-based, technology-enabled organizations will have to aim their human resource policies in this direction as well.

What Are Lateral Career Paths?

Lateral career moves can take place in two ways: team to team, and job to job within a team. Earlier chapters have described and illustrated the latter; local gurus and trainers are examples. In these cases, the individuals themselves do not necessarily move from one job to another. What does move, to a higher level in this case, are their skills and the complexity of the tasks they perform. The field service technician at SWP&L adds software development, systems support, and user training to his repertoire of skills and tasks. Secretaries now operate and maintain computers and other office equipment, manage information flows, and create data bases. The data managers in our example in chapter 10 can now perform data analyses—except that their managers are too rigid and narrow in their thinking to recognize the benefits associated with this job reinvention.

Lateral moves from team to team can also serve multiple interests. Employees acquire valuable experience and skills from each team they work on or each unit they rotate through. In the words of Robert Waterman, Judith Waterman, and Betsy Collard, they become "career-resilient." The teams, the units, and the overall organization also gain from the experience, skills, and perspectives employees acquire as they move from one assignment to the next. In the words of Waterman and his colleagues: "These days, both companies and employees are healthier if employees have multiple skills, if they can move easily across functional boundaries, if they are comfortable switching back and forth between regular duties and special projects, and if they feel comfortable moving on when the right fit within one company can no longer be found."[9]

Given the themes of this book, one type of lateral career path that is of particular interest is the "hybrid career," described by Peter Keen. This career combines "technical fluency" with "business literacy," a combination well suited to addressing the information needs of business users. According to Keen, there are at least two hybrid roles emerging in business today: "business support" and "development support." The first role requires strong functional business skills plus an "adequate" understanding of information technology. In finance, for example, "this might be an individual who works in foreign exchange but has enough technical knowledge to evaluate software and hardware and work effectively with the corporate IS department to develop dealer information systems."[10] This role, he believes, will characterize most of the management, staff, and professional positions in the years to come.

The development support role reverses this picture by layering an adequate understanding of business onto the strong technology foundation of the typical information technology professional. For example, client-focused information technology departments are creating "business analyst" positions, senior professionals who are assigned to serve the ongoing information technology needs of major business units. The SWP&L system consultant who was assigned to help with the gas emergency team project (see chapter 5) is an example.

Policies and Programs That Help Foster Lateral Careers

Individuals and organizations can do a number of things to foster lateral career paths. For example, to cultivate the kind of people who can "bridge the cultural gap" between the information technology department and the business teams it serves, Keen says that "firms must make crossing the 'cultural divide' a requirement for advancement."[11] He proposes assigning selected individuals from information technology to a business department or team for periods ranging from six months to two years. Similar transfers would occur in the opposite direction as well—for example, local gurus could take a temporary assignment in information technology to develop their contacts and skills.

Eventually, these employees return to their original departments or units with the broadened perspectives and lateral skills they acquired during their transfer assignments. They are now well positioned to facilitate collaboration between historically separate parts of the organization. The applicability of this policy extends beyond information technology. It can be used to build other bridges, cross other boundaries, develop other skills. Lateral career moves from one team, project, or department to another should be encouraged, regardless of the cultures or functions involved.

Other formal policies, programs, and systems can also support lateral career movement. Human resource information systems that track people—skill levels, current assignments, etc.—and job opportunities—requirements, salary, etc.—are a good example. Either on their own or with the help of career counselors, employees can use these systems to search for work assignments that match their experience, training, and interests. Similarly, teams can scan for potential new members who meet the skill and other requirements of the team.

Training is important for lateral career movement because it enables individuals to acquire the skills they need for new assignments. Skill-based pay can provide additional incentives for the acquisition of these skills via formal training programs or lateral moves from one team or project to another. Of course, none of this would be much use unless managers allow individuals to take advantage of these opportunities. As the Waterman group notes: "Managers must be receptive to lateral transfers and even to employees' taking a step back to broaden their experience or to be happier and more productive. Indeed, an employee should have the right to switch jobs within the company provided there is a need and he or she readily qualifies to fill it. An employee's manager should not have the power to block such a move unilaterally."[12]

The same can also be said about job reinvention. In chapter 10, we discussed the dilemma and the challenge of reinvention—what to do about individuals who on their own initiative acquire new skills, take on new tasks, and essentially redefine their jobs, even if it means neglecting their formal job responsibilities. We presented examples of two organizations where reinvention was discouraged. In both cases, it was made clear to the "reinventors" that stepping beyond the bounds of their formal job descriptions would not be tolerated.

But there is another, ultimately more productive approach. When possible, organizations and managers should build some slack time and resources into their daily schedules and change efforts.[13] This will give users the psychological "space" they need to explore and experiment with their new ways of working. Management can encourage users to take advantage of the opportunities offered by their new tools and work arrangements to do things they have not been able to do before. In time, these new functions and tasks can be formally incorporated into their jobs, then their job and pay levels upgraded to reflect their new responsibilities and skills. Opportunities for learning and professional development could be especially rewarding for local gurus. For example, liaison and dotted-line relationships with the corporate information technology function can enhance local gurus' access to technical seminars and colleagues; temporary assignments and job rotation into the information technology department would develop their skills and network of contacts even further.

Job reinvention often occurs but is rarely rewarded. Those organizations with the foresight and flexibility to support the boundary-busting initiative and creativity of their more inventive employees will reap significant benefits. Cost savings and quality improvements are the most obvious, new products and services that emerge as users tinker with the technology and push the envelopes of their jobs are the most dramatic. Nurturing these activities may rub against the grain in many companies, but for those who can develop the necessary culture, structures, and policies, the potential payoff will be well worth the effort.

Implications: New Roles for Human Resources

Lateral careers, performance and skill-based pay, teams, and new information systems have similar consequences. They all help break down formal, well-defined specializations and categories. At the very least, they make the boundaries that separate them less relevant. By increasing interdependence and collaboration, one team member's tasks become inseparable from another's. The same holds for technology: access by some users to information and tools previously available only to others blurs the boundaries between specializations and changes professional identities. New reward systems separate pay from formal job categories and attach it instead to performance, skill, and knowledge. Lateral careers reduce the barriers of job, function, and hierarchy. Together, they add up to a new logic for work and organizations.

The essence of this new logic—which argues for flexibility, permeable boundaries, and uncertainty—has significant implications for human resource practice. Over the years, the HR function has been the antithesis of this new logic. The very tasks and tools of the trade (affirmative action plans, the *Dictionary of Occupational Titles,* functional job analysis, compensation packages, etc.) reflect the largely formal, specialized, reactive, and hierarchical nature of traditional human resource work. Like many staff professionals, HR practitioners are "rooted in their functional specialties and resist change. The result often is that the very people who think of themselves as agents of change may act as inhibitors of change because of the way in which they ply their trade."[14]

But new kinds of organizations require new ways of working for human resource professionals as well as for those they typically support. We first addressed this issue in chapter 5, where we argued that HR professionals need to take a more proactive role in MDI and briefly described a number of specific ways they can contribute to these projects. But the challenges to the profession do not stop there. The dynamic and ambiguous nature of team-based, technology-enabled organizations means that HR professionals will be working under very different and potentially unsettling circumstances. As if that were not enough, the issues they will address—information technology and organization design—are largely unfamiliar and go well beyond their traditional scope. Fortunately, they will not be alone in navigating, adapting, and shaping this unfamiliar territory. In the next two sections we look at two other groups who will join them in exploring this new and difficult terrain.

NEW ROLES FOR THE INFORMATION TECHNOLOGY FUNCTION

Probably no corporate entity is changing as rapidly as the centralized information technology function. Indeed, no function has been in greater need of change. Arrogant, aloof, patronizing, and uncommunicative are just some of the expressions used to describe corporate IT staff over the years. Narrow and overly specialized are others.[15] Criticisms of their "technology *uber alles*" attitude suggest a profession under siege. What was said earlier about human resource professionals being rooted to their professional specialities and inhibiting change applies to corporate IT staff as well. In this section we look at how the role of IT expert is changing and at what the organization can do to foster that change.

From IT Expert to Cross-Functional Collaborator

The onrushing waves of technological change sweeping over the IT function in progressively shorter intervals is changing the way some IT staff members view their role and go about their business. They are leading the way for their beleaguered colleagues through the brave new world of networks, end-user applications development, and client-server architecture. We have described a number of these role changes throughout the book.[16] The model that is emerging from these leading-edge efforts is proactive, collaborative, integrative, and customer focused.

An excellent description of these new roles and behaviors is offered by Lynne Markus and Daniel Robey, who apply Peter Block's work on consultant-client relationships to the specific case of IT staff professionals.

> In what Block calls the collaborative role, consultants work with clients, actively applying their knowledge and skill to *help* clients diagnose and solve problems. Rather than separating out and distributing the roles of expertise, direction, and effort to either the client or the consultant, collaboration involves both parties sharing the responsibility for performance improvement. Communications between the partners is intense and bi-directional; conflicts are resolved in a constructive fashion. The outcome of a collaborative relationship between client and consultant is a more thorough understanding by both parties of the problem being addressed and the solution being designed. This understanding forms the basis for future collaborations and future improvement efforts.[17]

Clearly, a different kind of IT staff professional is needed to work in partnership with the business units and user teams the department serves. The kind of person who will fit comfortably in this new role can:

- reach out to clients and help them identify potential problems and opportunities that would otherwise go unrecognized;
- speak the client's language and interpret his or her needs in terms amenable to technological solutions;

- adopt a cross-functional perspective—that is, work effectively in cross-functional teams and be able to integrate different functional systems across critical processes; and

- focus on client needs rather than on his or her own particular technological preferences.

In the words of systems integration and reengineering consultant Dan Heitzer, these professionals will have to shift from MIS to MSI—from "management information systems" to "management systems integration."[18]

How to Change IT Staff Behavior and Roles

Changing the roles and behavior of IT departments and their staff requires initiatives at several levels—from the overall organization as well as from the IT department and its staff. Several of these initiatives have already been discussed: for example, rotating corporate IT staff through business units and creating dotted-line relationships with team-based IT experts. Other initiatives can also be pursued that will help develop the consultant/collaborator skills, behaviors, and perspectives of the corporate IT staff.

Redeploy Resources to User Teams One of the most important initiatives that centralized IT departments can pursue is to redeploy some of their resources—money and people—to user departments and teams. For example, IT can physically and functionally locate some of its staff in user departments. Or, that portion of the corporate IT budget normally devoted to applications development can be distributed to the user units for whom these applications are intended. The portion of the budget reserved for development of IT infrastructure would remain with the centralized IT department. User teams could then use their own IT budget to contract with external vendors to develop their applications, especially if the IT department is too busy or lacks the specific expertise to address their needs adequately.[19] With the purse strings clearly in the hands of the user teams, they can exercise more control over what they get and minimize contractor's confusion about who their customer is. If the IT department is initially reluctant to transfer some of their resources to the user teams they serve, senior management may have to pressure the department to make these changes and demonstrate how they will ultimately be to the department's advantage.

The role of the internal IT function would be to broker the relationship between the user teams and the external IT experts. Specifically, it could:

- help identify potential contractors,
- assist in the contracting process,
- facilitate the relationship and act as advisors during the project,
- insure compatibility with existing systems, and
- help the user teams maintain the applications after the contract has been concluded.

Build Collaborative Relationships Other initiatives can focus on building collaborative relationships throughout the organization. For example, the information technology department can initiate activities to reach out and connect with local IT experts to capitalize on their shared interests in information technology. This might include holding seminars and publishing newsletters. These activities do not need to be associated with particular MDI projects and in fact will probably be most effective if they are in place before the projects begin. In effect, they lay the groundwork for subsequent IT/local expert collaborations as these projects emerge.

Another form of outreach that has proven successful in some organizations is the proactive help line. Most everyone has some experience with computer help lines. The typical scenario looks something like this: *You can't figure out how to do something or are experiencing difficulty in getting an application to work the way it's supposed to. You call the help line and the user consultant/technical support person walks you through the necessary steps and operations.* This kind of help line can be very effective for the user who wants to learn basic operations and solve technical problems. But it cannot address the next and most important level of need, applying the system capabilities to actual work tasks and requirements. As J. D. Eveland and his colleagues point out, "central support personnel are always going to lack the work group context that is needed for help on even moderately complicated issues to be truly effective."[20]

That's where the proactive help line comes in, as is shown in this example from World-Wide Resources, an international nonprofit organization.

> Like the lonely, bored appliance repairman in those familiar TV commercials, the applications development staff for World-Wide Resources received only infrequent calls from frustrated users looking for help with their new system. They finally decided to take matters into their own hands. They began to call the new users to see if they needed help with anything. They also asked if they could come by to see how the new system was working out for them. These occasions provided opportunities for IT staff to show the users how to apply the more advanced features of the system to their work. After several months of this over-the-shoulder "here, let me show you an easier way to do that," or "here's something else you can do," many of the users had progressed rapidly up the learning curve and were routinely demonstrating their newly discovered capabilities to coworkers.

Without this proactive help, the users in this example may never have progressed beyond acceptable but suboptimal knowledge of the few obvious features they latched onto in their first few weeks with the new application. Highly qualified support staff can play a critical role in encouraging users to push the envelope of their jobs, capabilities, and tools. Selecting, training, and rotating IT professionals through this crucial but undervalued function is an important step toward realizing the bang from the many bucks companies are spending on the latest technology.

Before moving on we should note that building collaborative relationships is not just an issue for IT staff. The senior-level manager responsible for the corporate IT function—the chief information officer—will also have to change. The key to developing this new role is building relationships, engaging in dialogues, and helping colleagues understand new technologies.[21] If information technology departments need to change their relationships with the business units they serve, so must senior IT managers change their relationships with their colleagues on the senior management team.

Introduce Organization-Level Initiatives Ultimately, the organization needs to encourage, enable, and reinforce the initiatives undertaken by the IT department and its staff. Probably the most important corporate-level initiative is the one discussed in the first half of this chapter:

changing performance assessment practices and reward systems. The best way to change behavior is to stop rewarding old behavior and begin rewarding desired new behaviors. What this means for information technology professionals is to assess how well they serve the needs of customers and to reward them for their good performance.

As logical as this may sound, and as much as particular departments may espouse customer service, actual assessment and reward practices often belie the logic and the rhetoric. For example, IT staff members are often rewarded for increased levels of technical proficiency regardless of whether these advanced technical skills actually bear any relationship to their ability to serve customers. We do not mean to suggest that they should not develop their technical skills, only that this should be balanced with measures that assess the quality of the services they deliver. Other initiatives and policy changes might include skill-based pay for learning lateral skills, incentives for acquiring knowledge about the work of the user teams they serve, and policies that make lateral career moves into business units and teams as attractive as moving up into IT management. Without these policies and programs, preaching to information technology staff about customer service and collaboration will have little long-run impact on its actual behavior.

NEW ROLES FOR THE SENIOR MANAGEMENT TEAM

The changes described throughout this book have significant implications for the senior management team. This team provides the vision and direction that will lead the organization into the twenty-first century. To do this effectively, senior management must appreciate the significance of two of its most important strategic resources—people and technology—and of the synergies that can result from integrating them. The senior management team cannot do this unless the members themselves are committed to learning about these resources in a very personal way. All members of the senior management team have to model the very behaviors they expect from those they manage; they have to use the technologies and work together as a team. By doing so, they will not only better understand the nature and implications of the changes they are leading, but they will lead the way for the rest of the organization by their example.

In addition, they must either serve as the principal integrating mechanism for individual MDI projects or create a mechanism that can serve that function. Because it sees the "big picture," the senior management team is the only one in the organization that can ensure that the team and technology designs implemented in one area are consistent with changes made in other areas. It can also help integrate and incorporate the new designs into the existing fabric of the organization—its ongoing structure, processes, and work flow. When necessary, the management team will need to alter that fabric—in ways described in this chapter—in order to create and support a culture of technology-enabled teamwork.

The management team will also have to address the consequences of the changes such a culture brings about. One potential consequence that strikes fear in the hearts of employees at almost all levels of the organization is downsizing. Whether that is the intention of the changes or not, it is surely a reasonable concern in this era of less is more, where lean is as important for corporations as it is for movie stars. No wonder then that employees may be inclined to view any organizational change effort as an excuse to trim the workforce and, as a result, resist change at every opportunity. Given such expectations and fears, anything less than honesty and candor on the part of senior management will jeopardize the project. Whatever it is called—downsizing, rightsizing, RIF (reductions in force), restructuring, or reengineering—job changes, often accompanied by periods of unemployment, are a fact of organizational life. Pretending otherwise will fool no one and immeasurably damage the credibility of the change effort and ultimately its chance of success.[22]

If job losses are likely, the senior management team needs to make that clear, with no sugarcoating. The challenge is dealing with the issue in as open, equitable, and supportive a fashion as possible. Communication and openness about what may happen is essential for creating an environment of fairness and trust. Offers of training, education support, and career counseling are also important to help those who may be laid off compete more effectively in the job market. With this information and support, employees can begin to consider other options. This in turn will give them a sense of control over their future, mitigate stress and resentment, and make it easier to gain their commitment to the change effort once the dust has settled. Given the potential consequences, we can see why learning how to communicate candidly and openly may be one of the most important—as well as one of the most difficult—challenges senior managers will have to face.

CONCLUSION

Teams of all types and purposes; new information technologies; flexible, open-ended change processes; new human resource policies, practices, and systems; collaborative roles, behaviors, and cultures—what we are really talking about is a new kind of organization. This topic is au courant among writers, management gurus, and leading-edge consultants. In the next chapter we will examine what they have been saying about the organization of the future—a future that is, in many cases, already here. We will explore what these visions have in common and see how well they mesh with the framework and recommendations described throughout this book. Finally, we will pull all of this together and offer our own vision of the organization of tomorrow.

◆ ◆ ◆

ONE YEAR LATER, the Wings and Things MicroBrewery Pub near the Paws & Claws plant . . .

Chris, Bill, Cindy, Calvin, Kirby, and several others from the team rewards task force and the SICIM project team are celebrating their success over spicy buffalo wings and pitchers of a heavy local brew. Their recommendations for the new team-based assessment and reward system have been in place for only a few months, but the results can already be seen in the quarterly reports and in worker morale.

Both Calvin and Cindy will shortly become the beneficiaries of one of the other task force recommendations. Calvin has just accepted a one-year assignment in the MIS department to receive advanced IT training and gain experience working on IT projects. At the end of the year he will return to the plant as a "business support analyst," a new position that has been created to provide convenient, business-focused information technology support for all of the teams in the plant. Cindy will be moving in the other direction—from information technology into a series of three-month rotations through various divisions. Eventually she will return to MIS as a "development support consultant." In that role she will contract with one of the divisions to serve their ongoing IT needs. Calvin and Cindy are just the first of many, the "guinea pigs," who will test the concept and help work out the kinks.

This is just one of several ideas that the task force, in conjunction with the SICIM project team and others, is considering to help break down the barriers between divisions, functions, and units throughout Paws & Claws. A subtle but especially significant shift in this direction seems to have already begun at the highest levels of the company. Kirby's boss, Mary Curtis, VP of human resources, has initiated a team-building effort with her colleagues on the senior management team. Her goal is to get them to think and act collaboratively with each other and with their direct reports. Mary's other goal is even more ambitious—to help them adopt a more hands-off management style to support creativity and innovation from the bottom up. They largely seem to buy the concept but, not surprisingly, resist the idea that they should allow their subordinates more slack and room for "play." "But, at least they're talking about it," Kirby said as she tried to encourage Mary following one especially frustrating meeting earlier this month.

Cindy's boss, the VP of information services, is having more success with his colleagues on the senior management team. They have embraced his proposal for an executive information system, and several members of the team have become almost evangelical in pushing their colleagues to lead the technological edge at Paws & Claws.

The glow of success, heightened no doubt by the several pitchers of beer they have consumed, touches all of them, but most of all Chris. "Speech, speech," the others implore, but not for long—Chris requires little encouragement to speak on such occasions. For the next several minutes, he reviews the high points as well as the low points of the entire project, its circuitous route, its unexpected destinations, toasting each and every one of them as appropriate. He finally reaches the end of his impromptu remarks.

". . . But this is no time to rest on our laurels. Our competition isn't standing still. The technology is changing, and so are we. We can't afford to think of this as the end point, but as the beginning of the next project. So what do you say we all get together in my office tomorrow morning at 8 o'clock to talk about our next directions? The future won't wait for us, so we might as well get started on making it happen." They all groan, then lift a glass in salute to Chris and each other.

12

Organizations without Boundaries: New Forms for the Twenty-first Century

T̲ʜᴇ ɴᴇxᴛ ᴅᴀʏ, Los Angeles . . .

The unmistakable rattle of the dishes, creaking of the house, and shaking of the bed wake Mark with a jolt. "That one felt like a 5.0. I wonder where the epicenter was?" The ringing of the phone jolts him again, like an aftershock of the aftershock that had just awakened him. "I must be getting frazzled," he muses to himself as he literally vibrates from the pounding of his heart.

"Mark, this is Chris. How are you doing? Any fires or mudslides out there?"

"No, just a few aftershocks—or maybe they're foreshocks for the next one. Who can tell? I must admit I'm getting a bit rattled by all of this, if you catch my (continental) drift."

"Hey, that's funny. Remind me to tell that to your old friends here at Paws & Claws. Which brings me to why I'm calling you . . . " Without so much as a pause or shifting of gears, he continues. "So, what do you know about new organizational forms?"

For the next 20 minutes Chris describes the meeting that has just concluded. It seems that a growing network of organizational futurists has emerged from the SICIM project team and spread well beyond its borders. This informal collection of very different people with widely varying backgrounds and positions is tied together by a shared belief, that Paws & Claws can't just fit revolutionary technology, new ways of working, and innovative practices into the old structures.

They realize that what has been implemented over the last few years is just the first step toward a new kind of organization. They want Mark to come back to Baltimore to help them brainstorm what this new kind of organization might look like—in Chris's words, "Something really radical." ("Is he back in the 60s or picking up his son's surfing lingo?" Mark wonders.)

"Are you interested?" Just then another tremor hits. "They're getting stronger and more frequent," he thinks nervously.

"What, are you kidding?" he says to Chris. "I'm on my way . . . "

◆ ◆ ◆

THROUGHOUT THIS BOOK we have offered recommendations on how organizations can use teams and information technology to compete effectively in a rapidly changing world. We first presented a framework for integrating the design of teams and new information systems and for reinforcing these designs with new human resource practices and other high-level organizational changes. We also proposed that a collaborative open-ended, and iterative learning process be used to achieve these mutual designs. This process should also embrace different interests and perspectives and the creative conflict and tension that will emerge from these differences; place as much emphasis on the implementation of change as on its design; and encourage play, support tinkering, and reward reinvention. In effect, the kinds of changes we have recommended require no less than a new way of thinking and behaving—for individuals who must now act as part of a team, for information technology staff members who must learn how to better serve their customers, and for senior managers who must model the kind of behavior they expect from those who work for them.

The cumulative effect of these recommendations suggests no less than a new and different kind of organization. We can't just fit revolutionary technology and innovative practices, processes, and programs into the old structures. The changes we have proposed here require what David Nadler, Marc Gerstein, and Robert Shaw describe as a new organizational "architecture" that looks beyond the formal structure of the organization—"what is in the boxes and which lines connect them"—and includes work processes and practices, social relationships, and culture.[1] In other words, what they and a growing number of managers, researchers, writers, and consultants are describing are new organizational forms for the twenty-first century.

The names and descriptors for this organization of the future vary widely—*virtual, networked, lateral, adaptive, boundaryless, flat, participative, learning,* and *horizontal* are among the most familiar. The different expressions belie what they share in common:

- flatter hierarchies, where formal and vertically defined reporting structures are replaced by layers of integrative, cross-functional teams;
- flexible, dynamic, overlapping, and broad categories that replace rigidly bound functional areas and specializations;
- offices and work spaces defined by where workers can actually generate, process, and communicate information (at home, in a client's office, or on the road in an airport, plane, or hotel room) rather than by the location of buildings and plants;
- working relationships defined by interaction needs and functional interdependencies rather than by organizational boundaries; and
- flexible, reconfigurable information infrastructures made up of interconnected webs and matrices of information and integrated data bases. Teams and individuals can reach in and pull out the information they want, along with the tools they need to analyze, use, and add value to it.

These are some of the most notable characteristics of emerging organizational forms. The common thread is flexibility—unnecessary boundaries are eliminated and constraints that inhibit innovation and change reduced. Almost all speculations about organizations of the (near) future offer a vision of work free of artificial and counterproductive boundaries. New technologies combined with new understandings about management, organization, and the psychology of work behavior create options never before feasible. In the next several pages we take a closer look at the traditional constraints on work and how the new developments outlined above and described throughout this book can help organizations move beyond these limits.

OLD BOUNDARIES, NEW OPPORTUNITIES

A number of boundaries and constraints limit how, where, when, and with whom we work, ranging from the nature of the work itself to distrust of others. New technologies and new models for work can help lower these barriers, create opportunities, and help fulfill the promise of the new organization.

The Nature of Work: From the Physical to the Abstract

Work in industrial economies requires metal, steel, machinery, and muscle. The sheer physicality of the work is its defining characteristic. In postindustrial economies, the raw material is information, the product is knowledge, the machinery is the computer, and physical labor is replaced by intellectual effort. Most knowledge-based work involves the manipulation of symbols and abstractions, not things. Inventory and stores are represented in data bases on disks several inches in diameter, not in warehouses covering acres of land. The defining characteristic of postindustrial work, in short, is its lack of physicality. Nowadays, it often involves little more than eyes scanning a computer screen, fingers moving across a keyboard, and the occasional furrowing of a brow.

The critical difference is flexibility. The design of knowledge-based work is not constrained by unwieldy physical materials and objects. The raw material, information, is infinitely manipulable. Even the machinery is flexible and can be "retooled" by writing new software code. Work can thus be designed, structured, and organized in any number of ways. For example, expert systems can deskill work by automatically generating decisions; or they can upgrade it by providing information to help individuals or teams make the decisions. Computers can be used by managers as an instrument of control, or by teams as a means for self-control.

The conclusion is clear. Information technology puts no constraints on where, when, and how we work. Quite the opposite. Technology expands the options for work design. The limits are more likely to be imposed by the values, culture, expectations, and imagination of the designers than by the technology or the raw material on which it operates.

Limits on Where and When to Work

Telecommuting is possibly the most visible demonstration of the inherent flexibility of knowledge-based work. Many of the examples and much of the discussion in this book show how information technology can help people transcend the traditional constraints of space and time.

With new communications technologies employees and independent contractors alike can work at home or in neighborhood satellite work centers. They can communicate with others in real time when necessary, or asynchronously by responding to E-mail messages, downloading reports and analyses, and writing memos as needed. Their schedules are set by due dates and milestones, not by the availability of team members.

The images are now commonplace—working at home, sometimes at great distance from the office and coworkers, sending out and responding to messages, memos, and reports at any hour of the day or night by fax or E-mail. Whether actual or conjectured, the benefits associated with lowering the work barriers of time and space are many. Workers can go at their own pace, adapt their work schedules to fit their lives rather than the other way around, and save money on clothes and commuting expenses. Their increased productivity contributes to the company's bottom line. We all gain from reduced traffic and auto emissions. While evidence concerning the ultimate economic impact of time- and space-independent work is still emerging, its potential impact on our lives and the flexibility and options it offers are unmistakable.[2]

Spanning Functions and Departments

The relatively impenetrable boundaries of department and function have become less formidable in recent years. In many organizations they now serve primarily as indicators of position, role, and level of expertise rather than as barriers to collaboration. Competitive pressures are behind this development, just as they have driven many of the other enlightened developments that have swept the business world in recent years. At the very least these pressures have helped sensitize managers to the benefits of cross-functional collaboration. Innovation, adaptability, time to market—it's the rare manager these days who does not recognize how rigid intraorganizational boundaries can threaten a firm's long-term viability.

It is no coincidence that this awareness comes as new boundary-spanning technologies proliferate. As we have seen throughout this book, information technology breaks down barriers. As it becomes easier for people in different work units to communicate, it becomes easier for them to collaborate. Teams form and spread, reinforcing the perception that intraorganizational boundaries can be easily crossed. In time, the formal distinctions of department and function will act less as barriers to collaboration than as facilitators. They will serve as convenient indicators of useful expertise to be used as needed rather than as barriers that keep people with diverse areas of expertise from working together on issues of mutual concern and benefit.

The Emergence of the Metaorganization

Essentially the same information technologies can be used to cross boundaries that separate one organization from another. What better indicator of the growing importance of technology-based interorganizational communications than the business card? Not long ago, addresses and telephone numbers were enough. Then fax numbers were added. Now Internet E-mail addresses are almost as ubiquitous. Individuals need to communicate easily and rapidly not just with coworkers in their own companies but with customers, suppliers, strategic partners, and colleagues in other organizations.

The nature and makeup of teams are also beginning to reflect just how fuzzy organizational boundaries have become.

> Increasingly, work teams have external customers and suppliers as members. The voice of the customer is more directly heard as work teams develop products and services for specific customers, receiving online information about customer requirements from shared data bases that connect the customer and supplier organizations. Similarly, external suppliers are members of work teams with increasing frequency, integrating the development of their subcontracted components with the components developed by the work teams.[3]

Internet addresses and cross-organizational teams are just the early indicators of an organizational change of potentially far greater significance. The same business imperatives that have led to the deconstruction of so many organizations in recent years are now driving the formation of alliances, strategic partnerships, and joint ventures. In effect, the slimmed-down, reengineered organizations of the 1980s and 1990s are now being combined and reconstructed into metaorganizations for the twenty-first century. As described by Marc Gerstein and Robert Shaw, these "networks of suppliers, competitors, and customers"—linked together by shared "values, people, information, and operating styles"—will "cooperate with each other to survive in an increasingly competitive marketplace. . . . The days of rigid boundaries . . . will end as new forms of collaboration emerge."[4]

Authority, Power, and Influence

New team and technology designs can also change the political dynamics of the workplace and of the organization. Teams often decentralize authority and distribute power. By increasing access to information, new technologies have similar effects. The consequences are most easily seen with networked designs, both technological and social. Instead of the static, one-directional, hierarchical relationships of more traditional work structures, network relationships tend to be dynamic, diffuse, and lateral. Technical expertise, access to information, and the ability to apply these to the tasks at hand take the place of formal roles and job titles (supervisor or manager, for instance) as the primary source of power.

The net result can be quite profound. For example, new power relationships can change how work gets done and who does it. In traditional, hierarchical organizations the formal organizational charts and process flow diagrams indicate—in theory, at least—the pathways to be followed and the individuals to contact to accomplish certain tasks. In a readily discernible series of straight lines one moves the forms, pursues the inquiries, and so forth from point A to point Z. In practice, of course, there are frequent end runs around the formal organization via unofficial networks of people and unwritten rules that do not show up on charts or in policy manuals. In addition, the results often run counter to the company's overall goals and objectives.

Teams and new information technologies help close the gap between the informal and formal organization and align the outcomes of one with the goals of the other. In networked organizations the pathways are designed as webs rather than straight lines. Since power is diffuse and collective, approaching one individual or pursuing one particular path may not be enough to get things done. Instead, "working the room" is the more appropriate metaphor—moving around, making contact with many individuals and groups, and pursuing several alternative pathways, never sure that you are getting to the right one, in the hopes that one will pay off. While the uncertainty may be unsettling, the potential payoff is well worth it in terms of higher levels of knowledge throughout the organization, better solutions to problems, broader commitment to actions pursued, and more effective implementation of change.

In sum, the role of traditional boundaries and formal distinctions, such as hierarchical and functional position, are greatly diminished. Access to power and influence is unfettered by such often irrelevant symbols of authority and based instead on knowledge and skill. The ability to enhance knowledge and skill by collaborating with new colleagues and using new technologies becomes critical. For those used to navigating traditional corridors of power, the new terrain of work may be quite unsettling, even more so for those who are well placed within these corridors. They have a lot to lose with the advent of new team and technology designs. But they also have a lot to gain if they can learn to collaborate and use the new information tools that have been literally placed at their collective fingertips.

Constraints on Change: Resistance, Inertia, and Inattention

The barriers to change are both psychological and institutional. They include inertia, active resistance from individuals and work units, and the failure to recognize that change requires explicit mechanisms and planned effort. To adapt effectively to a rapidly changing environment, organizations must move beyond occasional, unrelated projects to make change a part of their everyday work. To achieve ongoing high performance and innovation, organizations need to institutionalize change processes that continue after individual projects have concluded. They should create environments in which each project leads to other projects, building a momentum that carries change throughout the entire organization. Then they will be able to introduce, redesign, and integrate teams and new technologies as needed. Eventually, the process will become commonplace, ongoing, and minimally disruptive. Organizations cannot get to this point unless they create a culture that supports change and the mechanisms for carrying it out.

The characteristics of the emerging organizational forms described earlier, along with the teams and technologies they reinforce and reflect, can create a culture of continual change. As people gain experience with the new organizational structures and processes, they will learn—about the organization, their work, and themselves as well as about how to use their knowledge to work smarter. Then they will be able to modify and adapt the very structures and processes that lead to this learning.

Abilities want to be used. Just as a well-developed athletic skill contributes to the motivation to use the skill, the ability to create change will increase pressures for change.

Team-based, technology-enabled organizations are "changing organizations." Their culture, processes and mechanisms all work together to make change an ongoing fact of organizational life. Today's new organizational forms will be tomorrow's dinosaurs. Organizations do not have to figure out what new forms they should take. If they focus on developing and using their most important resources—people and technology—the new forms will eventually evolve from their efforts.

Toward the Learning Organization

In the opening pages to this book we argued that knowledge is the key strategic resource of the postindustrial organization. If so, the ability to acquire knowledge, to learn, will be the competitive advantage of the organization of the future.[5] Learning is the basis for effective organizational change. Organizations need to know what works and what doesn't work as they try to adapt to a world that seems far more threatening, turbulent, and interconnected than ever before. They must be able to learn from their failures as well as from their successes. They must be able to disseminate and share their knowledge with everyone—internal and external to their (increasingly permeable) boundaries—who can help them achieve their goals. They must be able to act on what they know, to carry out in practice the principles that often sound deceptively simple: "we must work together as a team," "we should involve users in systems development," "we need to take risks and learn from our mistakes" and so on.

Given its critical role in organizational change, it is not difficult to see why the subject of organizational learning, or its corporeal counterpart, the learning organization, is so popular today.[6] Shaw and Perkins define the "learning organization" as "the capacity of an organization to gain insight from its own experience and the experience of others and to modify the way it functions according to such insight."[7] What is the relationship of organizational learning to individual learning, and how do the two differ? While organizations ultimately learn from their individual members, organizational learning is more than the sum of its parts, more than the accumulated learnings of the individuals within the organization.[8] As Mohrman and Mohrman argue:

The training and development of individuals with new skills, knowledge bases, theories and frameworks does not constitute organizational learning unless such individual learning is translated into altered organizational practices, policies or design features. Individual learning is necessary but not sufficient for organizational learning. It may enable an individual to more effectively enact a role in the organization, but it will not lead to fundamentally altered patterns of behavior.[9]

Teams enabled by new information technology can be one of the most effective mechanisms for organizational learning. With these tools team members can experiment with and analyze work processes, then disseminate their knowledge throughout the organization. The constraints on learning will dissolve. The key is to provide technology-empowered teams with mechanisms for capturing, organizing, and storing the unstructured electronic communications that are so critical to this kind of analysis and learning.[10] They also need time to explore and reflect, the authority to act on their knowledge, and the motivation to share their learnings with others. Knowledge can then grow and spread, unrestrained by unnecessary boundaries, creating a learning organization in every sense of the expression.

Control versus Trust: The Ultimate Boundary

Lack of trust may be the most daunting boundary of all. It creates inefficiency, blocks commitment, and inhibits change. Without trust, no organization can work well and, as we can see in the following quote from management philosopher Charles Handy, the virtual organization can not work at all.

[M]ost of our organizations tend to be arranged on the assumption that people can not be trusted or relied on. . . . Oversight systems are set up to prevent anyone from doing the wrong thing, whether by accident or design. . . . [T]hat sort of attitude creates a paraphernalia of systems, checkers, checkers checking checkers—expensive and deadening. . . . [W]e no longer trust people to act for anything but their own short-term interests. That attitude becomes a self-fulfilling prophecy. "If they don't trust me," employees say to themselves, "why should I bother to put their needs before mine?" If it is even partly true that a lack of trust makes employees untrustworthy, it does not bode well for the future of virtuality in organizations. If we are to enjoy the efficiencies and other benefits of the virtual organization, we will have to rediscover how to run organizations based more on trust than on control. Virtuality requires trust to make it work: Technology on its own is not enough.[11]

The kind of technological, team-based, organizational change recommended throughout this book can help build trust. Technology that supports collaboration will by its very nature create shared understandings: these shared understandings will in turn increase trust among collaborators.[12] The same is true for well-designed teams. And the kind of supportive organizational environment described in chapter 11 will reinforce trust within the teams and help it spread well beyond their borders to eventually encompass the entire organization.

BUT NO LIMITS HAS ITS LIMITS

In a *Harvard Business Review* article Larry Hirschorn and Thomas Gilmore argue that the "boundaryless" organization is a myth. As old boundaries come down, new ones emerge in their place.

> Managers are right to break down the boundaries that make organizations rigid and unresponsive. But they are wrong if they think that doing so eliminates the need for boundaries altogether. Indeed, once traditional boundaries of hierarchy, function, and geography disappear, a new set of boundaries becomes important. These boundaries are more psychological than organizational. They aren't drawn on a company's organizational chart but in the minds of its managers and employees.[13]

As the authors suggest, it's not possible to create a completely boundaryless organization—and we wouldn't want one if it were. In many organizations pushing their employees toward virtuality, some employees are already beginning to push back. Some, perhaps many, want to get out of their houses at least a couple of days a week, to come into the office and schmooze with coworkers. They want what Stuart Schmidt and David Kipnis refer to as "the easy give and take of conversation which is rich in both information and emotionality" and "the emotional relationship building" that comes from "face-to-face organizational contact."[14] Or, as Handy notes: "E-mail and voice mail have many attractions, including immediacy, but they are not the same as watching the eyes of others."[15]

Employees also want an office or work space they can call their own, where they can leave their work on their desktop and know that it will be there, in the same orderly or chaotic fashion they left it, when they return. In the face of continual and often dramatic change, they want some constancy, a safe harbor where they can withdraw from the turmoil around them. Most people need to identify with some entity— if not the organization, at least the team members they work with on projects. But like everything else, the projects and team members can change all too often.

Even trust has its limits. Without certain conditions and reciprocal expectations, trust can be misplaced and abused. As Handy writes:

> When trust proves to be misplaced—not because people are deceitful or malicious but because they cannot live up to expectations or cannot be relied on to do what is needed—then those people have to go. Where you cannot trust, you have to become a checker once more, with all the systems of control that involves. Therefore, for the sake of the whole, the individual must leave.[16]

If there are no mechanisms for dealing with situations such as these, the organizational pendulum will eventually swing back in the other direction and may even swing well past the position it started from.

What people really want, what is too often lost in the rhetorical excess of futuristic speculation, is a flexible organization, not a chaotic one. Our point is not that the boundaries, constraints, and limits typically imposed by work and organizations can or should be completely eliminated. Our position is that the constraints can be far more flexible than they are now. We are talking not about barriers but guidelines and indicators that structure our environments so that we can find our way. These guidelines will be far more effective if the people who will have to live by them participate in their design. The limits we help set on our own individual behavior as a member of a team work better than limits imposed on us by others.

In any case, no one really knows for sure what the organization of the future will look like. We have identified a few critical features, raised several key issues, and asked a number of intriguing questions. But ultimately all of this is new territory. Although a handful of organizations are bravely exploring this new frontier, they have barely begun the trek. The way will be difficult and uncertain, and no one knows for sure where their trip will take them. As they make the journey, they will become the new organizational forms that will point the way for the others to follow.

One thing we can say for sure is that the potential is great. The organization's performance can be as unrestrained as the conditions that help produce it. Knowledgeable people working together, armed with powerful new tools, supported by a flexible, nurturing environment— capitalizing on this synergy will help fulfill the promise of the new organization.

◆ ◆ ◆

Fɪᴠᴇ ʏᴇᴀʀꜱ ʟᴀᴛᴇʀ, Los Angeles . . .

Mark didn't know what woke him up. The howling wind or his creaking house—whatever, it was not the most restful way to emerge from an unsettled sleep. Just a quick glance in the direction of his videotext screen confirmed his worst suspicion. The up-to-the-moment electronic edition of the LA Times was predicting a very hot day—115 degrees, 7 percent humidity, Santa Ana winds gusting at 60 miles an hour. "Could be a shake and bake weekend," he noted to no one in particular, using an old gag line to mask his uneasiness over the many tremors that have been jolting LA for the last several weeks.

After pouring himself a cup of freshly brewed coffee—"how did I ever manage without that robotic kitchen aide," he thought—he shuffles down the hall to his study. He sits down at his workstation, then meditates for a few minutes by gazing at the constantly shifting Zen Mandala™ screen saver he just installed the other day. Centered, focused, and relaxed, he is ready to work.

He first logs into the Paws & Claws ad hoc learning network on teams and technology. The network is a constantly changing collection of people who are at least loosely affiliated with Paws & Claws or one of its strategic partners. The purpose of the network is to share experiences and insights about how to manage the many new collaborative forms and technologies that seem to pop up every day within the entity now known as Paws & Claws Allied Partners.

He reads the many messages that have been posted to the network overnight, most by those whose time zones align their worktime with his sleeptime. He also can't help but notice that more and more messages are being posted by apparently workaholic insomniacs for whom time zones and work schedules seem increasingly irrelevant. He responds to several and saves the rest for later in the day when he can reflect on the issues they have raised.

His relationship with Paws & Claws has evolved over the last several years. Instead of consulting with the company on an occasional basis, he now contracts with it project by project, sharing in the gains resulting from the project along with the other project team members, rather than being compensated on the basis of billable hours or days. With this arrangement, he is able to maintain a great deal of flexibility and autonomy. He can still choose the projects he wants to be involved in. And the potential upside is great. If the project is very successful, he can make a lot of money. Of course, the downside risk is also great. If the project bombs, he has little to show for his time and effort.

It was now time for the videoconference on his latest project for Paws & Claws. Most of the other project team members are located at the Paws & Claws plant in Baltimore. Some work at other plants and a couple are partners with other companies. This has been a particularly contentious project, so the project leader, Chris DeManconi, now the VP of manufacturing for all Paws & Claws plants in North America, has arranged the videoconference to iron out some of the more difficult issues. Mark adjusts the camera atop his workstation monitor so that the others will not notice that he is still in his pajamas. One by one the faces of the others appear on his monitor screen. "Hmmm . . . looks like Calvin just got out of bed, too. He must be visiting the Vancouver plant . . . "

As the videoconference draws to a close an hour and a half later, the participants have decided that Mark and the other off-site members will have to "travel for trust," a guideline they use for deciding when face-to-face meetings should be called.[17] Bickering among the team members is on the rise, and trust is rapidly ebbing. They agree that it's time for all of them to get together for some fun and a lot of hard work. "A few late night meetings over crabs and pitchers of stout ought to get us back on track," was Chris's parting remark as they all signed off.

By the time Mark finally finishes packing, it's time for bed. He can't sleep at first—so much is on his mind. His life is anything but boring—he travels a lot, he works on interesting projects, he has a great deal of flexibility and autonomy. He likes the unpredictability, the variety, the challenge of it all. But he sometimes wonders about the price he has to pay for such a free-wheeling lifestyle. Freedom and uncertainty—the two seem inseparable. A little more predictability and stability, a greater sense of place would be welcome at times, he thinks.

The hot winds howling outside and the quaking earth ("whoops, there goes another one") suggest the appropriate metaphor for his life. "It's like living in LA," he realizes. "Life on the cutting edge. . . . The trouble is that the edge sometimes feels as if it's about to break off and crumble into the sea. . . ." Slowly, he drifts off into sleep.

Notes

Chapter 1

1. The first two lines of our continuing story are adapted from Raymond Chandler's *Red Wind* (New York: The World Publishing Co., 1946). The balance is a fictionalized composite based on the authors' research and consulting experience. All characters, organizations, and incidents depicted in this continuing story are fictitious, although they are inspired by and build upon real life.

2. National Research Council, *Information Technology in the Service Sector: A Twenty-first Century Lever* (Washington, D.C.: National Academy Press, 1994).

3. E. E. Lawler III, S. A. Mohrman, and G. E. Ledford, Jr., *Creating High-Performance Organizations: Employee Involvement and Total Quality Management* (San Francisco: Jossey-Bass, 1995).

4. Many writers over the years have discussed the growing role of knowledge in work and organizational performance. Among them, the authors particularly recommend D. Bell, *The Coming of Post-Industrial Society* (New York: Basic Books, 1973), and more recently, P. Drucker, "The Age of Social Transformation," *Atlantic Monthly,* November 1994, 53–80.

5. Drucker, "The Age of Social Transformation," 68.

6. J. R. Katzenbach, and D. K. Smith, *The Wisdom of Teams: Creating the High-Performance Organization* (Boston: Harvard Business School Press, 1993), 5.

7. Of course, not all of the forecasts were so rosy. Many futurists saw information systems as a new form of enslavement, a cruel electronic

assembly line that could be easily monitored by "Big Brother." Given the clarity of hindsight, neither forecast seems particularly accurate. For more discussion, see D. A. Mankin, T. K. Bikson, and B. A. Gutek, "The Office of the Future: Prison or Paradise," *Futurist* 16, no. 3 (1983): 33–36.

8. P. Attewell, "Information Technology and the Productivity Paradox" in *Organizational Linkages: Understanding the Productivity Paradox,* ed. National Research Council (Washington, D.C.: National Academy Press, 1994).

9. Sociotechnical strategies for change have a long and highly respected history. The "sociotechnical systems" (STS) tradition began at the Tavistock Institute in England, following World War II, with the work of A. K. Rice (see *Productivity and Social Organization: The Ahmedabad Experiment* [London: Tavistock Institute, 1958]), F. E. Emery, and Eric Trist (see their chapter, "Socio-technical Systems" in *Management Science: Models and Techniques,* ed. C. W. Churchman and M. Verhulst [New York: Pergamon, 1960]). STS approaches call for integrating the design of technical systems with complementary design of social systems (user needs, skills, interrelationships, etc.) so that each is compatible with the other. The goal is joint optimization of both. For more recent STS work, see C. Pava, *Managing New Office Technology: An Organizational Strategy* (New York: Free Press, 1983); W. A. Pasmore, *Designing Effective Organizations: The Sociotechnical Systems Perspective* (New York: Wiley, 1988); K. Eason, *Information Technology and Organizational Change* (London: Taylor and Francis, 1990); T. H. Davenport, *Process Innovation: Reengineering Work through Information Technology* (Boston: Harvard Business School Press, 1992); M. Hammer and J. Champy, *Reengineering the Corporation: A Manifesto for Business Revolution* (New York: Harper, 1993). This book falls squarely within the STS tradition but extends the approach to address social and technical systems explicitly designed for collaboration.

10. For example, see A. B. Shani and J. A. Sena, "Information Technology and the Integration of Change: Sociotechnical System Approach," *Journal of Applied Behavioral Science* 30 (1994): 247–70.

11. R. E. Walton, *Up and Running: Integrating Information Technology and the Organization* (Boston: Harvard Business School Press, 1989); T. K. Bikson, B. G. Gutek, and D. A. Mankin, *Implementing Computerized Procedures in Office Settings* (Santa Monica, Calif.: RAND Corporation, 1987).

12. For example, see B. Dumaine, "The Trouble with Teams," *Fortune,* September 5, 1994, 86–92.

13. As our title suggests, our primary focus is on the integrated development of teams and technology. Nevertheless, suggestions and recommendations for organizational change are offered when appropriate, especially in the last two chapters of the book.

14. The origins of this symbol to represent change comes from the early

alchemists. They used it because of its resemblance to a Bunsen burner flame, which produced the heat necessary for converting a mixture of chemicals into a different compound.

15. For more on this point, see R. Kling, "Cooperation and Control in Computer Supported Work," *Communications of the ACM* 34, no. 12 (1991): 83–88.

16. C. Ciborra, "From Thinking to Tinkering: The Grassroots of Strategic Information Systems," Proceedings of ICIS Conference, December 1991, 289.

17. Ibid., 288.

18. Doug Englebart was the first to use the concept of augmentation in this manner. See his paper "Augmenting Human Intellect: A Conceptual Framework," (Menlo Park, Calif.: Stanford Research Institute, 1962). In a similar vein, Shoshana Zuboff uses the expression "informate" in her book, *In the Age of the Smart Machine: The Future of Work and Power* (New York: Basic Books, 1988).

19. T. K., Bikson, C. Stasz, and D. A. Mankin, *Computer-Mediated Work: Individual and Organizational Impact in One Corporate Headquarters* (Santa Monica, Calif.: RAND Corporation, 1985).

20. Ibid., and T. H. Davenport, "Will Participative Makeovers of Business Processes Succeed Where Reengineering Failed?" *Planning Review* 23, no. 1 (1995): 24–29.

21. Personal communication with J. D. Eveland. While we agree wholeheartedly with Eveland, the typically linear flow of expository books such as this, from one chapter to another, has forced us to depict a process that looks far more linear than we intend.

Chapter 2

1. Zuboff, *In The Age of the Smart Machine,* 9.

2. While he was a Senator, Albert Gore, Jr., proposed the creation of the National Information Infrastructure in "Infrastructure for the Global Village," *Scientific American* 265, no. 3 (1991): 150–153. NII later became the focus of a federal initiative. Given the title of his article and the emerging international scope of this growing network of communications networks, "global information infrastructure" would seem to be a better descriptor.

3. Internet is an outgrowth of ARPANET, originally developed by the U.S. Department of Defense for use by researchers in universities, government labs, and other institutions nationwide. Since then, it has evolved into an international "metanetwork," a complex system of communication networks connecting information resources and users throughout the world.

With the development of such snazzy, easy-to-use, graphics-oriented components as the World Wide Web, the "Net" may soon become as familiar and ubiquitous to the typical business user as direct long-distance dialing is now.

4. For example, see M. Hopper, "Rattling SABRE—New Ways to Compete on Information," *Harvard Business Review* 68, no. 3 (1990): 118–25.

5. After the quake, Pacific Bell offered free installation of telecommuting services to area businesses and residents facing months of traffic delays because of damaged freeways and streets. Seven months later, the company surveyed 660 of the customers who had accepted the offer. Ninety-three percent were still telecommuting at the time of the survey. The authors would like to thank Julie Dodd-Thomas of Pacific Bell for providing the Executive Summary (dated September 15, 1994) of the survey.

6. Evidence for the business impacts of the NII can be seen in one of its earliest and best-known approximations, France's Minitel system. For example, by 1991, business services made up more than 50 percent of the services available on the system. And those businesses that used the system most often tended to be more profitable and efficient. (Robert Kraut, "The Impact of National Data Networks on Firm Performance and Market Structure," Presentation made at The RAND Corporation, November 19, 1993.)

7. Other sources offer different typologies. For example, Katzenbach and Smith in *The Wisdom of Teams* differentiate between "teams that make or do things," "teams that recommend things," and "teams that run things." Of the categories in our typology, work teams and project and development teams correspond to their "teams that make or do things," parallel teams to their "teams that recommend things," and management teams to their "teams that run things" category. Also see E. Sundstrom, K. P. De Meuse, and D. Futrell, "Work Teams: Applications and Effectiveness," *American Psychologist* 45, no. 2 (1990): 120–33.

8. See E. L. Trist and K. W. Bamforth, "Some Social and Psychological Consequences of the Longwall Method of Coal-Getting," *Human Relations* 4, no. 3 (1951): 3–38, and Emery and Trist, "Sociotechnical Systems," 1960.

9. S. G. Cohen, "New Approaches to Teams and Teamwork," in *Organizing for the Future: The New Logic for Managing Complex Organizations,* ed. J. R. Galbraith and E. E. Lawler III (San Francisco: Jossey-Bass, 1993).

10. E. E. Lawler III, *The Ultimate Advantage: Creating the High-Involvement Organization* (San Francisco: Jossey-Bass, 1992).

11. Lawler, Mohrman, Ledford, *Creating High-Performance Organizations.*

12. Parallel teams have also been used as a mechanism for creating learning organizations. See G. R. Bushe and A. B. Shani, *Parallel Learning Structures:*

Increasing Innovation in Bureaucracies (Reading, Mass.: Addison-Wesley, 1991).

13. Lawler, Mohrman, Ledford, *Creating High-Performance Organizations*.

14. Lawler, *The Ultimate Advantage*.

15. S. A. Mohrman, S. G. Cohen, and A. M. Mohrman, Jr., *Designing Team-Based Organizations: New Forms for Knowledge Work* (San Francisco: Jossey-Bass, 1995), 41.

16. From an internal presentation.

17. This is an actual example. To subscribe send your E-mail address to listserv@psuhmc.hmc.psu.edu.

18. R. E. Miles and C. Snow, "Organizations: New Concepts for New Forms," *California Management Review* 28 (1986): 62–73; P. F. Drucker, "The Coming of the New Organization," *Harvard Business Review* 66, no. 5 (1988): 45–53; C. M. Savage, *Fifth-Generation Management: Integrating Enterprises through Human Networking* (Bedford, Mass.: Digital Press, 1990); J. R. Galbraith, *Designing Organizations: An Executive Briefing on Strategy, Structure, and Process* (San Francisco: Jossey-Bass, 1995).

19. Some team-building practitioners do include these issues in their repertoire.

20. M. D. Dunnette and J. P. Campbell, "Laboratory Education: Impact on People and Organizations," *Industrial Relations* 8 (1968): 1–40; R. E. Kaplan, "The Conspicuous Absence of Evidence That Process Consultation Enhances Task Performance," *Applied Behavioral Science* 15 (1979): 346–60; and R. J. Wagner, T. T. Baldwin, and C. C. Roland, "Outdoor Training: Revolution or Fad?" *Training and Development Journal* 45, no. 3 (1991): 51–56.

21. For example, numerous research studies over the years have failed to demonstrate a consistent, causal relationship between job satisfaction and job performance. See, for example, A. H. Brayfield and W. H. Crockett, "Employee Attitudes and Employee Performance," *Psychological Bulletin* 52 (1955): 415–22; V. H. Vroom, *Work and Motivation* (New York: John Wiley, 1964); E. F. Lawler and L. W. Porter, "The Effect of Performance on Job Satisfaction," *Industrial Relations* 7 (1967): 20–28; M. T. Iaffaldano and P. M. Muchinsky, "Job Satisfaction and Job Performance: A Meta-Analysis," *Psychological Bulletin* 97 (1985): 251–273.

22. These are by no means the only design factors or steps, but they are among the most important and easy to implement at the team level. We will describe another design factor, team-based assessment and reward systems, in chapter 11 when we address organizationwide policies and programs.

23. Mohrman, Cohen, and Mohrman, *Designing Team-Based Organizations*.

24. The title of the book edited by J. R. Hackman, *Groups That Work (And Those That Don't): Creating Conditions for Effective Teamwork* (San Francisco:

Jossey-Bass, 1990), says it all. We recommend this book to anyone interested in creating more effective teams.

Chapter 3

1. As we will see in chapter 5, this IT expert can be a member of the user team who has developed some IT knowledge and skill. In many cases, he or she will have gained this knowledge by tinkering with existing systems on his or her own time or with a computer at home.
2. National Research Council, *Information Technology in the Service Sector: A Twenty-First Century Lever,* 19–20.
3. Ibid., 171.
4. Ibid., 186.
5. For a discussion of the problems inherent to organizational change approaches that are primarily IT or team-driven, see M. L. Markus, and D. Robey, "Business Process Reengineering and the Role of the Information Systems Professional," in *Business Process Reengineering: A Strategic Approach,* ed. V. Grover and W. Kettinger (Middletown, Penn.: Idea Group Publishing, 1995) 591–611.

Chapter 4

1. Bikson, Gutek, and Mankin, *Implementing Computerized Procedures in Office Settings.*
2. User teams may not necessarily exist as such at the time the project begins—that is, the individuals may not be using information technology and they may not yet be part of a team. Nonetheless, we will continue to refer to them as *user teams* throughout the book since the purpose of MDI is to design for what *will* be, not for what is.
3. The important role of user involvement in systems development is supported by the research literature as well. See Bikson, Gutek, and Mankin, *Implementing Computerized Procedures in Office Settings;* K. J. Klein and R. S. Ralls, "The Organizational Dynamics of Computerized Technology Implementation: A Review of the Empirical Literature," in *Advances in Global High Technology Management: Volume 5A,* ed. L. R. Gomez-Mejia and M. Lawless (Greenwich, Conn.: JAI Press, 1995), 31–79. D. Leonard-Barton, "The Case for Integrative Innovation: An Expert System at Digital," *Sloan Management Review* 29, no. 1 (1987): 7–19; Walton, *Up and Running.*
4. M. C. Pei, "Examining the Nature and Effects of User Involvement on User Acceptance of New Information Systems." Ph.D. diss., California School of Professional Psychology/Los Angeles, 1990.

5. Several of the qualifications are adapted from the work of Richard E. Walton and Dorothy Leonard-Barton.

6. Walton, *Up and Running*, 147.

7. Ibid., 148.

8. *American Heritage Dictionary*, 2d college ed., s.v. "empathy."

9. R. Hogan, "Development of an Empathy Scale," *Journal of Consulting and Clinical Psychology* 33 (1969): 307–16.

10. Walton, *Up and Running*, 147. See also J. E. Ettlie, "Implementing Manufacturing Technologies: Lessons from Experience," in *Managing Technological Innovation*, ed. D. Davis (San Francisco: Jossey-Bass, 1986).

11. Walton, *Up and Running*, 148.

12. User team delegates also risk squandering an unparalleled opportunity to develop their careers and to influence the future technological capabilities of their user teams. By acquiring the "developer's sophisticated understanding of the technology," a user team delegate can become a valuable, easily accessible source of technical knowledge for his or her user team during the implementation stage of the project. Furthermore, the delegate's combined technical skills and functional knowledge of the user team's work will enable him or her to play an important new role in future projects as the technical expert who helps transform the team's needs into useful tools and systems. (There will be more about this in the next chapter when we talk about information technology experts on the MDI team.)

13. D. Leonard-Barton, "Modes of Technology Transfer within Organizations: Point-to-Point versus Diffusion," Working paper 90-060 (Boston: Harvard Business School, 1990).

14. In chapter 8 we will discuss a design methodology—iterative prototyping—that can help users look ahead and anticipate potential uses for systems under development.

Chapter 5

1. Klein and Ralls, "The Organizational Dynamics of Computerized Technology Implementation."

2. A. C. Boynton, G. C. Jacobs, and R. W. Zmud, "Whose Responsibility Is IT Management?" *Sloan Management Review* 33, no. 4 (1992): 32.

3. P. G. W. Keen, *Shaping the Future: Business Design through Information Technology* (Boston: Harvard Business School Press, 1991), 155.

4. For more on local experts and gurus, see D. Lee, "Usage Pattern and Sources of Assistance for Personal Computer Users," *MIS Quarterly* 10 (1986): 313–25; J. D. Eveland, A. Blanchard, W. Brown, and J. Mattocks, "The Role of 'Help Networks' in Facilitating Use of CSCW Tools," in *Proceedings of the ACM 1994 Conference on Computer Supported Cooperative*

Work, ed. R. Furuta and C. Neuwirth (New York: ACM Press, 1994), 265–74; J. Rockhart and L. Flannery, "The Management of End User Computing," *Communications of the ACM* 26 (1983): 776–84.

5. One reason is that many organizations and managers strongly discourage home-grown expertise (e.g., see C. Stasz, T. Bikson, J. D. Eveland, and B. S. Mittman, *Information Technology in the Forest Service* (Santa Monica, Calif.: RAND Corporation, 1990)). This issue is discussed in more detail in chapter 10.

6. See W. Mackay, "Patterns of Sharing Customizable Software," In *Proceedings of the 1990 Conference on Computer-Supported Cooperative Work,* Los Angeles, September 1990, 223–36.

7. Since local experts are knowledgeable about both the team tasks and the technology for augmenting these tasks, can they wear two hats on an MDI team by also serving as user representative? The answer is . . . maybe. It depends on the degree to which they are still in touch with the day-to-day realities of their team's work and how closely identified they are with the technical issues of the project. If they are able to balance both perspectives, then they may be able to fulfill both roles. This said, we recommend caution in placing too many hats on the already overburdened heads of team-based IT experts.

8. See chapter 8 for a review of recent trends and references on end-user applications development.

9. For a particularly upbeat perspective on this increasingly popular practice, see James Brian Quinn's book *Intelligent Enterprise: A Knowledge- and Service-Based Paradigm for Industry* (New York: Free Press, 1992). For a more critical perspective, see M. C. Lacity and R. Hirschheim, "The Information Outsourcing Bandwagon," *Sloan Management Review* 35 (1993): 73–86.

10. The authors would like to thank Dan Heitzer of the UNISYS Corporation for his help in identifying the significance and nature of these political issues.

11. See National Research Council, *Information Technology in the Service Sector,* and T. K. Bikson and E. J. Frinking, *Preserving the Present: Toward Viable Electronic Records* (The Hague: Sdu Publishers, 1993).

12. A shared history of infighting or of failed past projects might impair such integration.

13. Keen, *Shaping the Future;* Bikson, Stasz, and Mankin, *Computer-Mediated Work;* Bikson, Gutek, and Mankin, *Implementing Computerized Procedures in Office Settings.*

14. Keen, *Shaping the Future,* 139.

15. We need to include this cautionary note, however. The MDI team should be careful about adding representatives too early in the process. This can

easily encumber the team with too many members to work efficiently and too much activity to maintain a clear focus. Besides, representatives and stakeholder groups who are involved too soon may feel that their time is being wasted and at least psychologically withdraw from the process.

16. Pei, "User Acceptance of New Information Systems"; B. J. Bashein, M. L. Markus, and P. Riley, "Preconditions for BPR Success and How to Prevent Failures," *Information Systems Management* 11, no. 2 (1994): 7–13.

17. The authors would like to thank J. D. Eveland for drawing our attention to this critical issue.

Chapter 6

1. The discussion of project teams in this chapter is adapted from Cohen, "New Approaches to Teams and Teamwork."

2. For a detailed discussion of timing issues in the life cycle of project teams, see C. J. Gersick, "Time and Transition in Work Teams: Toward a New Model of Group Development," *Academy of Management Journal* 31 (1988): 9–41.

3. See Mohrman, Cohen, and Mohrman, *Designing Team-Based Organizations*.

4. For example, see A. L. Delbecq, A. H. Van de Ven, and D. H. Gustafson, *Group Techniques for Program Planning: A Guide to Nominal Group and Delphi Processes* (Glenview, Ill.: Scott, Foresman, 1975); J. Hauser and D. Clausing, "The House of Quality," *Harvard Business Review* 66, no. 3 (1988): 63–73; P. R. Scholtes, *The Team Handbook: How to Use Teams to Improve Quality* (Madison, Wis.: Joiner Assoc., 1988).

5. For more information on specific techniques for and approaches to resolving conflicts, see R. E. Walton, *Managing Conflict: Interpersonal Dialogue and Third-Party Roles,* 2d ed. (Reading, Mass.: Addison-Wesley, 1987); W. L. Ury, J. M. Bett, and S. P. Goldberg, *Getting Disputes Resolved: Designing Systems to Cut the Costs of Conflict,* San Francisco: Jossey-Bass, 1988); and D. Tjosvold, *The Conflict Positive Organization: Stimulate Diversity and Create Unity* (Reading, Mass.: Addison-Wesley, 1991).

6. Gersick, "Time and Transition in Work Teams."

7. See D. G. Ancona and D. F. Caldwell, "Beyond Task and Maintenance: Defining External Functions in Groups," *Group and Organization Studies* 13 (1988): 468–94, for a detailed description of the various kinds of external connections that can help project teams in their work and of the implications of these connections for the roles played by project team members.

8. Pei, "User Acceptance of New Information Systems."

9. This may be more difficult when the MDI team is part-time. Even then, the team should consider establishing a project office on site.
10. Groupware is discussed in more detail in chapter 8.
11. L. Sproul and S. Kiesler, *Connections: New Ways of Working in the Networked Organization* (Cambridge, Mass.: MIT Press, 1991).
12. R. McLeod, Jr., *Management Information Systems: A Study of Computer-Based Information Systems,* 4th ed. (New York: Macmillan, 1990), 659.
13. To make this work, the MDI team, the IT department, and the user teams or external sources would have to address a number of issues: the relative roles and responsibilities of the IT representative and of the other IT experts on the MDI team; project deliverables and milestones; and—perhaps the thorniest issue of all—who pays for the IT representative's time on the project. Depending on the scope and scale of the project and, consequently, the level of the IT representative's involvement, a formal contract and budget specifying mutual agreements and understandings on these issues may be necessary. These contractual and budgetary issues do not go away when the project is concluded. Collaborations and agreements on these issues during the MDI process can lay the groundwork for achieving similar understandings concerning long-term maintenance, support, and upgrades once the system is fully implemented.
14. See for example, D. Dougherty, "Interpretative Barriers to Successful Product Innovation in Large Firms," *Organization Science* 3 (1992): 179–202. In this paper she presents evidence on the different "thought-worlds" of research and development, sales, manufacturing, and marketing representatives in new product development projects.
15. For further information on the contribution of diversity to creativity and on training programs for managing diversity, see D. Jamieson and J. O'Mara, *Managing Workforce 2000: Gaining the Diversity Advantage* (San Francisco: Jossey-Bass, 1991); L. Gardenswartz and A. Rowe, *Managing Diversity: A Complete Desk Reference and Planning Guide* (Homewood, Ill.: Irwin, 1993); and R. W. Brislin, and T. Yoshida, eds., *Improving Intercultural Interactions: Modules for Cross-Cultural Training Programs* (Thousand Oaks, Calif.: Sage, 1994).

Chapter 7

1. The MDI team need not automatically accept the status quo as given and design with these constraints in mind. MDI projects can help shape the organizational context by serving as examples that are replicated throughout the organization. They can also identify barriers to change that might inhibit the success of other projects. Gradually and incrementally, the critical mass of successful projects may eventually pressure senior management into

creating mechanisms, policies, and structures to support team-based, technology-enabled work (more about this in chapter 11).

Chapter 8

1. That we have chosen to address technology design before team design does *not* mean that we believe technology design should be addressed first. The order we have chosen here is strictly arbitrary. Depending on the initiating conditions and rationale for the project (see chapter 3), the MDI team may start with the technology or the teams or may address both simultaneously. Regardless of which one the team begins with, the other should be included before too long so that the development of both will be integrated and mutually reinforcing.
2. Bikson, Stasz, and Mankin, *Computer-Mediated Work,* 51.
3. Ibid.
4. R. I. Benjamin and J. Blount, "Critical IT Issues: The Next Ten Years," *Sloan Management Review* 33, no. 4 (1992): 14.
5. P. G. W. Keen, *Every Manager's Guide to Information Technology: A Glossary of Concepts for Today's Business Leaders* (Boston: Harvard Business School Press, 1991), 100.
6. Ibid., 141.
7. Ibid., 120.
8. For example, in the message protocol area, the OSI standard (X.400) faces serious resistance from a well-established and equally open competitor (TCPIP).
9. For example, see K. L. Kraemer and J. L. King, "Computer-Based Systems for Cooperative Work and Group Decision Making," *ACM Computing Surveys,* 20, no. 2 (1988): 115–46; J. Galegher, R. E. Kraut, and C. Egido, eds., *Intellectual Teamwork: Social and Technological Foundations of Cooperative Work* (Hillsdale, N.J.: Erlbaum, 1990); and R. Johansen, "Groupware: Future Directions and Wild Cards," *Journal of Organizational Computing* 2, no. 1 (1992): 210–27.
10. See the references listed in preceding footnote, as well as M. Schrage, *Shared Minds: The New Technologies of Collaboration* (New York: Random House, 1990); A. Alter, "Team Boosters," *CIO,* April 1, 1992; and D. Kirkpatrick, "Here Comes the Payoff from PCs," *Fortune,* March 23, 1992—to mention just a few.
11. We should note that serving group functions and needs is more difficult with user-modifiable software.
12. This is a paraphrase of the title of the monograph by M. Elden, V. Haun, M. Levin, T. Nilssen, B. Rasmussen, and K. Veium, *Good Technology Is Not Enough* (Trondheim, Norway: Institute for Social Research in Indus-

try, 1982). Although this monograph appeared well before the earliest published work on groupware, its conclusion, as expressed by the title, is still applicable.

13. C. Ciborra, *Teams, Markets, and Systems* (Cambridge: Cambridge University Press, 1993). A number of researchers are exploring an entirely different way that groupware may be used to "transform" organizations. Their focus is on the development of software tools to help design teams and organizations. For the most part, this work is in the early conceptual stages, and few actual tools are available as of this writing. We will discuss this topic in more detail and provide citations for relevant work in chapter 9.

14. "Software Transforms PC Networks," *USA Today*, May 24, 1994.

15. The processes referred to throughout this section apply to the development of new systems as well as the modification of existing systems.

16. P. Seybold, "How to Leapfrog Your Organization into the Twenty-first Century: Highlights from Patricia Seybold's 1994 Technology Forum," Patricia Seybold Group, 1994, 1.

17. R. Altman, "Traditional Waterfall Application Methodology: Can It Be Shaped to Suit End-User Development?" *Workgroup Computing Report* 17, no. 1 (1994): 9–12; D. Hussain and K. M. Hussain, *Information Processing Systems for Management* (Homewood, Ill.: Irwin, 1981); K. C. Laudon and J. P. Laudon, *Management Information Systems: A Contemporary Perspective* 3d ed., (New York: Macmillan, 1993); McLeod, *Management Information Systems,* 627–61.

18. Laudon and Laudon, *Management Information Systems,* 354.

19. Ibid.

20. Mcleod, *Management Information Systems,* 646. Although the emphasis is his, we would have added it if he hadn't.

21. Hussain and Hussain, *Information Processing Systems for Management,* 281.

22. Laudon and Laudon, *Management Information Systems,* 359.

23. B. Kantor, "Iterative Prototyping Model: How to Use Iterative Prototyping When Developing Lotus Notes Applications," *Workgroup Computing Report* 17, no. 1 (1994): 14–25.

24. Ibid., 14.

25. H. Takeuchi and I. Nonaka, "The New New Product Development Game," *Harvard Business Review* 64, no. 1 (1986): 137. The rugby metaphor seems much in favor these days for characterizing effective teamwork. For example, see also F. Becker and F. Steele, *Workplace by Design: Mapping the High-Performance Workscape* (San Francisco: Jossey-Bass, 1995).

26. Seybold, "How to Leapfrog Your Organization," 2.

27. J. M. Carey and J. D. Currey, "The Prototyping Conundrum," *Datamation* 35 (1989): 30.

28. For example, see Ross Altman, "End-User Application Development," *Workgroup Computing Report* 17, no. 1 (1994): 3–23.
29. That the line separating design from implementation is far more fuzzy in RAD than it is in the waterfall model reflects the more dynamic and iterative nature of this approach to systems development.
30. Kantor, "Iterative Prototyping Model."
31. R. Garner, "Why JAD Goes Bad," *Computerworld* 28, no. 17 (1994): 87–88.

Chapter 9

1. Much of the discussion in the remainder of this chapter is adapted from Cohen, "New Approaches to Teams and Teamwork."
2. Mohrman, Cohen, and Mohrman, *Designing Team-Based Organizations.*
3. For more discussion of the team leader's role in fostering self-management, see C. C. Manz and H. P. Sims, "Leading Workers to Lead Themselves: The External Leadership of Self-Managing Work Teams," *Administrative Science Quarterly* 32 (1987): 106–28, and K. Fisher, *Leading Self-Directed Work Teams: A Guide to Developing New Team Leadership Skills* (New York: McGraw-Hill, 1993).
4. R. A. Eisenstat and S. G. Cohen, "Summary: Top Management Groups," in *Groups That Work,* ed. J. Richard Hackman (San Francisco: Jossey-Bass, 1989), 78–86.
5. D. G. Ancona and D. Nadler, "Top Hats and Executive Tales: Designing the Senior Team," *Sloan Management Review* 31, no. 1 (1989): 24.
6. For more information on the importance of these "weak ties" for senior managers see M. Granovetter, "The Strength of Weak Ties," *American Journal of Sociology* 78 (1973): 1360–1386.
7. Bikson and Frinking, *Preserving the Present.*
8. For a more detailed discussion of the information needs of management teams and examples from actual organizations, see K. M. Eisenhardt and L. J. Bourgeois III, "Charting Strategic Decisions in the Microcomputer Industry: Profile of an Industry Star," in *Managing Complexity in High-Technology Organizations,* ed. M. A. Von Glinow and S. A. Mohrman (New York: Oxford University Press, 1990), 74–89.
9. Organizations can get a network started with a small number of members. Then, by its very existence, the network itself will pull in additional members and evolve and grow with little, if any, further intervention or intent.
10. J. Galbraith, *Competing with Flexible Lateral Organizations,* 2d ed. (San Francisco: Jossey-Bass, 1994), 44–45.

11. Ibid., 46.
12. Ibid., 50. An example of this is the building where much of this book was written, the headquarters of The RAND Corporation in Santa Monica, California. The building was explicitly designed to "increase the probability of chance personal meetings" to promote the formation of interdisciplinary ad hoc networks and project teams (from the wall display, "Designing a Building for Chance Meetings," on the first floor of the headquarters building at 1700 Main St., Santa Monica).
13. Galbraith, *Competing with Flexible Lateral Organizations,* 52.
14. Ibid., 45.
15. This is a composite case based on "best practices" observed in thirty-nine PCB manufacturing sites as part of a larger study of technology and work design integration in 100 companies in North America. See D. Mankin and E. Jacobs, *"Best Practices in American Manufacturing: Impressions from Site Visits of Thirty-Nine Manufacturing Plants,* Unpublished manuscript, 1994, A. Majchrzak and Q. W. Wang, "The Human Dimension of Manufacturing: Results of a Survey of Electronics Manufacturers," *The Journal of Applied Manufacturing Systems* 7, no. 1 (1994): 5–15.
16. See Mankin, Bikson, and Gutek, "The Office of the Future."
17. L. Dublin, "Learn While You Work," *Computerworld* 27, no. 35 (1993): 81.
18. Bikson, Stasz, and Mankin, *Computer-Mediated Work,* 51.
19. T. W. Malone, K. Crowston, J. Lee, and B. Pentland, "Tools for Inventing Organizations: Toward a Handbook of Organizational Processes," Sloan School Working paper 3562-93 (Cambridge, Mass.: MIT, 1993); K. D. Mackenzie, T. Shoemaker, and D. F. Utter, "Development of Organizational Design Support Systems," *Journal of Organizational Computing* 4 (1994): 241–70; J. J. Navarro, "Computer Supported Self-Managing Work Teams," *Journal of Organizational Computing* 4 (1994): 317–42.
20. Malone, Crowston, Lee, and Pentland, *Tools for Inventing Organizations,* 16.
21. Implementation is "final" to the degree that any organizational change process can ever reach a genuinely "final" stage.

Chapter 10

1. Bikson, Gutek, and Mankin, *Implementing Computerized Procedures in Office Settings.*
2. Ibid. See also Bikson, Stasz, and Mankin, *Computer-Mediated Work.*
3. Like most metaphors, this one too has its limits. Roads are linear and,

literally, fixed in concrete, an image that contrasts sharply with that of the kind of organizational change we have tried to convey throughout this book.

4. The title of this section is adapted from a book by Don Michael, *On Planning to Learn, and Learning to Plan* (San Francisco: Jossey-Bass, 1973), a seminal work that was one of the first to offer a model for what is now commonly referred to as "organizational learning."

5. S. A. Mohrman and T. G. Cummings, *Self-Designing Organizations: Learning How to Create High Performance* (Reading, Mass.: Addison-Wesley, 1989), 107.

6. Of course, if the pilot site is completely divorced from the rest of the organization, it will be harder to generalize from the pilot to the other implementation sites.

7. Mohrman and Cummings, *Self-Designing Organizations,* 133.

8. Ibid., 134.

9. Ibid., 135.

10. This example was adapted from Bikson, Stasz, and Mankin, *Computer-Mediated Work,* 27.

11. This section on training resources was adapted from D. Mankin, T. K. Bikson, B. A. Gutek, and C. Stasz, "Managing Technological Change: The Process Is Key," *Datamation* 34, no. 18 (1988): 68–80.

12. Ibid., 76.

13. For more on "reinvention," see R. E. Rice and E. M. Rogers, "Reinvention in the Innovation Process" *Knowledge* 1 (1980): 499–514; T. K. Bikson and J. D. Eveland, *New Office Technology: Planning for People* (New York: Pergamon Press, 1986); B. M. Johnson and R. Rice, *Managing Organizational Innovation* (New York: Columbia University Press, 1986); D. Leonard-Barton, "Implementation as Mutual Adaptation of Technology and Organization," *Research Policy* 17 (1988): 251–67; and E. Von Hippel, *The Sources of Innovation* (New York: Oxford University Press, 1988).

14. As typically used, *reinvention* does not mean fundamental, global redesign of the technology and its functions but refers instead to relatively modest and focused modifications of its operations, interface, etc. Our use is consistent with this interpretation.

15. M. J. Tyre and W. J. Orlikowski, "Windows Of Opportunity: Temporal Patterns of Technology Adaptation in Organizations," *Organization Science* 5 (1994): 98.

16. Johnson and Rice, *Managing Organizational Innovation.*

17. This example was adapted from Bikson, Stasz, and Mankin, *Computer-Mediated Work,* 47.

18. Mankin, Bikson, Gutek, and Stasz, "Managing Technological Change," 74, 76.

19. J. D. Eveland, personal communication, 1995.

20. This does not mean that there are no limitations on this process. When one user's reinventions begin to impinge on another user's tasks, the team should step in, take ownership of the process, and guide it when necessary. The team as a whole may need to resolve incompatibilities between interdependent tasks, reinvented and otherwise.

21. Ciborra, "From Thinking to Tinkering," 289.

22. While the time taken for full implementation may vary from one group to another, each group should be made aware of when the changeover will occur.

23. L. G. Tornatzky, J. D. Eveland, M. G. Boylan, W. A. Hetzner, E. C. Johnson, D. Roitman, and J. Schneider, *The Process of Technological Innovation: Reviewing the Literature* (Washington, DC: National Science Foundation, 1983), 135.

Chapter 11

1. The discussion in this section is adapted from Cohen, "New Approaches to Teams and Teamwork"; Mohrman, Cohen, and Mohrman, *Designing Team-Based Organizations;* and E. E. Lawler, and S. G. Cohen, "Designing Pay Systems for Teams," *ACA Journal: Perspectives in Compensation and Benefits* 1, no. 1 (1994): 6–19.

2. Mohrman, Cohen, and Mohrman, *Designing Team-Based Organizations.*

3. Ibid.

4. Lawler and Cohen, "Designing Pay Systems for Teams," 15.

5. Cohen, "New Approaches to Teams and Teamwork," 20.

6. In gainsharing plans the rewards are usually tied to gains in performance that exceed a specified target, such as an established goal or the unit's accomplishment in years past. Also, gainsharing is tied to the performance of a business unit rather than the profits of an entire organization. This way individual teams and performers can see a connection between their efforts and the performance of the unit. In a large corporation, this connection is often hard to see. For more on gainsharing, see J. R. Schuster and P. K. Zingheim, *The New Pay: Linking Employee and Organizational Performance* (New York: Lexington, 1992).

7. When applied to managers and professionals, the term *competency-based pay* is often used instead of *skill-based pay*. See G. E. Ledford, Jr., "Paying for the Skills, Knowledge, and Competencies of Knowledge Workers," *Compensation and Benefits Review* 27, no. 4 (1995): 55–62.

8. A. M. Mohrman, Jr., S. A. Mohrman, and E. E. Lawler III, "The Performance Management of Teams" in *Performance Measurement, Evaluation, and Incentives*, ed. W. T. Bruns, Jr. (Boston: Harvard Business School Press): 235.

9. R. H. Waterman, J. A. Waterman, and B. A. Collard, "Toward a Career-Resilient Workforce," *Harvard Business Review* 72, no. 4 (1994): 88.

10. Keen, *Shaping the Future*, 121–22.

11. Ibid., 126.

12. Waterman, Waterman, and Collard, "Career-Resilient Workforce," 91.

13. Admittedly, this can be difficult to do in a downsized, competitive business environment.

14. Markus and Robey, "Business Process Reengineering," 595.

15. The authors' personal favorite is "high priest of the machine god," offered by former "high priest" Jim Tidwell of the Hughes Corporation.

16. For example, partitioning of labor between centralized IT staff and team-based experts; having centralized IT staff work in close collaboration with the people they serve on the MDI team to integrate team and technological change. See chapter 5, particularly the citations by Boynton et al., "Whose Responsibility Is IT Management?"

17. Markus and Robey, "Business Process Reengineering," 607.

18. Personal Communication with Dan Heitzer, 1993.

19. Even if the IT department is not too busy and does have the expertise, there are still good reasons for it to market and sell its services internally and compete with external sources for the user teams' business—better-quality and lower-cost services, in particular.

20. Eveland, Blanchard, Brown, and Mattocks, "The Role of Help Networks in Facilitating Use of CSCW Tools," 272.

21. Keen, *Shaping the Future;* M. J. Earl and D. F. Feeny, "Is Your CIO Adding Value?" *Sloan Management Review* 35, no. 3 (1994): 11–20.

22. As a sobering counterpoint to the self-congratulations with which many organizations laud their own downsizing efforts, James Brian Quinn offers the following comment in the December 1993 issue of *Catalyst,* the newsletter of the Centre for Corporate Change (published by the Australian Graduate School of Management, University of New South Wales): "I am personally very concerned at the U.S. tendency to think managers have done some great managing when they downsize an enterprise radically. I think that's basically wrong. It means they (or their predecessors) haven't done the job right. They haven't built new markets or groomed people with the skills customers want." See also S. Roach, "The Perils of a Productivity-Led Recovery," Special economic study published by Morgan Stanley, January 7, 1994.

Chapter 12

1. D. A. Nadler, M. S. Gerstein, and R. B. Shaw, *Organizational Architecture: Designs for Changing Organizations* (San Francisco: Jossey-Bass, 1992), 4.

2. J. M. Nilles, *Making Telecommuting Happen: A Guide for Telemanagers and Telecommuters* (New York: Van Nostrand Reinhold, 1994).

3. Mohrman, Cohen, and Mohrman, *Designing Team-Based Organizations*, 350.

4. M. S. Gerstein and R. S. Shaw, "Organizational Architectures for the Twenty-first Century," in *Organizational Architecture,* ed. D. A. Nadler, M. C. Gerstein, and R. B. Shaw, 265.

5. A. M. Mohrman and S. A. Mohrman, "Organizational Change and Learning," in *Organizing for the Future: The New Logic for Managing Complete Organizations,* ed. J. R. Galbraith and E. E. Lawler, III, and Associates (San Francisco: Jossey-Bass, 1993): 87–108.

6. R. Cyert and J. March, *The Behavioral Theory of the Firm* (Englewood Cliffs, N.J.: Prentice-Hall, 1963); C. Argyris and D. Schon, *Organizational Learning* (Reading, Mass.: Addison-Wesley, 1978); P. M. Senge, *The Fifth Discipline: The Art and Practice of the Learning Organization* (New York: Doubleday, 1990).

7. R. B. Shaw and D. N. T. Perkins, "Teaching Organizations to Learn: The Power of Productive Failures," in *Organizational Architecture,* ed. D. A. Nadler, M. C. Gerstein, and R. B. Shaw, 175.

8. See Mohrman and Mohrman, *Organizational Change and Learning,* and D. H. Kim, "The Link between Individual and Organizational Learning," *Sloan Management Review* 34, no. 1 (1993): 37–50 for a discussion of the relationship between individual and organizational learning.

9. Mohrman and Mohrman, *Organizational Change and Learning,* 89.

10. Bikson and Frinking, in *Preserving the Present,* find that this information need is frequently overlooked. Few organizations in their study were creating mechanisms for retaining and documenting E-mail messages for subsequent analysis and learning.

11. From C. Handy, "Trust and the Virtual Organization," *Harvard Business Review* 83, no. 3 (1995): 44.

12. Schrage, *Shared Minds.*

13. L. Hirschorn and T. Gilmore, "The New Boundaries of a 'Boundaryless' Company," *Harvard Business Review* 70, no. 3 (1992): 104–5. Although we quote from their article, the authors go on to make a point that is somewhat different from what we discuss here. Their focus is on the new boundaries that will replace the old, traditional boundaries. Our point is that there are countervailing factors working against the complete elimination of the old boundaries.

14. S. Schmidt and D. Kipnis, "Electronic Communication: E-Mailing to Empowerment or Autocracy," Synergy Session on E-mail, Eastern Academy of Management, 1995.

15. Handy, "Trust and the Virtual Organization," 42.

16. Ibid., 46.

17. For more on this guideline, see M. O'Hara-Devereaux and R. J. Johansen, *Global Work: Bridging Distance, Culture and Time* (San Francisco: Jossey-Bass, 1994).

Index

Organizations
defined, 22–23
learning, 247–248
Organizations, future team-based, technology-enabled, 218–219, 237, 240–242, 247, 249–251
assessing and rewarding team performance in, 219–226
authority, power, and influence in, 245–246
and constraints on change, 246–247
and control versus trust, 248–249
creating lateral career paths in, 226–230
as learning organizations, 247–248
limits on where and when to work in, 242–243
as metaorganization, 244–245
nature of work in, 242
new roles for information technology function in, 230–235
new roles for senior management team in, 235–236
spanning functions and departments in, 243–244
Orlikowski, Wanda, 204

Pacific Bell, xiv
Parallel teams, 35, 37
assessing and rewarding, 224–225
challenges presented by, 76, 77
characteristics of, 27–30
composition of, 175–176
designing, 174–177
external connections of, 176
information resources of, 177
leadership of, 176
training of, 177
Participation, of user delegates, 72–75, 76
Pasmore, W. A., 8n 9
Pava, C., 8n 9
Pei, M. C., 68n 4, 97n 16, 109n 8
Pentland, B., 191n 19,20
Performance management, by work team leaders, 172
See also Team performance
Perkins, D. N. T., 247

Pilot test, 156, 165, 200
conducting, 197–199
Porter, L. W., 36n 21
Power, in organization of the future, 245–246
Princess Cruises, xiv
Process, definition and illustration of, 51
Procter & Gamble, 26
Profit-sharing, 222
Project and development team(s), 35, 37
assessing and rewarding, 224
challenges presented by, 76–77
characteristics of, 26–27
composition of external connections, 102–103
information resources for, 115–116
leader's role, defining, 103–105
training programs of, 116–118
See also MDI team
Project management, defined, 103
Project sponsors, 92–93
Project teams, see Project and development team(s)
Prototypes
iterative, 158–161
for linking MDI team with user teams, 111–112
Public Service Company of Colorado, xiv

Quinn, James Brian, 85n 9, 236n 22

Ralls, R. S., 67n 3, 69n 1
Rapid application development (RAD), 157–158
iterative prototyping, 158–161
model, comparing waterfall model and, 164–165
modular, concurrent development, 161–164
Rasmussen, B., 153n 12
Reengineering, 14
Reinvention, 203–204
dilemma and challenge of, 207–209
job, 203, 204–206, 228–229
task, 204–205

User Team(s) *(continued)*
  redeploying resources to, 232–233
  relationship between information technology experts and, 82, 97
  type, implications of, 76–78
  versus MDI team, 67
  See also User delegates
U.S. Forest Service, xiv
Utter, D. F., 191n 19

Values and objectives, identifying MDI project, 129–132
Van de Ven, A. H., 104n 4
Velum, K., 153n 12
Vendors, external, as source of information technology experts, 85–86, 89–91
Ventana GroupSystems, 150
Videoconferencing, 21, 190
Voice mail, 110, 206, 249
Von Hipple, E., 204n 13
Vroom, V. H., 36n 21

Wagner, R. J., 36n 20
Walton, Richard E., 10n 11, 67n 3, 69n 5, 71, 72, 73, 105n 5
Wang, Q. W., 187n 15
"Waterfall" model of systems development, 154, 198
  comparing RAD model and, 164–165

(see also Rapid application development)
  designing and building, 155–156, 165
  establishing functional requirements, 154–155, 164–165
  problems with, 156–157
  testing and evaluating, 156, 165
Waterman, Judith, 227
Waterman, Robert, 227, 228
Work, in organization of the future, 242–243
Workflow systems, 151
Work teams, 35, 37
  assessing and rewarding, 223–224
  challenges presented by, 76
  characteristics of, 24–26
  composition of, 169–171
  designing, 169–174
  external connections of, 172
  information resources of, 172–173
  leadership of, 171–172
  training of, 173
World Bank, xiv

Yoshida, T., 117n 15

Zingheim, P. K., 222n 6
Zmud, R. W., 83n 2
Zuboff, Shoshana, *In the Age of the Smart Machine,* 13n 18, 19–20

About the Authors

Don Mankin is the dean of Organizational Psychology Programs for the Los Angeles campus of the California School of Professional Psychology. He teaches, consults, and writes on issues of organization design, team effectiveness, and the management of technology, innovation, and human resources. He is the author of *Toward a Post-Industrial Psychology: Emerging Perspectives on Technology, Work, Education, and Leisure*, co-author of *Classics in Industrial and Organizational Psychology* and has written many articles on these and related themes.

Susan G. Cohen is a research scientist at the Center for Effective Organizations, Graduate School of Business, University of Southern California. Her research and consulting focus on team effectiveness and empowerment, employee involvement, human resource management, implementation of information technology, organization development and change, and self-management. She is the co-author of *Designing Team-Based Organizations: New Forms for Knowledge Work* and has written numerous articles and book chapters on self-management and teams and teamwork.

Tora K. Bikson is a senior scientist in behavioral science at RAND. She is a visiting professor at THESUS (an international business school in France), where she teaches classes on computer supported cooperative work; she has taught at University of Missouri, UCLA, and Stern School of Business at NYU. Tora heads research projects funded by NSF, OTA, OECD, the USDA Forest Service, the Markle Foundation, and other institutions regarding innovative technologies, with an emphasis on advanced information and communication technologies. She has published widely on this topic.